Hosea

The Broken Hearted Prophet

O'Neil K. Russell

Scripture quotations are from The ESV® Bible (The Holy Bible, English Standard Version®), copyright © 2001 by Crossway, a publishing ministry of Good News Publishers. Used by permission. All rights reserved.

Copyright © 2021 O'Neil K. Russell

All rights reserved.

ISBN:9798486222726

DEDICATION

This volume is dedicated to Jesus Christ, my Saviour, who chose me as His own and called me unto Himself by His magnificent grace.

TO GOD BE ALL GLORY!

TABLE OF CONTENTS

    Acknowledgements   i
    Series Prologue   3
    Introduction   5

1   Broken Hearts—Broken Dreams   Pg7

2   Forsaking God   Pg19

3   Divine Reversal   Pg27

4   Amazing Love   Pg37

5   From Pleasure to Pain   Pg49

6   Corrupt to the Core   Pg57

7   Taken for Granted   Pg67

8   The Lion from Zion   Pg77

9   Running in Rebellion   Pg85

10   Hard-Headed Hebrews   Pg95

11   The Silly Season   Pg103

12   Reaping the Whirlwind   Pg113

13   Give Me the Real Thing   Pg123

14   Floods of Fury   Pg133

15	Guardians of the Truth	Pg141
16	A Dried-Up Root	Pg151
17	The Dark Side of Success	Pg163
18	When the Hammer Falls	Pg175
19	The Folly of Fallow Ground	Pg183
20	Torn By Love	Pg195
21	Mercy Multiplied	Pg207
22	U-Turn	Pg217
23	One And the Same	Pg229
24	Dead Man Walking	Pg241
25	Demolition Day	Pg253
26	Homecoming	Pg265

ACKNOWLEDGMENTS

Gratitude is expressed to the following individuals for their indispensable assistance in producing this volume:

Kayvanna A. Russell, Editor
Audrey Davis, Proofreader/Formatting
Owen Moss, Graphic Design

SERIES PROLOGUE

This *Devotional Commentary* series functions as a union of the best of two worlds. On one side of the chasm is the daily devotional. Its strength is that it is easily understood and provides practical instruction on how the Christian ought to live daily to the honour and glory of God. However, its weakness is that it does not permit the reader to probe deeply enough into the immense theological foundation of the Christian faith, with the added danger of Scripture sometimes being effortlessly taken out of context. On the other side of the chasm is the commentary. Its undeniable asset is that it expounds major swathes of Scripture verse by verse—often even engaging with the original biblical languages (Hebrew and Greek) to bring the reader to an understanding of what the biblical text actually meant to its original audience. The challenge is that the average Christian is overwhelmed by such technically verbose literature and may even be discouraged at the sight of a Hebrew/Greek reference. Furthermore, the commentary is usually deficient of personal application to the believer's life.

The devotional commentary endeavors to take the superior of each world and fuse them into one hybrid unit—not falling hard to one extreme or the other but striking middle ground. As a definitive goal, God's people should find in the devotional commentary a bridge between the devotional and the commentary that would effectively enable them to make a safe journey across that gulf, shaking off the remnants of spiritual infancy and pressing forward to sanctification and spiritual maturity.

Succinctly, the philosophical objective of this series is to be:

- Textually Faithful
- Theologically Sound
- Clearly Written
- Readily Applicable

INTRODUCTION

Title

The title of this book is taken from its primary figure and author whose name means "salvation". This is the first of the 12 "minor prophets". "Minor" is a term which suggests that these books are shorter prophetic works and does not imply lesser importance.

Date

All that is known about Hosea is extracted from the work itself. When the reigning Jewish kings mentioned in the book are examined, it can be determined that Hosea's ministry was conducted during the second half of the 8th century B.C. around the region of 755-715.

Background

The prophet's ministry was carried out chiefly to the Northern Kingdom of Israel of which he may have been a resident. Material prosperity and spiritual degradation was extensive when Hosea began his prophecies and in 722 B.C., the capital of the Northern Kingdom, Samaria, fell to the Assyrian Empire.

Theme

Hosea clearly depicts God's unfailing, steadfast love for Israel despite her unfaithfulness and stubbornness of will, demonstrated by Hosea's marriage to Gomer.

Hosea's Marriage

The three main perspectives concerning Hosea's union to Gomer are:

1. It was only allegorical (symbolic).
2. Hosea married a woman who was already a prostitute.
3. Gomer became a prostitute after her marriage to Hosea.

No logical reason exists to assume the marriage was not historical fact, although Hosea's marriage to Gomer unquestionably illustrates God's affection for rebellious Israel.

1

BROKEN HEARTS—
BROKEN DREAMS
1:1-11

¹The word of the Lord that came to Hosea, the son of Beeri, in the days of Uzziah, Jotham, Ahaz, and Hezekiah, kings of Judah, and in the days of Jeroboam the son of Joash, king of Israel. ² When the Lord first spoke through Hosea, the Lord said to Hosea, "Go, take to yourself a wife of whoredom and have children of whoredom, for the land commits great whoredom by forsaking the Lord." ³ So he went and took Gomer, the daughter of Diblaim, and she conceived and bore him a son.⁴ And the Lord said to him, "Call his name Jezreel, for in just a little while I will punish the house of Jehu for the blood of Jezreel, and I will put an end to the kingdom of the house of Israel. ⁵ And on that day I will break the bow of Israel in the Valley of Jezreel." ⁶ She conceived again and bore a daughter. And the Lord said to him, "Call her name No Mercy, for I will no more have mercy on the house of Israel, to forgive them at all. ⁷ But I will have mercy on the house of Judah, and I will save them by the Lord their God. I will not save them by bow or by sword or by war or by horses or by horsemen."⁸ When she had weaned No Mercy, she conceived and bore a son. ⁹ And the Lord said, "Call his name Not My People, for you are not my people, and I am not your God."¹⁰ Yet the number of the children of Israel shall be like the sand of the sea, which cannot be measured or numbered. And in the place where it was said to them,"You are not my people," it shall be said to them, "Children of the living God." ¹¹ And the children of Judah and the children of Israel shall be gathered together, and they shall appoint for themselves one head. And they shall go up from the land, for great shall be the day of Jezreel.[1]

---

[1] Unless otherwise indicated, all Scripture quotations are from the *English Standard Version* (ESV).

There was a time in the United States of America when the name Lance Armstrong was a household one. This gentleman was a professional road cyclist who had won a number of road racing championships even before the age of twenty-four. Unfortunately, at twenty-five, while still in his prime, he was diagnosed with stage three testicular cancer. By the time the cancer was discovered, it had already spread to his brain, lungs, and abdomen. The future for Mr. Armstrong looked bleak.

Nevertheless—amazingly—within six months of receiving chemotherapy, he was declared cancer-free. The indomitable sportsman bounced back onto the world stage and won several more racing titles.

Sadly, however, an earth-shattering doping scandal would follow closely behind. In 2012, the United States Anti-Doping Agency came to the conclusion that Armstrong had used performance-enhancing drugs over the course of his career and he was christened the mastermind behind one of the most elaborate and prosperous doping scandals that cycling has ever seen.

This left the hearts of countless American people both stunned and crushed. He was a "knight in shining armor". He was a "comeback king". Needless to say, the relationship between Lance Armstrong and his fan base would never be the same as he left them all with broken hearts.

As the first chapter of Hosea begins, Yahweh, the eternal God of the Bible, also has a broken heart because of the betrayal of His people.

Hosea's Context

"The word of the Lord" which begins verse 1 should be recognized as a clear communication that came from the Almighty God. Consequently, everything that is explained thereafter is the unraveling of that distinct message through the mouth of the prophet Hosea. Indeed, Hosea was the vehicle through whom the words came, but in the end, the words themselves are the direct product of God. He is the source and first cause of what is contained in this prophetic book.

The Scripture continues **"that came to Hosea."** Hosea's name means "salvation". It is an alternative rendering of the Hebrew name Joshua. Interestingly, the name

Jesus also means "salvation" or, more specifically, "Jehovah's salvation". Hence, Jesus was the New Testament name for God's salvation while Joshua and Hosea are the Old Testament names for the same.

The text notes that he was **"the son of Beeri."** Nothing of significance is known of his father or even about the prophet himself. His tribe, occupation, age, and activities prior to his call to prophetic ministry all remain a mystery. Such forsaken facts lead to the logical assumption that Hosea was plausibly not of significant stature in his day. In spite of this, God was going to use this unknown personality as His instrument.

Sometimes Christians feel that their existence is of no significance whatsoever. There are believers who wrestle with not coming from well-known families, and there are others who struggle with a lack of prestigious occupation. Still, others encounter the unhappiness that a lack of financial steadiness may produce. In spite of these occurrences, God wants to significantly use His saints as His instruments just as He used Hosea.

The timespan of Hosea's prophecy must be observed. It took place **"in the days of Uzziah, Jotham, Ahaz, and Hezekiah, kings of Judah, and the days of Jeroboam the son of Joash, king of Israel."** This gives clear insight into the historical context. At this period in the nation's story, the country was split into two kingdoms. The Northern Kingdom consisted of the ten northern tribes (Asher, Dan, Ephraim, Gad, Issachar, Manasseh, Naphtali, Reuben, Simeon, and Zebulun) and its capital was the city of Samaria. This Northern Kingdom was officially called "Israel". Across the border, the Southern Kingdom incorporated only two tribes: Judah and Benjamin. Its capital city was Jerusalem and this kingdom was named "Judah".

Hosea's prophetic ministry was performed predominantly to the wealthy, prosperous, and spiritually complacent Northern Kingdom. Idolatry and human injustices were deeply engrained into the very fabric of Jewish society. These are the people whom Hosea must boldly confront with God's truth.

Hosea's Commissioning

The biblical text in verse 2 begins **"When the LORD first spoke through Hosea"** to identify that this is the commencement of the prophet's ministry. It can be assumed that prior to this occasion, he never received direct revelation from God. Therefore, God was now speaking; but no one—especially not Hosea—would be prepared for what God was about to say. According to the rest of the verse **"the LORD said to Hosea, 'Go, take to yourself a wife of whoredom'."** The Lord's command was that Hosea go immediately, without any courtship or betrothal (engagement) period, and marry a known prostitute in Israel. Bible scholars are divided on whether this individual was a prostitute before Hosea encountered her or whether she would eventually become a prostitute after she married Hosea. I take the position that she was previously a prostitute before even marrying Hosea. The words "become" or "will become" or "became" are not even hinted to in the verse. It gives the impression that her lifestyle was already recognized as one of harlotry. This unusual ordeal may not seem to be a big issue when casually reading Hosea, but the thought of one of your own relatives—or even children—being asked to give the same level of sacrifice and obedience today would bring any reader face to face with the gravity of such a matter. Hosea was someone's relative and son; yet, he took on the mantle of obedience wholeheartedly and unflinchingly.

It is also stated that he must **"have children of whoredom."** Marriage was only the first step of compliance. The bearing of children was to follow closely behind. The intention of the phrase is not to suggest that the children were also guaranteed to conduct themselves in such a vile manner. Rather, it submits that the children would be produced from the marital union.

But what is God's motivation? Why should a man be subject to such a daring act of obedience, even if he was a prophet?

God acknowledges that **"the land commits great whoredom by forsaking the LORD."** In reality, God also had a bride. His bride was Israel, the Northern Kingdom. God's bride strayed and prostituted herself with lovers from a host of other nations. As a result, God commands His servant to marry a harlot in order to illustrate in real time how unfaithful and treacherous His bride had been to Him. Theologically, this is known as a "sign act". Sign acts are actions performed by Old Testament prophets in order to illustrate a message to His people. Prophets like Isaiah, Jeremiah, and Ezekiel also engaged sign acts during their ministries.

Verse 3 begins **"So he went and took Gomer, the daughter of Diblaim."** What God demanded, Hosea delivered. In spite of her repulsive lifestyle, Hosea—God's man—took Gomer as his wife. He showed clearly that he was both fully surrendered and fully obedient to God's plans and desires for his life. Hosea was not remotely concerned about his reputation in the court of public opinion.

Those who identify as children of God must be fully surrendered and fully obedient to God's plan and purposes for their lives. The Christian life can be unpredictable, and often God calls us to areas and actions that may not be inscribed on the personal agenda we have set for our own existence. If God's agenda clashes with our agenda, obedience requires that we be willing to subject ours to His. Christians must obey because God is the one who has saved us in the first place. It is He who calls. It is He who saves. Therefore, it is He who must have the final say in the direction of our lives. If He is truly King, then those who are citizens of His kingdom must submit to His rule. Even though we may not be called to the same act of obedience that Hosea was called to in his lifetime, we *will* be called to obedience. If God demands, will you, as a Christian, deliver?

Hosea's Children

It continues on by acknowledging **"and she conceived and bore him a son."** "Conceived" comes from a root word that seems to suggest a swelling. It paints the picture of a woman becoming pregnant. "Bore" means she gave birth to the baby—the first child being a male. The book of Hosea informs **"And the LORD said to him, 'Call his name Jezreel'"** (vs. 4). Jezreel was the name of a valley located in the Northern Kingdom of Israel. Countless battles and bloodshed had taken place in that location. Why would God want Hosea to name his child Jezreel? The text makes it clear by stating **"for in just a little while I will punish the house of Jehu for the blood of Jezreel."** The assertion is made that someone named Jehu shed blood in Jezreel.

This verse recalls the events of 2 Kings 10:1-11.

> [1]*Now Ahab had seventy sons in Samaria. So Jehu wrote letters and sent them to Samaria, to the rulers of the city, to the elders, and to the guardians of the sons of Ahab, saying,* [2]*"Now then, as soon as this letter comes to you, seeing your master's sons are with you, and there are with you chariots and horses, fortified cities also, and weapons,* [3]*select the best and fittest of your master's sons and set him on his father's throne and fight for your master's house."* [4]*But they were exceedingly afraid and said, "Behold, the two kings could not stand before him. How then can we stand?"* [5]*So he who was over the palace, and he who was over the city, together with the elders and the guardians, sent to Jehu, saying, "We are your servants, and we will do all that you tell us. We will not make*

anyone king. Do whatever is good in your eyes." ⁶Then he wrote to them a second letter, saying, "If you are on my side, and if you are ready to obey me, take the heads of your master's sons and come to me at Jezreel tomorrow at this time." Now the king's sons, seventy persons, were with the great men of the city, who were bringing them up. ⁷And as soon as the letter came to them, they took the king's sons and slaughtered them, seventy persons, and put their heads in baskets and sent them to him at Jezreel. ⁸When the messenger came and told him, "They have brought the heads of the king's sons," he said, "Lay them in two heaps at the entrance of the gate until the morning." ⁹Then in the morning, when he went out, he stood and said to all the people, "You are innocent. It was I who conspired against my master and killed him, but who struck down all these? ¹⁰Know then that there shall fall to the earth nothing of the word of the Lord, which the Lord spoke concerning the house of Ahab, for the Lord has done what he said by his servant Elijah." ¹¹So Jehu struck down all who remained of the house of Ahab in Jezreel, all his great men and his close friends and his priests, until he left him none remaining.

Jehu, the courageous army officer, brought down the house of the evil northern king, Ahab. This narrative has both a positive and negative aspect to it. The positive is that Jehu was executing the divine will of God. The fact that he was blessed by the prophet Elijah before all of these events took place confirms this. The negative is that Jehu and his associates overplayed their hand and overstepped their boundaries in their desire for bloodshed. No restraint was exercised. Thus, the moral of the story is that God is not only to be obeyed; He must be obeyed in the manner that pleases Him. Even in our obedience, we cannot be autonomous; we must execute God's will in God's way.

The script continues **"and I will put an end to the kingdom of the house of Israel."** In approximately the year 722 B.C., this prophecy was fulfilled when the Northern Kingdom of Israel came crashing down at the feet of the Assyrian Empire and they were dragged away into captivity. For the sake of clarity, it must be understood that these foretold judgements were not irrevocable indictments. Rather, God intended for them to function as warnings for Israel to return to her Master. Only when the call to repentance went unheeded did God unleash His judgement upon them.

Similarly, today the clarion call to repentance is still echoing. The book of Revelation warns of another judgement—an eternal judgement. Revelation 20:15 maintains "And if anyone's name was not found written in the book of life, he was thrown into the lake of fire." This "book of life" secures all the names of those who will inherit eternal life forever with God in Heaven. Those who lack this eternal life by refusing to believe on Jesus Christ alone, completely, and wholeheartedly for salvation and reject the opportunity to find refuge in His sacrifice on Calvary's cross will be cast into the lake of fire for everlasting punishment and torment. Dear friend, you are also warned to do the same and follow the Lord Jesus Christ because if the warning is not heeded, judgement will be the result, as was the case with Israel.

Verse **5** reads **"And on that day I will break the bow of Israel in the Valley of Jezreel."** The bow in this verse is a reference to a war bow, similar to the "bow and arrow" with which the modern mind would be familiar. The bow was a weapon of choice for the Israelites during this period. Typically, in the Old Testament, when God said He would "break the bow" of a people, it meant He was hastening to Israel's rescue. However, in the current discussion, it is—ironically—Israel's bow which He would shatter.

Furthermore, the valley of Jezreel was a location of significance for the Jews. In this same valley in the book of Judges, Gideon and his army gained victory over the Midianites. As such, the valley of Jezreel had a name of prestige and honor attached to it. Unfortunately, God was now going to do the direct opposite with the valley of Jezreel.

"She conceived again and bore a daughter. And the LORD said to him, 'Call her name No Mercy'", (vs. 6). The term used for 'No Mercy' in some English translations is Lo-ruhama. It is the transliteration of a Hebrew word which literally means "no mercy" or "no pity". Hence, most modern translations give the English rendering outright.

It continues **"for I will no more have mercy on the house of Israel, to forgive them at all."** Israel had been drenched in God's mercy and forgiveness from time immemorial; now, that mercy and forgiveness was reduced to only faint droplets which would soon come to an abrupt halt.

This should give great caution to believers who surmise they can be involved in habitual, unrepentant sin and not receive the due penalty for their actions. It is clear from Scripture that God heavily chastens even those whom He loves by sometimes ushering judgement into their life experiences. The Lord's clemency must never be trodden under foot by those that bear His name throughout the Earth.

God notes through His prophet (vs. **7**) **"But I will have mercy on the house of Judah and I will save them."** Judah will be spared such harsh realities. God treated the Southern Kingdom of Judah differently because they behaved differently. To be clear, there was sin in Judah, but it had not reached the heights of that in Israel. Because God is just in nature, He always distributes discipline in a manner that is both fair and right.

Judah will be saved **"by the hand of their God. I will not save them by bow or by sword or by war or by horses or by horsemen."** Yahweh is going to save the South by His mighty, omnipotent hand from the Assyrians—the same Assyrians that crushed Israel. God Himself will deliver Judah and not by the measly weapons of war.

Certainly, this promise was fulfilled as 2 Kings 19:30-36 records.

> *[30]And the surviving remnant of the house of Judah shall again take root downward and bear fruit upward. [31]For out of Jerusalem shall go a remnant, and out of Mount Zion a band of survivors. The zeal of the Lord will do this. [32]"Therefore thus says the Lord concerning the king of Assyria: He shall not come into this city or shoot an arrow there, or come before it with a shield or cast up a siege mound against it. [33]By the way that he came, by the same he shall return, and he shall not come into this city, declares the Lord. [34]For I will defend this city to save it, for my own sake and for the sake of my servant David." [35]And that night the angel of the Lord went out and struck down 185,000 in the camp of the Assyrians. And when people arose early in the morning, behold, these were all dead bodies. [36]Then Sennacherib king of Assyria departed and went home and lived at Nineveh.*

God's angel annihilated 185,000 of the Assyrians! No weapons or warriors had accomplished this. God did it by Himself.

Appropriately, one must pause and take stock of who gets the glory when miracles are performed in our own lives. How easy is it to give glory to family members, friends, doctors, and even pastors for the blessings we encounter from time to time.

Yet, God alone is fully deserving of the praise for the bountiful blessings He bestows. James 1:17 is careful to remind us that *"Every good gift and every perfect gift is from above, coming down from the Father of lights..."* Who have you been praising lately? If it's not the Almighty God, you are in error.

According to verse 8, **"When she had weaned No Mercy, she conceived and bore a son."** It must be assumed that some time has passed. In Old Testament eras, it was not uncommon for mothers to breast feed their children up to two years of age. As an estimate, about two years after No Mercy (Lo-ruhama), another son was begotten.

God gave the command to (vs. 9) **"call his name Not My People."** The name in some older translations is written as Lo-ammi. Again, this is the Hebrew terminology that translates into English as "not my people".

Hosea continues **"for you are not my people, and I am not your God."** God distances Himself from Israel and verbally disowns them. They worshiped countless gods from numerous nations and were unrecognizable to him. Repeatedly in violation of the covenant, God would have none of it any longer.

Hope and Comfort

Verse 10 informs **"Yet the number of the children of Israel shall be like the sand of the sea, which cannot be measured or numbered."** This recalls the promise God made to Abraham, the father of the nation, in the book of Genesis. Here, Hosea affirms that the promise still stands and that God had not reneged on His word or changed His mind.

Certainly, the Lord always keeps His promises, even today. His commitment to doing so is not equal to that of close kindred or politicians. His faithfulness—like His personhood—is infinite and perfect. The promises revealed in His Word will be kept through thick and thin.

It further reads **"And in the place where it was said to them, 'You are not my people', it shall be said to them, 'Children of the living God'."** What a change! The same population God has rejected are going to be called children of the living God. Who are these people? Undoubtedly, judgement is still pensively pending for the Northern Kingdom of Israel, but the future remains hopeful for an alternative group of Jews.

Romans 9:22-26 a parallel passage of Scripture gives greater insight into this dilemma.

> ^{22}What if God, desiring to show his wrath and to make known his power, has endured with much patience vessels of wrath prepared for destruction, ^{23}in order to make known the riches of his glory for vessels of mercy, which he has prepared beforehand for glory– ^{24}even us whom he has called, not from the Jews only but also from the Gentiles? ^{25}As indeed he says in Hosea, "Those who were not my people I will call 'my people,' and her who was not beloved I will call 'beloved.'" ^{26}"And in the very place where it was said to them, 'You are not my people,'

It must be maintained that both Hosea's and Paul's writings are God-breathed. Nevertheless, Paul, coming into existence further down the corridor of time, obtained a more precise understanding of what God's plan was all along. According to Romans 9:22-26, Jews and Gentiles (non-Jews) are included in what Hosea wrote concerning "sons of the living God". Hosea had in mind every Christian who would be converted to Christ whether Jew or Gentile. The saints of God, both Jew and Gentile, should be the focus and if you are a believer in Jesus Christ, this verse is fulfilled in you. God had you in mind even while speaking through a prophet thousands of years ago. What a blessing it is to be a child of the living God!

Also, (vs. 11) **"the children of Judah and the children of Israel shall be gathered together, and they shall appoint for themselves one head."** I concur with most Bible scholars that the assertions of this verse are still yet to take place. The entire nation (both North and South) will be united as one in a way that they had not been beforehand. Their one head and leader will be the Lord Jesus Christ. As Christ's return nears, so does the fulfilment of this promise.

Finally, **"they shall go up from the land, for great shall be the day of Jezreel."** Jezreel means "God sows". In other words, God sows seeds that will produce an abundant harvest. Marvelous will be that day of sowing. Let us not be discouraged as Christians because even a cursory survey of Scripture will reveal that the best days of God's workings are yet ahead of us and we must remain focused and faithful.

> Discuss

1. Were the words of Hosea his words or God's words? What implication does that have for the entire book of Hosea? What implications does that have for the entire Bible?

2. Is there anything written in the Holy Scriptures that is not from God? How should Christians respond to parts of the Bible that appear unpleasant, offensive, or discriminatory?

3. What do you think Hosea's family thought of him after marrying a woman like Gomer and how would you have responded if you were his father/mother?

4. Why did God treat Israel and Judah differently during the time of Hosea's ministry?

5. What are your feelings toward Gentiles being "grafted in" to God's plan of salvation. Is it fair or not? Discuss Jesus' conversation with the Canaanite woman in Matthew 15:21-28.

2

FORSAKING GOD
2:1-13

¹Say to your brothers, "You are my people," and to your sisters, "You have received mercy." ² "Plead with your mother, plead for she is not my wife, and I am not her husband— that she put away her whoring from her face, and her adultery from between her breasts; ³ lest I strip her naked and make her as in the day she was born, and make her like a wilderness, and make her like a parched land, and kill her with thirst. ⁴ Upon her children also I will have no mercy, because they are children of whoredom. ⁵ For their mother has played the whore; she who conceived them has acted shamefully. For she said, 'I will go after my lovers, who give me my bread and my water, my wool and my flax, my oil and my drink.' ⁶ Therefore I will hedge up her[d] way with thorns, and I will build a wall against her, so that she cannot find her paths. ⁷ She shall pursue her lovers but not overtake them, and she shall seek them but shall not find them. Then she shall say, 'I will go and return to my first husband, for it was better for me then than now.' ⁸ And she did not know that it was I who gave her the grain, the wine, and the oil, and who lavished on her silver and gold, which they used for Baal. ⁹ Therefore I will take back my grain in its time, and my wine in its season, and I will take away my wool and my flax, which were to cover her nakedness. ¹⁰ Now I will uncover her lewdness in the sight of her lovers, and no one shall rescue her out of my hand. ¹¹ And I will put an end to all her mirth, her feasts, her new moons, her Sabbaths, and all her appointed feasts. ¹² And I will lay waste her vines and her fig trees, of which she said, These are my wages, which my lovers have given me.' I will make them a forest, and the beasts of the field shall devour them. ¹³ And I will punish her for the feast days of the Baals when she burned offerings to them and adorned herself with her ring and jewelry, and went after her lovers and forgot me, declares the LORD.

One Sunday after church, my wife and I travelled to have dinner with a fellow ministerial pal and his family. In the course of that visit, we observed that his household had a precise method of eating their supper. They ensured that all attendees at the table completed their meals before desserts were introduced. The reason for this regulation was that he had two young sons: a six year old and a four year old. It was imperative that the youngest (especially) finished his dinner before a dessert was served. If not, he would lose focus of eating his dinner the very moment he spotted the dessert. In essence, he would forsake and depart from his dinner at the sheer sighting of anything sweet—he would leave never to return. In the verses under examination, the act of forsaking also takes place. It is not the forsaking of a thing, but of a person. God is deserted by His people, and, as a result, there will be dire consequences.

The text begins (vs. 1) **"Say to your brothers, 'You are my people," and to your sisters, 'You have received mercy'."** This first verse fits more with the end of chapter 1 than the beginning of chapter 2. It must be recognized that ancient manuscripts (hand-written copies) of biblical writings did not include chapter and verse designations. Therefore, as far as writing is concerned, these were all one large continuously flowing script without any separation of sections. Nothing is violated, however, by attaching these words to chapter 2 of Hosea. Verse 1 is a reiteration of the great reversal mentioned in chapter 1. Those who were not God's people would become God's people, and those who did not receive mercy will eventually encounter it.

This serves as an encouraging reminder that in life—even in the midst of darkness—there is always hope. Ecclesiastes 9:4 reminds us *"But he who is joined with all the living has hope, for a living dog is better than a dead lion."* Nonetheless, all semblances of hope will evaporate as the journey into the second chapter begins.

Humiliation

Hosea urges Israel to (vs. 2) **"plead with your mother, plead—for she is not my wife and I am not her husband."** The marriage relationship between Hosea and Gomer from the previous chapter is still in view. "Plead" here conveys the idea of "to strive" or "to grapple" or "to wrestle with". Hosea demands that his children take hold of their mother to make her come to her senses.

"For she is not my wife and I am not her husband" does not intend to suggest that Hosea had officially divorced his wife. As a prophet, Hosea presumably had strong convictions about divorce and knew that it was not what God wanted for his life or this union that He joined together. Instead, Hosea was implying that the reality of the relationship was not present. Gomer had been so grossly unfaithful to her husband that he no longer felt married. Yet, Hosea and Gomer's marriage was an illustration of a much larger predicament. Their union was a sketch of God's marriage to the nation of Israel.

The verse continues **"that she put away her whoring from her face"** in order to highlight that Gomer's adulterous escapades were always in front of her as a priority, and she never ceased to entertain them. Instead, she ought to shove such atrocities out of her view and life. **"And her adultery from between her breasts"** paints the picture of her infidelity being coddled closely to her like something precious—the same way a mother coddles her infant.

Let us not be excessively critical of Gomer because this is precisely the way we sometimes treat sin. It's held squarely in front of our faces for entertainment or we hold it close to our chest like a precious or dear keepsake. Sin and iniquity should be treated like a rattlesnake instead of like a teddy bear. Christians must take drastic measures to avoid the infectious—and often deadly—disease of sin.

This must be done (vs. **3**) **"lest I strip her naked and make her as in the day she was born."** Full-fledge humiliation comes into view. Utterly embarrassing is the deed of having one's clothes completely seized from his/her body. Does this text still have Gomer in view? I would argue that it does not. I support this position because the rest of the verse says **"and make her like a wilderness, and make her like a parched land, and kill her with thirst."** The mention of land here probably suggests that He has the Northern Kingdom of Israel in His sights. "Wilderness" and "parched land" paint the picture of a desert where little, if anything, flourishes. Many things perish in the desert, but few things grow there.

Yet, for those who have been saved by God's grace and eventually end up wandering away from Him, the only thing that remains is a spiritual desert. There will be no spiritual water or food—only deterioration and death. What a fearful thing it is to forsake the Lord.

Desperation

It is learned from the prophet that (vs. **4)** **"Upon her children also I will have no mercy, because they are children of whoredom."** If Gomer represents the nation of Israel in the passage, then the children must correspondingly represent a group or groups as well. The identity of these "children" can only be determined by investigating chapter 1 afresh. In that chapter, "No Mercy" (Lo-ruhama) and "Not My people" (Lo-ammi) both represented Israel (1:6, 9). Therefore, both Gomer and her children are pictures of Israel. Gomer, the mother, represents Israel in a more holistic, combined sense—the nation as one. The children, however, represent Israel in an individual sense—person by person. Still, they both signify the Northern Kingdom of Israel. Yahweh asserts firmly that the children who are the individual Israelites will not have the arm of mercy extended to them. Every single person without exception will feel the blow of this judgement in some way and none will escape.

This happens because (vs. **5) "their mother has played the whore; she who conceived them has acted shamefully."** Israel's marriage with God has been abandoned, and she has passionately pursued numerous false gods of various forms and names. Included in this list are several of the Baals and Ashteroth.

Neither is it an impossibility for followers of Christ to be guilty of worshipping false gods. It can be a possession. It can be progress in life. Maybe it's intelligence or degrees and accomplishments. Almost anything is capable of becoming an idol in our lives. What's noticeable is that, usually, before a Christian begins to stray, they are guilty of some aspect of whoredom. There is something or someone they are in love with more than God Himself.

"For she said, 'I will go after my lovers, who give me my bread and my water, my wool and my flax, my oil and my drink' " is the continuation. Such lovers are obviously the false deities that Israel is worshipping and she is desperately pursuing material possessions. Bread, water, wool, flax, oil, and drink all have one thing in common. These objects are material goods that provide some aspect of satisfaction for the human life.

What is your primary source of satisfaction? Is it bread? Is it water? Is it wool or some other modern variation of these items? Is your primary satisfaction found in the fleeting pleasures of this life? Every follower of Jesus must find primary satisfaction in their own personal relationship with Him. Furthermore, this spiritual relationship can only be obtained by being converted from within and trusting completely in the finished work of Jesus Christ on Calvary's cross for salvation.

Frustration

The Lord promises that (vs. 6) **"Therefore I will hedge up her way with thorns."** He envisioned Israel strolling down a narrow pathway which is flanked on both sides with thorns as its hedge. While Israel travels through, there is constant pain, discomfort, pricks, cuts, and bruises. The types of thorns located in Israel were thick and long and unlike the thorns in most other localities across the globe. This journey for Israel will be filled with excruciating pain.

He also threatens to **"build a wall against her, so that she cannot find her paths."** After walking down a thorny way, Israel comes to a wall that she cannot overcome. In addition to pain, there are obstacles. Tragically, not only is the nation unaware of where her destination is, she is unaware of how to arrive there.

Perhaps you as a reader are presently contending with the same situation. You identify well with a pathway of thorns. You constantly peer back over your shoulder with regret after regret. Know that God always yearns to receive those who repent; and the door to forgiveness, for the believer, will never shut.

Note that (vs. 7) **"she shall pursue her lovers but not overtake them, and she shall seek them but shall not find them."** Much energy and effort will be exerted in chasing worthless idols, but God will hinder success. Israel, like Tom, will never catch Jerry. Her strivings will be an indiscriminate waste of time.

Because of this **"Then she will say, 'I will go and return to my first husband, for it was better for me then than now'."** The language used is similar to that of the prodigal son in Luke's gospel who, leaving home, lived a fast and wild life (Luke 15:11-32). After falling on hard times, he realized what he possessed at home was a thousand times better than what he was chasing in the world.

Are you, dear friend, a prodigal son or daughter who needs to return to the Father? Are you a Jew who needs to be reconciled to your first husband? Such important matters should not be postponed to future possibilities. Tomorrow is promised to no man. The Father awaits even now with open arms.

Delusion

Verse 8 further explains **"and she did not know that it was I who gave her the grain, the wine, and the oil, and who lavished on her silver and gold, which they used for Baal."** Every—single—blessing that the Northern Kingdom experienced was a gift to her from God—without exception. This included the grain, the wine, the oil, the silver, the gold and everything between.

Similarly, every single blessing that we as human beings possess has been laid at our feet by the Almighty Father— without exception. James 1:17 submits that *"Every good gift and every perfect gift is from above, coming down from the Father of lights with whom there is no variation or shadow due to change."* Who, therefore, receives the praise for that which you possess? Is it yourself? Is it your job? Is it your government? Ultimate glory always belongs to God for His relentless showers of blessing.

On the other hand, the consequences of not giving God the glory for these showers is that (vs. 9) **"I will take back my grain in its time, and my wine in its season, and I will take away my wool and my flax, which were to cover her nakedness."** The exact benefits that God bestowed to His people, He will revoke. Grain, wine, wool, and flax will be retracted from their nation's table.

Equally, the same advantages that have been transferred to us can be rescinded. What a terrible gaffe it is to be deluded in knowing from whom all blessings truly flow.

Dejection

Verse 10 threatens that **"Now I will uncover her lewdness in the sight of her lovers."** This warning mirrors the "stripping naked" terminology from earlier in the passage (vs. 3). Shame will be made evident in the presence of other heathen nations and **"no one shall rescue her out of my hand."** Israel is in a frightening predicament. Most often in Scripture, God is coming to Israel's rescue and victoriously saving the day. Unfortunately, the text suggests that, on this occasion, God is whom Israel will need to be rescued from—and no other being has even the slightest capability of rescuing from God's unstoppable hand. The moral of the story is difficult to overlook. Indeed, God and His attributes must be taken seriously and as Hebrews 10:31 exclaims *"It is a fearful thing to fall into the hands of the living God."* With Israel now falling into those same hands, things are about to get ugly.

"And I will put an end to all her mirth, her feasts, her new moons, her Sabbaths, and all her appointed feasts." (vs. 11) All Jewish seasons of rest and joyfulness will come to a screeching halt. As a modern rendition, this would be the equivalent of cancelling Christmas, Easter, summer and national holidays, along with Saturdays and Sundays. All opportunities of enjoyment and festivities have vanished into thin air.

Depression

It continues (vs. 12) **"And I will lay waste her vines and her fig trees, of which she said, 'These are my wages which my lovers have given me'."** Vegetation and produce of the land will be utterly obliterated. Even the gift received from her lovers for her adultery will be destroyed. In addition, **"I will make them a forest, and the beasts of the field shall devour them."** No stone is left unturned and everything is demolished. Israel is left with absolutely nothing. It should never be doubted that God can perform the same acts today with professed believers who do not live according to their calling and stray off into oblivion forsaking the Lord.

Finally, it is prophesied (vs. 13) **"And I will punish her for the feast days of the Baals when she burned offerings to them and adorned herself with her ring and jewelry, and went after her lovers and forgot me declares the LORD."** The Northern Kingdom proudly enjoyed the sin and satisfaction of heathen nations by indulging themselves in reprehensible Baal worship and sacrifice. All that has happened to them thus far can be summarized into one word—punishment—and they are at the cliff edge of destruction.

Have you fallen on hard times? God permits such difficulties in the lives of Christians for two reasons only. Testing times can be either a trial or a thorn. A trial serves as a means for God to strengthen, complete, and conform us into the image of His Son, Jesus (James 1:2-4). However, a thorn serves to prick us with pain in the midst of sin and transgression so that we can return to Him (1 Corinthians 7:27-31). The latter was the reason for Israel's difficulty and we must painstakingly examine whether our season of difficulty is a trial or a thorn.

> Discuss

1. List four consequences Israel faced for forsaking God.

2. In verse 8, what might grain, wine, wool, and flax correspond with in today's world?

3. Is having to be rescued from God an intimidating thought to you? Why or why not?

4. Discuss trials from James 1:2-4. Discuss thorns from 1 Corinthians 7:27-31.

5. Give examples of trials you have faced in your lifetime. Give examples of thorns you have faced in your lifetime.

3

DIVINE REVERSAL

2:14-23

¹⁴"Therefore, behold, I will allure her and bring her into the wilderness and speak tenderly to her. ¹⁵And there I will give her her vineyards and make the Valley of Achor a door of hope. And there she shall answer as in the days of her youth, as at the time when she came out of the land of Egypt. ¹⁶"And in that day, declares the LORD, you will call me 'My Husband,' and no longer will you call me 'My Baal.' ¹⁷For I will remove the names of the Baals from her mouth, and they shall be remembered by name no more. ¹⁸And I will make for them a covenant on that day with the beasts of the field, the birds of the heavens, and the creeping things of the ground. And I will abolish the bow, the sword, and war from the land, and I will make you lie down in safety. ¹⁹And I will betroth you to me forever. I will betroth you to me in righteousness and in justice, in steadfast love and in mercy. ²⁰I will betroth you to me in faithfulness. And you shall know the LORD. ²¹"And in that day I will answer, declares the LORD I will answer the heavens, and they shall answer the earth,²² and the earth shall answer the grain, the wine, and the oil, and they shall answer Jezreel, ²³ and I will sow her for myself in the land. And I will have mercy on No Mercy, and I will say to Not My People, 'You are my people'; and he shall say, 'You are my God.'"

Recently, I encountered someone who had a peculiar dilemma with his car. The issue was not with the typical essential parts of the vehicle like the engine, battery, or tires. Instead, the problem was with the gearbox. The car could no longer be put in reverse. Certainly, that is not a desirable problem to have because the time inevitably comes when the automobile absolutely must be put in reverse in order to go the opposite direction. In this section of Hosea's prophecy, Israel has been driving in the wrong direction for an extensive period of time. Yet, God promises to—one day—put them in reverse and send them in the right direction.

An Effective Reversal

God firstly says through His prophet (vs. 14) **"Therefore, behold, I will allure her."** Israel, rather than Judah is still the intended audience of God's speech. "Allure" means to persuade or influence. Its roots are grounded in a word in the Hebrew which means "open". It bears the notion of having an open mind and heart that can be easily persuaded by another. In addition, He promises to **"bring her into the wilderness."** Why would He want to do such a thing? At face value it seems like punishment, judgement, and retribution. The mention of wilderness in this instance, however, is meant to be a positive notion rather than a negative one. A brief survey of Israel's history brings to memory that the wilderness is the exact location where Moses mediated God's covenant to Israel. It is also where God sustained Israel by His mighty hand before ushering them into the Promised Land. Hence, the use of the term "wilderness" here is intended to provoke nostalgia, for the Jews to remember the time when the nation had been birthed. The marriage between God and Israel was fresh, new, and vibrant in that early season of their history.

The Lord also promises to **"speak tenderly to her."** In the Hebrew, it reads literally "speak to her heart". God is alluring Israel and He will be successful because He will stir her from within. Effectual calling, a doctrine found heavily in the New Testament, is being highlighted here. Effectual calling refers to God personally working in someone's heart so that they ultimately respond to His message i.e. the Gospel. Several examples of this principle can be found in Scripture. The clearest one concerns what happened to Lydia during one of Paul's missionary journeys.

Acts 16:14-15.

> [14] *One who heard us was a woman named Lydia, from the city of Thyatira, a seller of purple goods, who was a worshiper of God. The Lord opened her heart to pay attention to what was said by Paul.* [15] *And after she was baptized, and her household as well, she urged us, saying, "If you have judged me to be faithful to the Lord, come to my house and stay."*

God opened Lydia's heart in the book of Acts. He is going to speak to the heart of the Jews in the current text, and He must also speak to any human's heart before he can come to believe on Jesus Christ. Jesus echoes the same sentiment in John 6:44a saying *"No one can come to Me unless the Father who sent Me draws him."* This is the essence of the effectual call of God. He must awaken spiritually dead sinners before they can believe on Him. As physically dead men have never lived unless someone intervened, so spiritually dead men can never live unless someone intervenes (Ephesians 2: 1,4-5). What can a dead man do? Nothing but stink!

Verse **15** continues **"And there I will give her vineyards."** Vineyards are fields with plants of high, profitable quality including various kinds of grapes and anything else that grows on a vine. Take note of the distinct contrast to what he has promised a few verses earlier in the chapter. In verse 12 it is read, "And I will lay waste her vines and her fig trees of which she said, 'These are my wages which my lovers have given me.' I will make them a forest and the beasts of the field shall devour them." Previously, God was destroying their vines and vineyards, but here, He is providing vines and vineyards. Filling the cup some more, He promises to **"make the Valley of Achor a door of hope."** The epithet "Achor" means trouble. Thus, the valley of Achor is "the valley of trouble". What is the valley of Achor? Its initial mention is in Joshua 7:24. Israel (united as one) was victorious in battles when it first entered the Promised Land. At the town of Ai, however, they were defeated for the first time, and God informed Joshua that they lost the battle because someone had stolen forbidden items. Through a series of events, it was discovered that a man named Achan was guilty of the theft. Disobedience led he and his family to be stoned to death in this same valley. Unsurprisingly, the Valley of Achor is a metaphor for the valley of trouble because of the distress that Achan brought upon Israel. In spite of its history, this valley will be converted into something different. The present verse uncovers that it will become instead a door of hope.

From this, it can be clearly gleaned that, with God, hope is never out of reach. No "lost cause" exists in His realm. No situation is too hard for God to turn around and there is no heart too hardened for the Lord to transform. In Matthew 19:26, Jesus maintained that "With man this is impossible but with God all things are possible." Perhaps you are in a valley of trouble and see no way through it. You cannot perceive any possible solution to the problem. Take comfort in the fact that with God, the reality of a divine reversal is never out of reach. The possibility of a drastic turnaround is as achievable with God as your next breath of air. The same verse continues **"And there she shall answer as in the days of her youth, as at the time when she came out of the land of Egypt."** Feelings of nostalgia still flood

God's mind as He recalls the delightful times in the past when Israel was a much younger nation. He remembers how excited and obedient they were as they trusted Him walking through the Red Sea on dry ground.

Is it possible that as you assess your past years as a Christian, you sense you were more excited, obedient, and trusting then than you are currently? If that's your situation, God wants you back where you once were. He wants continuous progression in your relationship with Him—a persistent vibrancy. Forward ever. Backward never.

A Religious Reversal

Hosea continues in verse **16 "And in that day, declares the LORD, you will call me 'My Husband'."** God revisits and reminds them of the initial relationship He intended to have with the nation of Israel from its inception. Theoretically speaking, Israel, being God's chosen people, were like a bride to Him and He was her groom. Furthermore, He continues the analogy from the first chapter where Hosea and Gomer's marriage was a representation of God's marriage to Israel. The present text makes clear that there is yet a coming season when Israel will return to acknowledging God as her husband. Intimacy and fellowship will be renewed once again. **"And no longer will you call me 'My Baal'."** Baal was the primary god/idol worshipped by the Jews during this period. They had set the true God, Jehovah, on the back burner and, thereby placed Baal, an idol, and false deity to the front of the stove. Yet, God has in His plans a time when that will no longer be the case. Verse **17** states **"For I will remove the names of the Baals from her mouth."** Notice that "the Baals" is plural. What's the purpose? The Jews did not only worship one Baal statue, they were ensnared by all kinds and forms of Baals. Such included Baal-Peor and Baal-Zebub. Jehovah was pushed far into the background. It concludes **"they shall be remembered by name no more."** These false deities will be erased even from the very memory of the Jews. They will be deleted like emails from a computer or pictures from a cellphone. Talk about change! Talk about a reversal!

However, what must not be overlooked is that there is no mention of the Jews repenting in this chapter. That is astounding! The second chapter moves directly from punishment to blessing and renewal without crossing the river of repentance. Can it be assumed that these Jews will repent? Yes, I think it is right to assume so, because God will not bless iniquity. But why will these Jews repent? It is through

God activating repentance within them. It is God who will transform their hearts. It is God who will turn them around. Other portions of Scripture support this.

2 Timothy 2:24-26 declares *"²⁴ And the Lord's servant must not be quarrelsome but kind to everyone, able to teach, patiently enduring evil, ²⁵ correcting his opponents with gentleness. God may perhaps grant them repentance leading to a knowledge of the truth, ²⁶ and they may come to their senses and escape from the snare of the devil, after being captured by him to do his will."*

From this passage, it must be realized that God must grant sinners repentance, implying that they cannot merely do it themselves. Repentance is God-dependent. Also, take note of how much the phrase "I will" is used in these verses. It screams not "you will", but "I will". The phrase is used 14 times in a short space of verses. With an exclamation point, this stamps that it is God who does this transformative work. To be clear, this biblical truth does not endorse a fatalist, "do-nothing" mindset where the believer's only recourse is to raise his hands to the sky and shout "even so come Lord Jesus". The Gospel must be faithfully and fervently proclaimed from shore to shore until His return because it is the divinely-ordained means whereby He will rescue rotten rebels.

What God's people cannot do is forecast who will or won't genuinely respond to the Gospel—that is totally up to the sovereign will of God (Romans 9:14-18). The Christian's obligation is to dispense the Gospel to the ears of men. Only God can transport that message from men's ears to men's hearts. Born-again saints should be bursting at the seams with thankful humility because it is only through God's initiative that we possess a changed heart. He has saved us and not us ourselves. Salvation is all of grace—this is the grace that is truly amazing.

A Circumstantial Reversal

The text records in verse **18 "And I will make for them a covenant on that day with the beasts of the field, the birds of the heavens, and the creeping things of the ground."** The Lord intends to make an oath of peace with the animal kingdom. Thus, it appears that neither the beasts of the field, the birds of the heavens, or the creeping things on the ground will endanger anyone anymore. Diverse opinions exists among Bible scholars concerning what period this verse refers to and its implications for end-times eschatology. I personally believe these events will be enacted during the one thousand year Millennial Reign of Christ. Even the animal kingdom will experience an absence of treachery. Poisonous snakes and spiders will not be a source of fear during that period. People will no longer fear lions, tigers, and bears because they will be at complete peace with humankind. Isaiah 11:6-9 further expands on this idea.

> [6]*The wolf shall dwell with the lamb, and the leopard shall lie down with the young goat, and the calf and the lion and the fattened calf together; and a little child shall lead them.* [7]*The cow and the bear shall graze; their young shall lie down together; and the lion shall eat straw like the ox.* [8] *The nursing child shall play over the hole of the cobra, and the weaned child shall put his hand on the adder's den.* [9] *They shall not hurt or destroy in all my holy mountain; for the earth shall be full of the knowledge of the Lord as the waters cover the sea.*

The thought of a child leading a lion is dumbfounding. All will be brought back into order as it was in the Garden of Eden where man exercised complete dominion over the animal kingdom.

Added to that is the promise that **"I will abolish the bow, the sword, and war from the land, and I will make you lie down in safety."** Peace will prevail among humanity as well. All wars, battles, and fighting will cease and the entire globe will dwell secure and safe. Such a state is hard to envision. Only God can bring such promises to fruition. Despite the dark, dreary days we experience in this world, God has the power to set things right at the snap of His fingers. Nothing is too hard for Him.

A Heart Reversal

He persists in announcing that (vs. 19) **"I will betroth you to me forever."** Marriage terminology makes its way back to the front of the pack. Although "betroth" describes the Jewish engagement period, it must not be assumed that Jewish engagement is identical to the engagement period of most Western societies. For the Jews, betrothal was nothing short of sacred. So sacred was the custom that by all intents and purposes those betrothed were essentially considered to already be married to one another. This is the precise reason why Joseph considered "divorcing" Mary even though he was only betrothed (engaged) to her (Matthew 1:9). Only microscopic differences existed between betrothal and marriage.

Therefore, God is asserting that He will unite Himself with these individuals and become one with them.

When an individual believes on the Lord Jesus Christ alone for salvation, this is precisely what happens. Spiritually speaking, a new creation is born. The Christian is placed in Christ (positionally) and Christ is placed in the Christian (i.e. the Holy Spirit). Have you been united with the Lord? Have you received the amazing grace He offers?

Furthermore, Hosea unveils that **"I will betroth you to me in righteousness and in justice, in steadfast love and in mercy."** Righteousness, justice, steadfast love, and mercy are the qualities that God brings to the marriage as well as what He implants into His people. He will not only be these characteristics, but will implant these characteristics so that His redeemed will never again be at enmity with Him.

Verse **20 "I will betroth you to me in faithfulness."** Yahweh will remain faithful to this marriage even when His bride is not faithful. In biblical salvation, someone is not only holding onto God, God is holding onto the individual (John 10:27-29). Salvation is eternally secure because the God who saves is eternally faithful, and He never "unsaves" those He saves or "unloves" those He loves. He also promises that **"you shall know the Lord."** This is a concise summary of these two verses and describes a true believer. A genuinely converted Christian "knows the Lord". Jeremiah 31:33-34 echoes these sentiments when foretelling the arrival of the New Covenant.

> *[33] For this is the covenant that I will make with the house of Israel after those days, declares the Lord: I will put my law within them, and I will write it on their hearts. And I will be their God, and they shall be my people. [34] And no longer shall each one teach his neighbor and each his brother, saying, 'Know the Lord,' for they shall all know me, from the least of them to the greatest, declares the Lord. For I will forgive their iniquity, and I will remember their sin no more."*

God promised that the advent of the New Covenant would enable people to know the Lord personally and intimately. All regenerate believers are shareholders in this covenant.

A Prosperous Reversal

Hosea's prophecy continues (vs. 21 and 22) **"And in that day I will answer, declares the LORD, I will answer the heavens, and they shall answer the earth, and the earth shall answer the grain, the wine, and the oil, and they shall answer Jezreel."** Now, a chain reaction is performed. Firstly, God answers—meaning He speaks. His speech is toward the "heavens" or skies initially. Then, the "heavens" speak to the earth. Hence, rain is showering the land. When the land receives rain, it answers the grain, wine and oil which all need soil and rain in order to grow.

A Hopeful Reversal

He further cries aloud (vs. 23) **"And I will sow her for myself in the land. And I will have mercy on No Mercy, and I will say to Not My People, 'You are my people': and he shall say, 'You are my God'."** "No Mercy" and "Not My People" are the fruit of Gomer's womb which, in the first chapter symbolized the individual Israelites.

Nevertheless, when we look at all of Scripture it is abundantly clear that God has made this applicable beyond the nation of Israel. He is extending mercy and calling a people to Himself all over the globe. It is incumbent upon every individual to examine himself and ensure that they personally have received His mercy to become a child of God.

> Discuss

1. In Hosea, Israel, God's nation, is frequently compared to being God's bride. Are there New Testament examples of the church regarding the same? If so, give examples.

2. List all 14 "I wills" of this passage.

3. What are your thoughts on Isaiah 11:6-9?

4. Besides Jeremiah 31:33-34, where else is the new covenant hinted at in the Old Testament?

5. Discuss John 10:27-29 in relation to the believer's eternal security.

4

AMAZING LOVE
3:1-5

¹And the LORD said to me, "Go again, love a woman who is loved by another man and is an adulteress, even as the LORD loves the children of Israel, though they turn to other gods and love cakes of raisins." ² So I bought her for fifteen shekels of silver and a homer and a lethech of barley. ³ And I said to her, "You must dwell as mine for many days. You shall not play the whore, or belong to another man; so will I also be to you." ⁴ For the children of Israel shall dwell many days without king or prince, without sacrifice or pillar, without ephod or household gods. ⁵ Afterward the children of Israel shall return and seek the LORD their God, and David their king, and they shall come in fear to the LORD and to his goodness in the latter days.

Two young, engaged lovers were strolling through Phoenix Park in Dublin, Ireland one evening holding hands. Anticipating being married in only two short months, they only looked at one another in blushing glances and then looked down at the green grass at intervals as they went along swinging their arms joyously. After about three minutes of silence, the young lady asked her fiancé,

"Do you love me?"

The lad shot back almost immediately, "Yes, dear; of course, I love you!"

Enraptured by his response, she then asked,

"Would you die for me?"

He then retorted as quickly as he did the first time, "No, I wouldn't!"

He said, "My love is an undying love!"

When we observe the text at hand, we see the kind of love that God has for His people Israel. The most suitable way to describe that love is with the word "undying". God's love for His people is constant and unceasing.

A Resilient Love

The first unit launches with (vs. 1) **"and the Lord said to me."** God not only spoke through Hosea, God spoke to Hosea. God not only called Hosea's audience to submission; He called Hosea to obedience as well. It is a grave act of hypocrisy to urge someone to follow God's demands, when you are not falling in line yourself. Those who serve as God's mouthpieces today are not exempt from obedience. Pastors, preachers, and ministers of God's Word must practice what they proclaim. Hosea set the example by being obedient in his own life first. Paul travels down the same lane of thought when he said to the Roman believers in Romans 2:21-22,

> ^{21} you then who teach others, do you not teach yourself? While you preach against stealing, do you steal? ^{22} You who say that one must not commit adultery, do you commit adultery? You who abhor idols, do you rob temples?

Christians must always be cautious of holding others to standards that they themselves don't keep. Hosea's obedience was on par or—perhaps even more radical—than the very conformance God was requiring of Israel at the time. The next phrase is **"go again."** Yahweh requires for his manservant to return, continue, persist and persevere because he was to **"love a woman."** The word "love" in the Old Testament has its roots in the idea of breathing after or longing after something. This is the difficult feat Hosea must accomplish. Although she is not named, the reference to "a woman" here must be Gomer, his wife. All the ensuing specifics of the chapter make it recognizable that Gomer is the woman identified in the chapter. Thus, Hosea is directed to exercise affection for his wife. Under normal conditions this should be an effortless endeavor, but Hosea is not under typical circumstances because she is one **"who is loved by another man and is an adulteress."** God wants Hosea to passionately love Gomer although she is now loved by another man who is not her husband. She has returned to her unfaithfulness. She has resumed her wickedness. To be clear, her infidelity was not only emotional, it was physical as well. The text calls her an adulteress meaning she was sexually entangled with this man. Still, from God's perspective, it is imperative that Hosea takes her back and loves her.

God's view of love stands in direct contrast to that of the world's view. The world's idea of love is built solely upon the underpinning of fleeting emotional stirrings; it is built upon how an individual feels from day to day. God's concept of love is erected upon commitment and promise; it is constant and unchanging throughout the varying circumstances of life. The world's idea of love is "up and down" while God's idea is one straight, continuous line without fluctuations.

A prime reason many marriages fail today, even in the church, is because the typical believer is entrenched in the world's concept of love rather than in God's. When Christians do this, they are exchanging diamonds for dirt. What are your personal thoughts on love? Are they God-based or are they world-based? Are they Bible-based or are they Hollywood-based?

Why should Hosea love Gomer this way if she is ill-deserving of such? It is because this kind of love accurately represents the love of God. The writer adds **"even as the Lord loves the children of Israel."** Hosea's persistent, unfailing love was to represent God's love for His nation. This is how much He breathed after them and longed for them. This is the extent to which He desired them. His covenant people Israel were the apple of His eye, and He longed for them in spite of their betrayal.

He adores His new covenant people (Christians) who have been transformed by the Spirit of God similarly. His love is just as unfailing and constant. His love is just as persistent. Contrary to popular belief, Christians are not faultless individuals. We fail and embarrass ourselves and are often unfaithful. Nevertheless, even though we are often unfaithful, God never is. Furthermore, not only is He never unfaithful, He never falls out of love with His people. Paul makes this undoubtedly clear in Romans 8:31-39. Mark how often the term "love" is used.

> [31] *What then shall we say to these things? If God is for us, who can be against us?* [32] *He who did not spare his own Son but gave him up for us all, how will he not also with him graciously give us all things?* [33] *Who shall bring any charge against God's elect? It is God who justifies.* [34] *Who is to condemn? Christ Jesus is the one who died—more than that, who was raised—who is at the right hand of God, who indeed is interceding for us.* [35] *Who shall separate us from the love of Christ? Shall tribulation,*

> or distress, or persecution, or famine, or nakedness, or danger, or sword? ³⁶ As it is written, "For your sake we are being killed all the day long; we are regarded as sheep to be slaughtered." ³⁷ No, in all these things we are more than conquerors through him who loved us. ³⁸ For I am sure that neither death nor life, nor angels nor rulers, nor things present nor things to come, nor powers, ³⁹ nor height nor depth, nor anything else in all creation, will be able to separate us from the love of God in Christ Jesus our Lord.

God doesn't have an "in love out-of-love" relationship with His children and it is impossible for a true child of God to ever be cast off by Him, no matter how many seasons of disloyalty he tumbles into. The Lord's saints are eternally secure and their salvation can never be lost. Oh the incomprehensible and inexplicable love of our God!

Moreover, the verse continues **"though they turn to other gods."** The Northern Kingdom was guilty of embracing false deities. Observing the Decalogue, this was a violation of the first commandment. *"You shall have no other gods before me"* is its cry (Exodus 20:3). Added to that, Yahweh fully acknowledges that He is a God who is jealous. Exodus 34:14 affirms *"for you shall worship no other God, for the Lord, whose name is jealous, is a jealous God."* Their present condition was no small matter. The verse also informs that Israel **"loves cakes of raisins."** This serves as additional proof of their infidelity to the Lord. Although little is revealed in Scripture about raisin cakes, the context of Hosea suggests that they were used in idolatrous rituals and may have been utilized as offerings to Baal (Isaiah 16:7).

A Redeeming Love

In obedience, the prophet confirms (vs. **2**) **"so I bought her."** The reason Gomer needed to be purchased is not made clear in the biblical text. Some commentators believe she owed a debt. Others think she fell on hard times and became a slave. Still, others are convinced this was the bargaining cost to get her out of the arms of her adulterous lover having already purchased her services. Since the answer is not revealed in Scripture, the reason for her procurement should be deemed insignificant. She was bought **"for fifteen shekels of silver and a homer and a lethech of barley."** Hosea needed a combination of both silver and barley to purchase his wife. A homer was a large measure of grain in Old Testament times, but a lethech was smaller than a homer. Interestingly, Exodus 21:32 implies that the worth of a slave was around 30 shekels of silver: *"If the ox gores a slave, male or female, the owner shall give to their master thirty shekels of silver and the ox shall be stoned."*

It is supposed by some that a homer and a lethech of barley was worth about 15 shekels of silver in totality, which could be joined with the additional 15 shekels of silver Hosea already had in his possession. Altogether, this would amount to the price of a slave which may have been Gomer's current status. Whatever the situation, Hosea was obligated to wage a fee in order to retrieve his spouse again.

The Lord Jesus did the same to purchase His bride, the church. Salvation was not without cost. Forgiveness was not free. Redemption demanded an unfathomable price. The Saviour did not pay in terms of silver and gold, though. Rather, He paid with something infinitely more precious— His own physical blood.

1 Peter 1:18-19 states,

> [18] *knowing that you were ransomed from the futile ways inherited from your forefathers, not with perishable things such as silver or gold,* [19] *but with the precious blood of Christ, like that of a lamb without blemish or spot.*

Only Jesus' blood was satisfactory to appease the wrath of God that was invoked by the iniquity of wayward disobedient sinners like you and I. Have you been bought with His blood? If you have indeed taken hold of the mercy that He offers through His sacrificial work at Golgotha's Hill, then you have been bought back just as Gomer was. Conversely, if you have yet to grasp that lifeline of mercy, then you are still in the arms of adulterous lovers.

In verse 3 the communication continues with **"and I said to her, 'you must dwell as mine for many days'."** Gomer must faithfully live with Hosea for an unspecified time span in which she will refuse to partake in any of the activities that previously devastated her marriage. No more harlotry. No more whoredom. No more unfaithfulness. Hosea demands this of her. Take note of the small word "mine". It indicates possession and that she is Hosea's lover and no one else's.

People would do well to comprehend this when they commit to marriage. When you enter a matrimonial union, you are pledging to become someone else's possession—a prized possession hopefully— but nevertheless a possession. Your body, mind, and heart must belong to no one else. Such is God's ancient standard and any attitude other than this opens the door to the potential of adultery. Gomer was deficient of such conviction when she first married Hosea so it is no surprise that she ended up in this dilemma. Then Hosea urges **"you shall not play the whore or belong to another man."** The expectation, requirement, and standard was for her to be unquestionably loyal to her mate moving forward. Infidelity was to be flung out the window; unfaithfulness was to be guided down the shredder. No more would it be tolerable. Since Gomer is typology for Israel, what is being asserted is that the nation must not press on in spiritual unfaithfulness and idolatry. God demands their faithfulness.

The bride of Christ has an equivalent mandate to exterminate unfaithfulness and annihilate infidelity to her Lord. It is incumbent upon us to repudiate the world's standards and reject evil philosophies. There is necessity to incessantly wrestle with the temptations of the flesh because that is what it means to live as a Christian (Colossians 3:5-10). Christianity is not what the planet's masses want it to be; Christianity is what Holy Scripture declares it to be. Any Christian who embraces values sourced in the world's ungodly influence identifies more with a two-timing whoremonger than a faithfully devoted spouse. Scripture sings the same tune in James 4:4: *"You adulterous people! Do you not know that friendship with the world is enmity with God? Therefore whoever wishes to be a friend of the world makes himself an enemy of God."*

None who have been purchased by Christ should befriend the world's system. That must be relegated to whoremongers and adulterers. How can we identify the world's system? There is an easy litmus test. Any ideology that runs counter to the clear teaching of the Bible is of a worldly, sinful origin.

Hosea promises that **"so will I also be to you."** Essentially, the prophet is saying, "Here is the expectation. You be faithful to me and I will be faithful to you." This is by no means a condition; it serves only as a standard to be upheld. Hosea is not threatening that only if his wife is faithful to him will he return the same allegiance. As Gomer symbolized Israel, so Hosea symbolized God and it is manifestly evident that Hosea was faithful to matrimony even though Gomer was not. In the same vain, God is faithful to His true children, even when they are not faithful to Him. He doesn't cast us off in times of weakness, nor disowns us when we sin. His indwelling Holy Spirit resides within perpetually and His faithfulness remains constant through thick and through thin. Such marvelous truths should only plunge God's elect deeper in love with the magnificent God that we serve.

A Removing Love

The **fourth** verse embarks with **"for the children of Israel shall dwell many days."** The beginning of this verse makes it unmistakable that Gomer represents the Northern Kingdom of Israel. Just as she must dwell for many days, so the children of Israel shall dwell for many days. They will do so **"without king or prince."** "King" is directed to the highest office in the land. "Prince" probably refers to more than just a member of the royal family because its range of meaning can also include those who serve as administrative leaders. Thus, the reigning monarch and his administrative officials will be removed from the nation. The nuance in this phrase is futuristic and points to a time when Israel will be subject to national defeat. No longer will they be self-governing. The script adds **"without sacrifice or pillar."** Lack of sacrifices means that, in the future, Israel will not be routinely functioning. What they will endure for "many days" must be abnormal circumstances since customary acts of worship and devotion will cease. Also, it cannot be ruled out that some of these sacrifices may have been to heathen deities since, presently, Israel was deep in the trenches of idolatry. Pillars were a vital component of Canaanite worship that the Jews were ensnared by for centuries. In several instances in Deuteronomy, God strongly warned against tolerating them. The divine mandate was for the Jews to obliterate these objects when they first occupied the Promised Land.

Deuteronomy 7:5

"But thus shall you deal with them: you shall break down their altars and dash in pieces their pillars and chop down their Asherim and burn their carved images with fire."

Deuteronomy 12:3

"You shall tear down their altars and dash in pieces their pillars and burn their Asherim with fire. You shall chop down the carved images of their gods and destroy their name out of that place. ⁴ You shall not worship the Lord your God in that way."

Deuteronomy 16:22

"And you shall not set up a pillar, which the Lord your God hates."

Unfortunately, by Hosea's generation syncretism (the mixing of different religions) was the order of the day and God detested it. The text furthers with **"without ephod."** The ephod was the plate the Levitical high priest wore on the chest of his priestly robe. Fitted with a number of precious jewels, it housed the Urim and

Thummim within—two stones that gave divine direction (Exodus 28:6-43). Again, this suggests the sacrificial system will not be operational in the future, but the context in which it is set hints at more than this. The ephod had, at times, become an idolatrous hindrance as well. In Judges, Gideon created an ephod of golden earrings that the people worshipped and were led into sin by (Judges 8:27). During the period of the Minor Prophets, they may have been used for some form of divination or magical rights. Added to that are **"household gods"**. These were idols and statues of heathen gods that were cherished within individual homesteads. Both an ephod and household gods are mentioned in Judges 17:5 stating *"And the man Micah had a shrine, and he made an ephod and household gods, and ordained one of his sons, who became his priest."* Unsurprisingly, the sixth verse augments *"in those days there was no King in Israel. Everyone did what was right in his own eyes."*

In Hosea's lifetime, Israel was probably in an identical spiritual state that it was in during the period of the judges. That Israel will be without king or prince, without sacrifice or pillar, without ephod or household gods emphatically underscores one upcoming cataclysmic event—their exile to Assyria. God's penalty upon the head of His people will be their handing over to bondage, for a more than miniscule space of time. As the text informs, they will abide there "many days".

Sin has harmful consequences, even for believers in Christ. We reside in a contemporary climate where many who profess to be born of God seem decreasingly afraid of upsetting Him. Such arrogance does not come from a knowledge of God's holy writings. Even the New Testament proclaims this truth in Hebrews 12:6, *"For the Lord disciplines the one he loves and chastises every son whom he receives."* Iniquity must always be taken seriously— never trivialized and minimalized as in the current culture. Largely today, the only actions that appear to be branded as immoral are those one is sent to prison for committing. Nonetheless, God has not changed and neither has His Word. In the words of Augustine, "wrong is wrong even if everyone is doing it and right is right even if no one is doing it." Just as God's Old Testament people were chastised for their sin, His New Testament people will be penalized for the same.

A Returning Love

Verse **five** begins with **"afterward"**. Obviously the following comes to fruition sometime after the children of Israel have gone into exile under the Assyrian

Empire. Furthermore, call to mind that they were to dwell without their idolatrous paraphernalia for "many days" so this is not a short stint. It continues that **"the children of Israel shall return and seek the Lord their God."** During an approaching season, the Jews will return to a vibrant relationship with Yahweh, seeking and finding Him. Reunited they will be with their first love. The relationship which was once broken will be restored and they will return back to God as Gomer returned to the prophet. But not only will they return to Yahweh, the text says also **"and David their king."** How does this happen since David is not alive? Will he be miraculously resurrected from the grave? The reference to David here is not really about David; it is about the Lord Jesus Christ. Jesus Christ was of David's family lineage through both Joseph and Mary's family tree. Numerous New Testament passages attest to this. A good example is John 7:42, *"Has not the Scripture said that the Christ comes from the offspring of David, and comes from Bethlehem, the village where David was?"*

Hence, long after the actual King David was dead, the Old Testament testified that another David would rise up and be king over Israel. Ezekiel 34: 23-24 says,

> [23] *And I will set up over them one shepherd, my servant David, and he shall feed them: he shall feed them and be their shepherd.* [24] *And I, the Lord, will be their God, and my servant David shall be prince among them. I am the Lord; I have spoken.*

Ezekiel 37: 22, 24

> [22] *And I will make them one nation in the land, on the mountains of Israel. And one king shall be king over them all, and they shall be no longer two nations, and no longer divided into two kingdoms.* [24] *"My servant David shall be king over them, and they shall all have one shepherd. They shall walk in my rules and be careful to obey my statutes.*

While the first King David already laid in his grave as a heap of dust, the Old Testament prophets point to a David who was still yet to come. That David was Jesus of Nazareth.

Over two thousand years ago, the greatest David invaded our world as a Saviour to pay the penalty for sin and secure a people unto Himself. At His coming advent, He will set up His physical kingdom and judge all nations including yours. Have you personally received the final David? Have you submitted to His Kingship? You will never encounter the eternal Kingdom without first giving your allegiance to the King. Before you can have peace in your soul, you must give loyalty to royalty.

Further, it reveals **"they shall come in the fear of the Lord and to His goodness."** The word "fear" here literally means to tremble or be startled. Solemn reverential awe will descend upon them as they begin to worship anew God, the Father and God, the Son. This is quite remarkable since throughout Israel's history the overwhelming majority of its citizens never upheld Jesus Christ as the Messiah or as the David who was to come. What a monumental shift in Israel's religious future! The times described in this verse, which are obviously still to come, will be unlike anything Israel— or the world for that matter—has ever experienced. They will bask in God's goodness and beauty as never before. All of this takes place **"in the latter days"**. The latter days can also be translated as the "last days". These realities will come to fulfilment at the end of time, the return of Jesus Christ, and the consummation of all things. Thus, despite God's people wandering far from Him during Hosea's generation, they will eventually return in the end. All the while, His love remains constant.

> Discuss

1. Give a hypothetical example of hypocrisy in a believer's life.

2. Besides 1 Peter 1:18-19, give two more examples of verses that teach redemption.

3. Why would the absence of a king classify as judgement upon Israel?

4. Not using the verses referenced in this chapter, give biblical proof that supports Jesus Christ as the "second David".

5. Are there any New Testament verses/passages that support the future turning of Israel to Christ? List some.

5

FROM PLEASURE TO PAIN
4:1-10

¹Hear the word of the LORD, O children of Israel, for the LORD has a controversy with the inhabitants of the land. There is no faithfulness or steadfast love, and no knowledge of God in the land; ²there is swearing, lying, murder, stealing, and committing adultery; they break all bounds, and bloodshed follows bloodshed. ³Therefore the land mourns, and all who dwell in it languish, and also the beasts of the field and the birds of the heavens, and even the fish of the sea are taken away. ⁴Yet let no one contend, and let none accuse, for with you is my contention, O priest. ⁵You shall stumble by day; the prophet also shall stumble with you by night; and I will destroy your mother. ⁶My people are destroyed for lack of knowledge; because you have rejected knowledge, I reject you from being a priest to me. And since you have forgotten the law of your God, I also will forget your children. ⁷The more they increased, the more they sinned against me; I will change their glory into shame. ⁸They feed on the sin of my people; they are greedy for their iniquity. ⁹And it shall be like people, like priest; I will punish them for their ways and repay them for their deeds. ¹⁰They shall eat, but not be satisfied; they shall play the whore, but not multiply, because they have forsaken the LORD to cherish...

Growing up in The Bahamas, there was an axiom that was rather prevalent at the time—especially among parents. The adage was this: "If you don't hear, you will feel." What meaning did it convey? It implied that if you, as a child, did not heed and obey the instructions specified to you by your parents, the result would be some form of corporal punishment. Therefore, if you neglected to hear instruction, you would feel pain. This is precisely what is happening to the Northern Kingdom in this chapter, and since they have repetitively rejected the instruction that has been given them, agony will pursue.

A Lack of Godliness

The prophet begins by crying aloud (vs. 1) **"Hear the word of the Lord, O children of Israel."** These words are uttered by Hosea who is nothing more than a mouthpiece for God; Hosea is the waiter, not the cook in the kitchen. Still, his audience is the Northern Kingdom of Israel—the nation at this time being split. The overwhelming majority of Hosea's ministry is spent reprimanding Israel instead of Judah **"for the LORD has a controversy with the inhabitants of the land."** "Controversy" in this verse literally signifies an accusation or a dispute portraying the idea of a courtroom setting where allegations are cast against a defendant. Firstly, **"There is no faithfulness."** Faithfulness, in this instance, communicates "stability", "trustworthiness", or "reliability". In laymen's terms, God does not trust His people to do right and live in a manner that is godly. It then adds **"or steadfast love"**. This quality is a loving kindness or loving favor that the Jews were to express toward their Lord since He and the nation were in covenant union together. Unfortunately, there was **"no knowledge of God in the land."** Commitment to divine instruction and preserving covenant relationship was significantly lacking on Israel's part.

In the stead of these qualities, verse 2 reveals that **"there is swearing."** The act of swearing is speaking an oath in the form of a curse—synonymous with taking the Lord's name in vain—a violation of the third commandment of Exodus 20. In addition, there was **"lying."** Lying is any form of deception or failure to remain truthful and honest—a violation of the ninth commandment. Present as well was **"murder"**, the unsanctioned taking of a human life; the sixth commandment is violated when murder takes place. Furthermore, much **"stealing"** took place in Israel. Stealing is unlawfully taking away that which rightfully belongs to another. This violates the eighth commandment. Then, there was **"committing adultery"**, the act of having sexual relations with anyone who is not one's spouse which breaks the seventh commandment. Israel was completely submerged in the oceans of rebellion and vice. How could they deteriorate into such a horrific state of affairs? As verse 1 suggests, there was no faithfulness to God, love for God, or knowledge of God in the land.

Thus, all followers of Christ must be careful to cultivate faithfulness to God, love for God, and the knowledge of God in their lives. If not, we will find ourselves in the same position and committing the identical sins of Israel. This is a classic cause and effect equation; because godliness was lacking, ungodliness inescapably takes its place. The soil of personal godliness must be repeatedly and unceasingly tilled in our lives to not give advantage to the great tempter. Also, **"they break all bounds."** The original Hebrew literally reads they "break out" or "break forth" assuming intentional and aggressive action. Their behaviour was no mishap; it was all premeditated rebellion. Unsurprisingly, **"bloodshed follows bloodshed."** The Hebrew text literally states "bloodshed touches bloodshed" and proposes that one pool of blood flows into another, pointing out the murderous rage and violence which consumed the populace of the land exhibiting a thirst for blood and a disdain for life.

God is also disgusted with the slayings that take place today. All human lives are created equal in His image. When one citizen of God's earth slaughters another, it is synonymous with striking down the Creator's masterpiece and arrogantly shaking a fist in His face.

After the lack of godliness, followed the lack of blessings, **"therefore the land mourns"** (vs. 3). When God and Israel sustain a healthy relationship, the land (plants and animals) thrive and produce bountiful fruit; however, because of the people's sin, the land is infected and sees deterioration. It will cease to be as bountiful as it was when it lived in humble obedience to its master. The text adds **"and all who dwell in it languish."** Logically, when the land suffers, the people suffer because all that human beings ingest (whether plant or animal) is a direct product of the physical land as the latter sustains the former.

If that were not enough, **"also the beasts of the field and the birds of the heavens, and even the fish of the sea are taken away."** Every species of beast, bird, and fish are impacted by this decline, and what they once overflowed with has now been withdrawn.

God can do the same today. The deeper a nation goes into sin, the more God can take away even its physical blessings. Proverbs 14:34 declares that **"righteousness exalts a nation, but sin is a reproach to any people."** Believers must get a firm grasp of shining forth the light of holiness, not only for the souls of unbelievers but also for the sanity of unbelievers. When God begins to judge a nation, both converted and unconverted alike feel the brunt of His fury.

A Lack of Knowledge

Verse 4 commences **"Yet let no one contend and let none accuse."** Speaking by divine inspiration, Hosea knew his audience would predictably begin pointing fingers, but he demands that none play the blame game and then focuses his sights on a particular group of individuals. He says **"for with you is my contention, O priest."** Clearly, he has a dispute and complaint against the priests of Israel; there is a bone to pick with those servants of God. **"You shall stumble by day; the prophet also shall stumble with you by night"** (vs. 5). Twice the word "stumble" is used in this verse and at this juncture, it is a metaphor for failing to achieve success along a path of action. Also, notice the mention of both prophet and priest. Both God-ordained offices fail in what they desire to achieve because of engrained disobedience.

He adds **"and I will destroy your mother."** "Destroy" presents the idea of making an end of something—meaning to cut down and cut off. Again, "mother" is a reference to the entire Northern Kingdom. To be clear to his listening audience, Hosea maintains that God will not only cut down prophets and priests, but all of Israel. Why are the people destroyed?

It further reveals that (vs. 6) **"My people are destroyed for lack of knowledge."** Northern territory will be cut off because they lack divine instruction since the priests' duty was to ensure the public was instructed in the knowledge of God through teaching them the Torah—the first five Old Testament books. Notably, God's people will be put to an end because they have not been sufficiently educated in the knowledge of the Scriptures.

How foolish for Christians to not be thoroughly acquainted with the truths of God's Word. Lack of scriptural knowledge hinders the believer's progress in godliness. 2 Timothy 3:16-17 affirms that *"all Scripture is breathed out by God and profitable for teaching, for reproof, for correction and for training in righteousness, that the man of God may be complete, equipped for every good work."* Consequently, knowing the Bible comprehensively and extensively enables us to effectively please God with our lives. It writes the cheque for us and all we must do is "cash" it by applying it to daily living. On the other hand, not knowing the Scriptures brings judgement upon Christians because there will not be sufficient awareness of how to faithfully live through the unpredictable complexities of life. In both Old and New Testaments, biblical teaching is of supreme significance. Never should one's spiritual maturity be compromised by remaining in a local church where there is a famine of theologically-sound, biblical teaching because the outcome will be nothing short of spiritual suicide.

In addition, it is **"because you have rejected knowledge, I reject you from being a priest to me."** The priests of Hosea's era are rejected because they refuse to accomplish one of their primary responsibilities. In the New Testament, it is the duty of those who lead the church to make teaching the Scriptures their foremost priority. The apostles affirmed in Acts 6:4, *"But we will devote ourselves to prayer and to the ministry of the Word."* Such is not only an Old Testament principle, but a New Testament one as well.

It continues **"And since you have forgotten the law of your God."** The mention of "the law of God" confirms that the teaching of the Hebrew Scriptures is the main source of their knowledge. **"I also will forget your children"** is probably addressed to the high priest. Hence the "children" of the high priest would be all the other priests under his authority. The entire Levitical priesthood is held responsible for the dearth of biblical knowledge. If you are a God-called preacher of the gospel of Jesus Christ and teacher of scriptural truth, you have a grave responsibility. Martin Lloyd-Jones unashamedly affirmed in his classic work, *Preachers and Preaching*, that "the work of preaching is the highest and the greatest and most glorious calling to which anyone can ever be called."[i]

A Lack of Respect

Verse 7 continues Hosea's speech with **"The more they increased, the more they sinned against me."** This occurrence is the opposite of what one would expect to take place since a greater number of priests should mean better accountability; and greater accountability should translate into less sin. Instead, the opposite happens and the more the priests increased, the more sin increased. Every priest was the same and no one was, seemingly, making a difference or standing for righteousness in the nation.

Are you making a difference as a Christian? Do you stand out? Are you distinct in your school, workplace, community, or family? If you were put on trial for being a Christian, would there be enough evidence to convict you, or would you be acquitted for lack of proof? It is impossible for those whom the Lord has redeemed with His precious blood to always fly under the radar without ever being detected. Countless are the multitudes that delude themselves into thinking they are the

Lord's sheep when in fact they are not.

As a result, God responds, **"I will change their glory into shame."** A level of prestige accompanied the priesthood and it is possible that the participants of that office felt untouchable. Nevertheless, God will invite shame into their calling because of their unfaithfulness.

Before God, not one individual in the universe is untouchable—whether believer or unbeliever. He who is no respecter of persons has the ability to observe humanity with flawless impartiality. Furthermore, believers should not be disheartened by the atrocities that take place across the globe because God can and does tumble the walls of evil men. He does it in His own way and in His own timing. Do names like Adolf Hitler, Saddam Hussein, or Osama Bin Laden still breathe fear in the ears of the masses? All have been prematurely silenced and transferred to the sleep of death. The word "untouchable" does not exists in the dictionary of the Sovereign Ruler, and both Christians and non-Christians alike should take note.

Yahweh is, also, vexed because (vs. 8) **"They feed on the sin of my people; they are greedy for their iniquity."** A plethora of Bible commentators are convinced, as am I that the word "sin" in this verse indicates the sin offering that was brought by the people to the priests under the Old Testament sacrificial system. The Levitical priests were permitted by God to receive small portions of the meat of that offering for themselves. During the season of Hosea's ministry, however, the priests, steeped in greed, confiscated more meat than was appropriate from the sin offering. Eli's sons were guilty of the same infractions in 1 Samuel 2:12-17. The reason this verse calls them "greedy for their iniquity" is because they grasped that the more they transgressed the more meat they could obtain. These men could not restrain their mischief for the "blessings" that it procured. **"And it shall be like people like priest; I will punish them for their ways and repay them for their deeds,"** says verse 9. Thus far, the majority of judgement in this book has been toward the citizens, but this verse informs the priests that they will receive the same judgement as well without any preferential favoritism to accompany their religious office.

Just as there was a coming reckoning in Hosea's day, there is still another imminent, future judgement. The good news about the judgement of Hosea's day was that it would be only temporal. Unfortunately, the judgement yet to come is eternal and everlasting and only those who have taken refuge in Jesus' sacrifice on the cross of Calvary will escape. There is not the slightest likelihood of any earthly soul dodging eternal damnation outside of Jesus' shed blood.

A Lack of Satisfaction

Next comes the warning that (vs. 10) **"They shall eat, but not be satisfied."** Hosea speaks with regard to the priests and their greed for the meat of the sin offering. Even though they are repetitive in consuming meat, they will not be filled to satisfaction. Also, **"they shall play the whore, but not multiply"** which explains them being involved in ungodly sexual activity but not being able to bear children; barrenness will become a national epidemic and children will not come forth anymore. Because God's hand is against them, they will not receive satisfaction in any way possible through any means—not even through the womb. It is all cotton candy—a chasing after the wind. Why does this happen? It's **"because they have forsaken the LORD to cherish whoredom."** God has been forsaken, sin is now loved, and the Israelites are found wanting.

> Discuss

1. How can a believer cultivate faithfulness to God, love for God, and knowledge of God?

2. Is material prosperity a sign of God's blessing upon a nation? Why or why not?

3. What effect does ignorance of God's Word have on today's Christian? What causes this ignorance?

4. Do Christians today, at times, think they are "untouchable"? In what ways?

5. Discuss 1 Samuel 2:12-17 and the iniquity of Eli's sons.

6

CORRUPT TO THE CORE
4:11-19

*¹¹ whoredom, wine, and new wine, which take away the understanding. ¹² My people inquire of a piece of wood, and their walking staff gives them oracles. For a spirit of whoredom has led them astray, and they have left their God to play the whore. ¹³ They sacrifice on the tops of the mountains and burn offerings on the hills, under oak, poplar, and terebinth, because their shade is good. Therefore your daughters play the whore, and your brides commit adultery. ¹⁴ I will not punish your daughters when they play the whore, nor your brides when they commit adultery; for the men themselves go aside with prostitutes and sacrifice with cult prostitutes, and a people without understanding shall come to ruin. ¹⁵ Though you play the whore, O Israel, let not Judah become guilty. Enter not into Gilgal, nor go up to Beth-aven, and swear not, "As the L*ORD *lives."¹⁶ Like a stubborn heifer, Israel is stubborn; can the* LORD *now feed them like a lamb in a broad pasture? ¹⁷ Ephraim is joined to idols; leave him alone. ¹⁸ When their drink is gone, they give themselves to whoring; their rulers dearly love shame. ¹⁹ A wind has wrapped them in its wings, and they shall be ashamed because of their sacrifices.*

One day, while in Bible college, I went to one of the school's cafeterias to have lunch with friends. I sat down and ate my meal as was typical, then, subsequently, proceeded to eat an apple. Taking a deep chump into that shiny, red apple, I immediately encountered a giant, brown blob of slime just sitting there at its core. The goo slid swiftly across my unsuspecting tongue. In an instant, I spat everything out of my mouth and across my tray. A few moments earlier, when I retrieved the apple from the fruit section, it was large and glossy on the exterior. However, once I bit into it, I realized it was foul and corrupt on the inside. In this section of Hosea's prophecy, the Israelites are just like that nasty apple. Even though they appear healthy and materially prosperous on the outside, they are rotten and corrupt within.

The Sin of Drunkenness

Hosea returns to his discourse (vs. 11), **"to cherish whoredom, wine, and new wine."** The word "cherish" means "to hold dear" or "feel affection" for something, also carrying the nuance of "to keep or cultivate with care and affection". In normal situations, the word carries a positive meaning, but in this text it elicits a negative connotation because of the object these people are cherishing. According to verse 11, they are cherishing wine and new wine which imparts the idea of them consuming wine and then going back to refill with more wine. In other words, they never have enough— more...more...more wine. The end result is that it will **"take away the understanding."** The Hebrew text literally reads "which take away the heart." What is the heart but the seat of the will? It is the moral compass and inner control center because from our hearts flow our actions. This text asserts that the habitual consumption of alcohol/strong drink will take away the ability to control one's self in a morally sensible manner. What an accurate depiction of drunkenness! When people are drunk, they look and act foolish simultaneously.

Proverbs 23:29-33 informs in this way...

> ^{29} Who has woe? Who has sorrow? Who has strife? Who has complaining? Who has wounds without cause? Who has redness of eyes? ^{30} Those who tarry long over wine; those who go to try mixed wine. ^{31} Do not look at wine when it is red, when it sparkles in the cup and goes down smoothly. ^{32} In the end it bites like a serpent and stings like an adder. ^{33} Your eyes will see strange things, and your heart utter perverse things.

Drunkenness is an offense to God and something that saints should take great pains to avoid. This is precisely why it has been the position of some throughout the centuries—and even many alive today—to totally abstain from alcohol. They are cognizant of the fact that it would be impossible to get drunk if one has never taken the first sip. Scripture, though, does not demand that all take this position. Every believer must make his own decision regarding the consumption of alcohol, but godliness mandates that serious standards be upheld in order to ensure the Lord's name is not mocked through the exercising of Christian liberties.

The Sin of Idolatry

Verse 12 begins with the phrase **"my people"**. Notice that this does not say "a people", but instead, it is "my people". The Jews were a chosen race—called out and set apart by God. Their paramount purpose was to display the glory and greatness of the Lord to all the other nations who were ignorant of the true God. The charge was that they **"inquire of a piece of wood."** Oddly and inappropriately, God's people are seeking guidance and spiritual inspiration from objects made of wood. The specific names of such idols are not mentioned but they can be accurately designated as idols because there is only one living God—Yahweh, the God of the Bible. Every other "god" is purely an idol or an idea that people worship. He is the only true, real, and living God. It is explained that **"their walking staff gives them oracles."** Difficulty exists in discerning exactly what transpires in this situation, but some conjecture can be made. Several biblical commentators surmise that this is a practice called rhabdomancy, a form of divination that uses rods or wands.[ii] In the execution of this practice, a stick would be seized and thrown up into the air at random and in whichever direction the stick landed, it was believed that some form of spiritual guidance was given from the heathen gods. Engaging in this practice was unacceptable for the people of God.

They do this **"for a spirit of whoredom has lead them astray."** The phrase "spirit of whoredom" does not suggest some form of demonic spirit. The word "spirit" here literally means "wind". Envision the wind blowing and moving leaves along its path. This spirit is a movement or influence of whoredom rather than an actual spiritual being. Yet, take note that the spirit has led them astray. God's intention was for Israel to be travelling a certain road, but now, they have taken an exit and are traversing in the opposite direction.

Today, there are spirits, movements, and influences that are alive and active, and would seek to lead the church of God astray. The LGBTQ agenda is taking many in Christendom by storm, so much so that in some denominations even leaders in the church are allowed to marry members of the same sex. The abortion agenda is also battering some churches like a hurricane by assemblies which were once pro-life now supporting the pro-choice position—which is literally a pro-death position. Then, there is the influence of those who hold to the rejection of any mention of sin or eternal hell in a sermon. "God loves you" is the only message that matters in the world today and to preach anything that is not in direct alignment with that communication is anathema and archaic. Since in a world such as ours, it is challenging to keep the body of Christ from straying and being led captive by such deceptive logic, the only avenue that can inhibit these devilish philosophies from becoming widespread is an unwavering, resolute commitment to the Word of God. The Church of Jesus Christ must stick with the Bible and stand by the Bible by affirming that it alone is the ONLY authority for faith and practice. The moment we begin compromising and apologizing for what the Scriptures clearly teach, we are in danger of being swept away by the seducing "spirits" of this age.

In addition, Hosea announces that **"they have left their God to play the whore."** Having removed themselves from under God's authority, they have become unfaithful to Him just as Gomer was unfaithful to Hosea. The two phrases, "left their God" and "play the whore", are necessarily compatible. If you have one, you will have the other; and if you don't have one, you will not have the other.

Is it possible that you have removed yourself from under God's authority? If you have, then you also play the whore. You cannot have the first option without having the latter. If you are committed to whoredom, now is the time to return to the Lord the Creator. Furthermore, those who have never come to repentance and trusted in the Lord Jesus Christ to be saved should turn now from the error of their whorish ways while the door to escape remains yet open.

Tension increases when verse 13 states **"they sacrifice on the tops of mountains and burn offerings on the hills, under oak, poplar, and terebinth, because their shade is good."** The activities mentioned in this verse gave honor to false gods. What's worse is that they had not an iota of shame in their debauchery, because under normal circumstances, people try to hide sin. Here, they violate God's covenant in locations where they are visible to everyone, worshipping heathen gods on mountains and hills—not valleys and ditches. This is as brazen as a midday murder. Blatant and rank is their idolatry.

We must be fair in acknowledging, however, that idolatry did not only occur in centuries gone by. Idolatry is just as alive and pervasive today as it ever was; the only thing that has changed are the identities of the idols. Children, lovers, money, possessions, politics, and countless more all serve as modern-day "gods". John Calvin correctly expressed that "Man's nature, so to speak, is a perpetual factory of idols." Society's idols may have changed, but mankind's fetish for idolatry has not.

The Sin of Sexual Immorality

The thought concludes that **"therefore your daughters play the whore, and your brides commit adultery."** Thus far in Hosea's prophecy, the terms "whoredom" and "adultery" are used as a metaphor for Israel's unfaithfulness to God. Notwithstanding, in this verse, literal whoredom and adultery is the intended meaning. Isaiah 57:4-7 is a near duplicate of this current text.

> [4]*"Whom are you mocking? Against whom do you open your mouth wide and stick out your tongue? Are you not children of transgression, the offspring of deceit,* [5]*you who burn with lust among the oaks, under every green tree, who slaughter your children in the valleys, under the clefts of the rocks?* [6]*Among the smooth stones of the valley is your portion; they, they are your lot; to them you have poured out a drink offering, you have brought a grain offering. Shall I relent for these things?* [7]*On a high and lofty mountain you have set your bed, and there you went up to offer sacrifice.*

In Isaiah 57, the mention of lust, oaks, and high mountains also occurs. The additional mention of "bed" in the Isaiah passage gives the additional hint as to the form of activity that was taking place at these locations. There was not only idol worship taking place, but sexually immoral ceremonies in honour of the heathen gods in tandem.

According to God (vs. 14), **"I will not punish your daughters when they play the whore nor your brides when they commit adultery."** Standing on its own, the first part of the verse can be quite confusing. Is God letting the females off the hook? The rest of the verse clears the smoke when He says **"for the men themselves go aside with the prostitutes and sacrifice with cult prostitutes."** In God's eyes, the men should be held responsible for the loose sexual culture of Israel because their example was like an avalanche of immorality bellowing down a mountainside at full speed. The women simply followed. This attitude goes totally against the grain of post-modern thinking. Post-modern society treats a man's sexual sin more leniently than a woman's, but in the current discourse, God is treating the women's sexual sin more leniently than their male counterparts. Sexual sin is equally immoral for both genders, but it is a further injustice to uphold a double standard concerning who is ultimately responsible for licentious activity.

It ends **"and a people without understanding shall come to ruin."** Those who do not obey God's demands on handling their sexuality will meet disaster and pay a high price.

The current culture of sexual freedom, sexual expression, and sexual confusion is diabolically opposed to the will and Word of God. Pornography, fornication, adultery, homosexuality, lesbianism, transgenderism, and everything else on that spectrum are all building blocks of the kingdom of darkness. Sexual purity matters to God. He does not turn a blind eye to how we use our bodies, and all who claim to be the children of God must set the example for the world by being blameless in this area of conduct. In 1 Thessalonians 4:3-8, Paul urged the believers by saying,

> *3 For this is the will of God, your sanctification: that you abstain from sexual immorality; 4 that each one of you know how to control his own body in holiness and honor, 5 not in the passion of lust like the Gentiles who do not know God; 6 that no one transgress and wrong his brother in this matter, because the Lord is an avenger in all these things, as we told you beforehand and solemnly warned you. 7 For God has not called us for impurity, but in holiness. 8 Therefore whoever disregards this, disregards not man but God, who gives his Holy Spirit to you.*

The Sin of Stubbornness

Verse 15 declares **"Though you play the whore, O Israel, let not Judah become guilty."** Although a major bulk of this prophet's ministry is to the Northern Kingdom of Israel, he gives a stark warning to the Southern Kingdom of Judah at the same time. This is similar to a parent reprimanding one child, while knowing that another child is listening and warning that second child simultaneously. They should not get any foolish ideas and learn from the mistakes of the first child.

Furthermore, he warns that they must **"enter not into Gilgal nor go up to Beth-aven."** Two named places are pushed to the forefront of Hosea's prophecy. While the exact location of Gilgal is unknown, it can be determined that it was in the vicinity of the west side of the Jordan River and was somewhere near Jericho. "Beth-aven", though, refers to the location more prominently known as Bethel. Bethel means "house of God" while, contrarily, Beth-aven means "house of wickedness". Hosea throws sarcastic jabs at Bethel by calling it a "house of wickedness" instead of a "house of God". What do these towns have in common? Both were the settlements where two major heathen shrines were erected. As a matter of fact, pilgrimages were made to Gilgal and Bethel (Beth-aven) to worship at those adulterous shrines. Therefore, God is explicitly prohibiting them from traveling to worship at those locations. He adds that they should **"swear not, 'As the LORD lives'."** The cry "As the LORD lives" was similar to exclaiming the more recent "Long Live the King". God was offended at their frivolous use of His name because they were entrenched in such hypocrisy.

Likewise, God is offended today when those who consistently bear verbal witness to knowing Him have unscriptural beliefs, ungodly lifestyles, and unappealing attitudes that are entirely divergent to the principles written in His Word. It amounts to nothing more than empty chatter and meaningless talk while degrading the Lord's name. If you do not live like a Christian, please kindly desist from attaching His name to yours. Enough damage has been done to the cause of Christ by such superficialities.

Even more embarrassing is the charge that (vs. 16) **"like a stubborn heifer, Israel is stubborn."** The nation resembles a headstrong cow. "Stubborn" here carries the meaning of "rebellious" or "a revolter". A stubborn cow wants to turn its own way and do its own thing because it abhors the farmer's direction and desire. Often, there is little difference between mankind and stubborn heifers. We often don't care about the truth or doing the right thing but rather prefer to follow our own self-deceived way. Sometimes there is a wave of bucking and butting against the Bible itself. At other times, the rebellion is camouflaged by pushing against those attempting to lead us in a scriptural, God-ward direction. If this sounds familiar to you then maybe this is your current state of affairs. I invite you on the authority of God's Word to disrobe those vestiges of obstinacy and to put on submission and humility towards God's will and way.

The text presses on with **"can the Lord now feed them like a lamb in a broad pasture?"** In other words, should the Lord treat a stubborn cow in the same way He would treat a little lamb? The answer to this rhetorical question is a resounding "No". Anyone who is even remotely familiar with the guardianship of animals would know that a stubborn cow does not deserve the tender nursing of an innocent lamb. Resistance should never be rewarded. Although the Shepherd of Israel wants to lead His people in wisdom, He must treat them as brute beasts who will not respond to their master.

The Sinfulness of Sin

"Ephraim is joined to idols," according to verse **17**. Ephraim is the largest tribe in the region of the Northern Kingdom, but, here, the label is used to designate the entire Northern Kingdom as a whole. They are drowning in the oceans of adultery. The warning to **"leave him alone"** implies that there should be no participation in his sins. There must be a separation from him. **"When their drink is gone"** (vs. **18**) suggests that they drank until the whole supply is dried up and they stumble intoxicated. Hosea reiterates the impact of their drunkenness. When that is done **"they give themselves to whoring."** This particular instance of the word "whoring" is literal and not just a metaphor for their unfaithfulness to God. It recalls the sexually immoral nature of the people. Furthermore, **"their rulers dearly love shame."** The passion they have for sinful acts shows their stubbornness.

The text goes on to explain that (vs. **19**) **"a wind has wrapped them in its wings, and they shall be ashamed because of their sacrifices."** There is a breeze that both wraps them as well as brings shame to them. The earlier verses of the chapter make clear what this wind is—the spirit of whoredom. Altogether, so far Hosea has presented a sad state of affairs. The prophecy has been a tsunami of bad news! So is there any good news? Is there any hope?

The book of Ecclesiastes submits that as long as there is life there is hope (9:4). Even in the Old Testament scriptures, God foretold the hope that was to come. Ezekiel 36:26-27 tell of that hope.

> [26] *I will give you a new heart and put a new spirit in you; I will remove from you your heart of stone and give you a heart of flesh.* [27] *And I will put my Spirit in you and move you to follow my decrees and be careful to keep my laws.*

The primary dilemma the Jews were facing was not just particular to their country or race, it is an issue that all human beings face no matter their place of origin. All are corrupt to the core. We all need a new heart. We all need a new spirit. We have hearts of stone and only our Creator can perform open heart surgery and replace the heart of stone with the heart of flesh (Ezekiel 11:19-20). Only when that change occurs can someone walk faithfully in God's statutes and obey His laws. How can this open heart surgery be accessed? Jesus explains how in Mark 1:15.

"The time is fulfilled, and the kingdom of God is at hand; repent and believe the Gospel."

Repentance is a change of mind and change of heart that, finally, changes the direction of one's life. If you are headed east you must now turn west. If you are running away from God you must now turn to Him and cast yourself fully upon the Lord Jesus Christ and His sacrifice for your corrupt sin nature that was accomplished through the shedding of His blood on the Cross of Calvary. All other forms of hope must be totally abandoned and Jesus Christ must be made the sole object of your trust in order to receive forgiveness and eternal life. This is the only pathway to receiving the new heart and new spirit which was foretold by the prophet Ezekiel.

> Discuss

1. How may drunkenness destroy a believer's testimony?

2. If there is only one true and living God, why are there so many "gods" represented in different religions today?

3. Can someone get to heaven by means of these other "gods"? Use Scripture to support your answer.

4. Identify another "spirit" (i.e. influence, agenda) that the modern church faces.

5. Identify and discuss a passage of Scripture, besides 1 Thessalonians 4:3-8, that gives commands regarding human sexuality.

7

TAKEN FOR GRANTED

5:1-7

¹Hear this, O priests! Pay attention, O house of Israel! Give ear, O house of the king! For the judgment is for you; for you have been a snare at Mizpah and a net spread upon Tabor.² And the revolters have gone deep into slaughter, but I will discipline all of them.³ I know Ephraim, and Israel is not hidden from me; for now, O Ephraim, you have played the whore; Israel is defiled.⁴ Their deeds do not permit them to return to their God. For the spirit of whoredom is within them, and they know not the LORD.⁵ The pride of Israel testifies to his face; Israel and Ephraim shall stumble in his guilt; Judah also shall stumble with them.⁶ With their flocks and herds they shall go to seek the LORD, but they will not find him; he has withdrawn from them.⁷ They have dealt faithlessly with the LORD; for they have borne alien children. Now the new moon shall devour them with their fields.

Undoubtedly, many people know at least one old, wise saying. These are proverbs and principles that transcend all countries and permeate all cultures. For example....

"A bird in the hand is worth two in the bush."

"Too many cooks spoil the broth."

"You can't have your cake and eat it too."

"Never judge a book by its cover."

"If you fail to plan, you plan to fail."

However, in my opinion, there is one old, wise saying that stands head and shoulders above the rest in popularity. It is this: "You never miss the water until the well runs dry." That particular proverb tells how easy it is to take both things and people for granted. In these verses, Israel has taken the Lord God Almighty for granted.

The Nobility has taken God for Granted

The fifth chapter commences (vs. 1) **"Hear this, O priests! Pay attention, O house of Israel! Give ear, O house of the king!"** As the prophet Hosea addresses the people, he includes three phrases that all basically render the same idea. He says they ought to "Hear this", "Pay attention", and "Give ear". Every hearer is urged to give their listening ear attentively to the communication from the prophet. To whom is he speaking?

"O priest" is addressed to the spiritual leaders of the nation of Israel—men who were obligated to teach the law of God and ensure that the children of Israel conducted themselves in accordance with it.

"O house of Israel" at face value appears to encourage the reader to imagine that every basic citizen of the nation is the intended audience. However, there are several biblical experts who are convinced that this term is used to designate the political leaders of that time by virtue of the contextual position in which it is set. Upon closer examination, it can be observed that the phrase is sandwiched between two other classes of leaders in Israel. As a result, there is a segment of Christian academia that asserts administrative or political leaders are intended by the phrase "house of Israel".

"O house of the king" addresses the king as the "top dog" and earthly ruler of the kingdom. Who was the king at this time? It could have been either Jereboam II or Zechariah. Hosea's prophetic ministry was likely launched at the ending of Jereboam II's lifetime and perhaps ran into the beginning of Zechariah's reign as well; thus, "The king" could have been either of these monarchs.

Moreover, take note of the fact that he warns these three categories of people with **"the judgement is for you."** It seems that retribution and punishment is right on their doorstep or just around the corner rather than in some distant land.

A false narrative is becoming popular today even in some Christian circles. It's one that assumes that since God is love, He will never hurt or harm anyone. To articulate it from a different perspective, no adversity will ever broach the Christian's presence. Therefore he can do what he desires and live as he pleases as rules and restrictions are totally unnecessary and irrelevant. Adherents to this position do not know God and are lost at sea without a compass. The fact that the God of the Bible is a God of love does not preclude that He is also a God of justice and wrath. These priests, administrators, and the king are on the cusp of meeting His indignation and fury.

The reason they will be judged is because **"you have been a snare at Mizpah and a net spread upon Tabor."** "Snare" describes to a trap of some sort, and the leaders of the North were trapping their citizenry; while "net" relates a similar idea—that of fish caught in a net incapable of escaping.

Furthermore, two locations are cited: Mizpah and Tabor (which is synonymous with Mount Tabor). It is believed that shrines were set up to heathen gods at both venues. So, the thrust of the verse is to inform that Israel's leaders were leading the people headlong into the trap of idol worship. The situation may not have been assessed as an atrocity had it been one of the "average Joes" leading them astray. Sadly, it was their leaders who guided them toward the abomination. With the way God organized the leadership of the nation, this should have never happened.

Serious is the responsibility of being a leader, whether it be in the home, workplace, church, or nation. All throughout scripture, God holds leaders to a higher level of accountability. Verse 1 is a perfect example of this. Although leadership is by no means a light task, anyone who leads must perpetually strive to ensure they are doing so in the way God expects.

Moving along he tells that (vs. 2) **"the revolters have gone deep into slaughter."** The revolters are those who have deviated from that which is right. Having led the population astray, the leaders are travelling a totally different direction than God intended for the nation. The charge is that they have gone deep into "slaughter". Less clear is the reference made to slaughter, but some have opined that it may refer to child sacrifice which was performed to honour heathen gods. Yahweh rebukes the Jews for this often through the Old Testament.

Isaiah 57:5 *"You who burn with lust among the oaks, under every green tree, who slaughter your children in the valleys, under the clefts of the rocks?"*

Ezekiel 16:20-21 *"And you took your sons and your daughters, whom you had borne to me, and these you sacrificed to them to be devoured. Were your whorings so small a matter that you slaughtered my children and delivered them up as an offering by fire to them?"*

Precious little lives were used for horrific, abominable, wicked, detestable acts.

Let us not pretend that, today, such folly has been removed from the human psyche. In those days, children were sacrificed to false gods. Today, children are being sacrificed in the womb to the god of self. Tragically, the murder of the unborn has been progressively normalized in many cultures across the globe and it is just as abominable, wicked, and detestable in the eyes of God today as it was three thousand years ago.

God's retort is that **"I will discipline all of them."** Like a parent disciplines his child, chastisement has saddled up his boots and is on His way. The use of "all" underscores that not one of them will escape. Christians should, also, be warned and afraid of persisting in unrepentant sin as, according to Hebrews 12:6, *"The Lord disciplines the one He loves, and chastises every son whom he receives."*

The Northern Kingdom has taken God for Granted

Verse 3 begins **"I know Ephraim."** God has an intimate knowledge of the country which in no way implies that Ephraim knows God because the reality is that they have distanced themselves. Nevertheless, He surely knows them in the same way He knows everyone who has ever been born. In addition, **"Israel is not hidden from me."** Here, God declares both His omniscience and His omnipresence. That God knows all things actual and possible is the essence of omniscience; He knows all things that are and all things that could be. Omnipresence implies that God is everywhere present at all times with every part of His being. It is just as impossible for Israel to escape from God's presence as it is for God to sin.

Similarly, no one can escape God's presence or successfully hide themselves from His view. Osama bin Laden, the terrorist mastermind behind the 9/11 Terrorist Attacks remained hidden from the whole world for almost an entire decade. Yet, at every nanosecond God knew exactly his precise location and the specific number of breaths he had drawn since the day he was hatched from his mother's womb. In somberness, we must conclude that absolutely nothing we can do in private is unknown to God.

Before progressing further, a vital question must be answered. What difference is there between Ephraim and Israel? Thus far in Hosea's prophecy, Ephraim and Israel were synonymous with one another. Technically, Ephraim was the largest tribe in the Northern Kingdom but it typified the entire Northern Kingdom. Nonetheless, here in verse 3 they are used as two distinct locations. What is the distinction?

Honestly, we cannot know with surety but some have speculated that something was transpiring within the country which only the residents of that region would be acutely aware of.

The text continues **"for now, O Ephraim, you have played the whore; Israel is defiled."** Israel and Ephraim have both been unfaithful to God, just as Gomer was to Hosea. Infidelity abounded. Whoredom reigned. Still, God's unceasing call to the inhabitants of Earth is for everyone everywhere to be faithful to Him and His laws.

Yet, today we are forced to admit that no one can accomplish this without first receiving a new heart. Only Jesus Christ, the Son of God, can transform the heart of stone into a heart of flesh when the unworthy sinner turns to Him, and fully embraces His person and finished work for their own deliverance from eternal punishment in the lake of fire. The gospel of God's grace through Jesus Christ is the only effective medicine for a whorish heart.

Verse **4** points out that **"their deeds do not permit them to return to their God."** Sinful actions have driven a wedge between them and Yahweh, breaking intimate fellowship. The Psalmist David declared *"If I had cherished iniquity in my heart, the Lord would not have listened"* (Ps. 66:18). Sin breaks the cords of our communion with the Father.

The Lord's flock must prioritize keeping a short account of sin. Daily confession, cleansing, and repentance clears the telephone lines of rubbish and debris, but a refusal to do so results in God's voice becoming increasingly faint.

The cause of this effect is that **"the spirit of whoredom is within them."** Recalling an earlier explanation, the label "spirit of whoredom" does not imply an evil spirit since the Hebrew word for spirit means "wind" or "breath". Rather, this is an influence, attitude, and mindset of whoredom. Observe, however, that it is not just with them—it indwells them. Every non-Christian fits this description. Unbelievers have not even the slightest capacity to be faithful to God.

The second cause is that **"they know not the LORD."** The behavior of these people are inseparably linked to who they are. They have no knowledge of God.

Numerous passages of Scripture make clear that when an individual operates with a lifestyle of ungodliness and wickedness, it is because they do not know God personally, even if they make claims to the contrary. The clearest and most potent example is 1 John 3:4-10.

> *⁴Everyone who makes a practice of sinning also practices lawlessness; sin is lawlessness. ⁵You know that he appeared in order to take away sins, and in him there is no sin. ⁶No one who abides in him keeps on sinning; no one who keeps on sinning has either seen him or known him. ⁷Little children, let no one deceive you. Whoever practices righteousness is righteous, as he is righteous. ⁸Whoever makes a practice of sinning is of the devil, for the devil has been sinning from the beginning. The reason the Son of God appeared was to destroy the works of the devil. ⁹No one born of God makes a practice of sinning, for God's[b] seed abides in him; and he cannot keep on sinning, because he has been born of God. ¹⁰By this it is evident who are the children of God, and who are the children of the devil: whoever does not practice righteousness is not of God, nor is the one who does not love his brother."*

Unquestionably, those who make a practice of sinning are unbelievers, unconverted, lost, in danger of hell, and in need of salvation. Does this describe your lifestyle? Are you in love with sin? Do you have a spirit of godliness? Is there a spirit of righteousness? Or is there a spirit of whoredom? Refuse to lie to yourself about your own spiritual condition because it is only by acknowledging the truth that you will be set free. As 1 John 3 assures, no one who loves sin has God's seed indwelling.

The Whole Nation has taken God for Granted

Verse **5** records that **"the pride of Israel testifies to his face."** Pride leads Israel to its downfall. As one commentator declared, this pride was "a nationalistic arrogance, a heedless sense of self-importance, and a related stubbornness of will".[iii] Because they were God's chosen race, the Jews perceived themselves to be untouchable. New Testament believers must beware of thinking they are untouchable being, also, God's chosen people. The "lashing" alert remains just as high today as it was for the Hebrews alive in Hosea's day.

Hosea adds to the thought that **"Israel and Ephraim shall stumble in his guilt."** Stumble implies that an individual cannot successfully walk down a path.

Today law enforcement officers use breathalyzers to determine if a driver is under the influence of alcohol. Before breathalyzers became the rave, some officers would require that an individual walk step-by-step, foot in front of foot, to determine if a driver was under the influence. If the motorist was drunk, he would stumble and fall over—unable to complete the task. The text paints an identical picture. God has a path marked out for Israel and Ephraim to follow, but instead they stumble like an inebriated bibber along that path because of their sin. When they should be walking onward step-by-step, they are faltering from side to side.

Likewise, God has a path of godly obedience for you to follow. Are you traversing that way victoriously or are you only stumbling through it from day to day?

The verse concludes that **"Judah also shall stumble with them."** The Southern Kingdom that was previously succeeding will eventually join the folly of the Northern Kingdom. The warning of Hosea 4:15 was not heeded: "let not Judah become guilty." Having received the warning, they failed to listen and, consequently, they will receive a day of reckoning as well.

Because someone in your personal circle may be enamored with a sinful lifestyle does not mean that you must mimic their example. A family member, co-worker, or classmate living rebelliously does not trump your accountability to God the Father. What you personally sow, you will personally reap and every human is accountable to God for His own actions. No attorneys will be present on the Day of Judgement outside of the Lord Jesus Christ, who will only judicially represent those who have turned to Him in faith during this lifetime. Just as Judah should have stood alone, even if Ephraim and Israel were sowing their wild oats, so the saints of God are called to stand alone in the face of what the world at large may be espousing. Augustine once emphasized that "wrong is wrong even if everyone is doing it, and right is right even if no one is doing it."

Pressing further (vs. 6), **"With their flocks and herds they shall go to seek the LORD."** "Flocks and herds" reflect the numerous creatures that would accompany them to the Temple to be sacrificed and highlights the various offerings through which they would seek the Lord. The burnt, meat, peace, sin, and trespass offerings are the focus of this verse.

However, Hosea warns that **"they will not find him; he has withdrawn from them."** God has vanished—not from the world—but from their presence and fellowship. Both North and South will pointlessly seek His protection, guidance, and help to no avail. In their place is disaster and destruction.

Christians can encounter matching experiences. God's shielding, direction, and assistance are not unvarying verdicts that cannot be reversed and His kindness should never be taken for weakness.

In verse **7**, the text proceeds that **"they have dealt faithlessly with the LORD; for they have born alien children."** "Faithlessly" is the expression of note. The opposite of "faithlessly" is "faithfully". In laymen's terms, they have not been faithful to the Lord. The language depicts a covenant marriage in which they have stepped out on God. They have cheated on Him and the product is ungodly. "Alien children" are the vile acts birthed by their betrayal and does not imply literal offspring. All children are a blessing from the Father and Hosea is not making disparaging remarks.

He recognizes, in addition, that **"Now the new moon shall devour them with their fields."** A new moon usually suggests a new month. In the subsequent months, damnation and destruction will overcome and overwhelm the inhabitants as they and their possessions will be annihilated by the approaching Assyrian army. The entirety of this devastation is the byproduct of their rejection of their God and taking Him for granted.

Discuss

1. Why is spiritual leadership a serious responsibility?

2. The word "whore" is used often in Hosea's prophecy. Is it unacceptable for him to use this terminology? Why or why not?

3. "No attorneys will be present on the Day of Judgement, outside of the Lord Jesus Christ, who will only judicially represent those who have turned to him in faith during this lifetime." Where is this principle located in Scripture?

4. According to 1 John 4:3-10, what distinguishes a child of God from a child of the devil?

5. How can God withdraw from a people if He is omnipresent?

8

THE LION FROM ZION

5:8-15

⁸*Blow the horn in Gibeah, the trumpet in Ramah. Sound the alarm at Beth-aven; we follow you, O Benjamin!* ⁹*Ephraim shall become a desolation in the day of punishment; among the tribes of Israel I make known what is sure.* ¹⁰ *The princes of Judah have become like those who move the landmark; upon them I will pour out my wrath like water.* ¹¹ *Ephraim is oppressed, crushed in judgment, because he was determined to go after filth.* ¹² *But I am like a moth to Ephraim, and like dry rot to the house of Judah.* ¹³ *When Ephraim saw his sickness, and Judah his wound, then Ephraim went to Assyria, and sent to the great king. But he is not able to cure you or heal your wound.* ¹⁴ *For I will be like a lion to Ephraim and like a young lion to the house of Judah. I, even I, will tear and go away; I will carry off, and no one shall rescue.* ¹⁵ *I will return again to my place, until they acknowledge their guilt and seek my face, and in their distress earnestly seek me.*

We all know what it means to do something by accident. Sometime ago, I was at a buffet preparing to have a meal about 15 minutes before a Sunday evening service. While I was waiting in line to take up my food, a young man standing next to me hit one of the cups from the top shelf that was filled with juice and it splashed all over my dress shirt. With there being only a short period of time before the service began, I did not have the opportunity to go back home, iron, and change my clothes. To say I was annoyed would be the understatement of the century. I spent the entire night counselling myself in order to stay calm.

"It was an accident."

"It was an accident."

"It was an accident."

Likewise, when it comes to the Sovereign God, there are no accidents. He does absolutely nothing by mistake and the events in this passage are no mistake either. God intentionally initiates and executes punishment upon those who revolt against Him.

A Warning Goes Out

Hosea's prophecy continues in verse 8 with **"Blow the horn in Gibeah, the trumpet in Ramah. Sound the alarm in Beth-aven."** Three commands are given by the prophet: 1) Blow the horn. 2) Blow the trumpet. 3) Sound the alarm. The purpose of these commands is to gain the attention of the public in order to dispense important information. In this situation, a threat was imminent, an army was approaching and destruction was on the horizon. Gibeah, Ramah, and Beth-aven, are all located in the territory of the tribe of Benjamin, just north of the location of the tribe of Judah. Therefore, it is likely that this is where the invading army has assembled itself. The Lord will use a degenerate, no-good army to execute payback upon His special people. This should come as no surprise since, all through the Bible, God raises up heathen armies by His own hand and utilizes them to smite Israel. The Assyrian, Babylonian, and Roman Empires all serve as pungent illustrations. Never should Christians neglect to take God in earnest because the same God who projects His people, pounds His people also. When the verse informs **"we follow you, O Benjamin!"** it can be surmised that Benjamin, a miniscule tribe, is expected to take the lead toward the South as the Northern Kingdom attempts to flee the pursuing army.

Furthermore, **"Ephraim shall become a desolation in the day of punishment"** (vs. 9). "Desolation" defines a position of horror and ruin to the point that an audience is left in astonishment. All the nation will be levelled to the ground and destroyed as if overcome by a natural disaster. Also, **"among the tribes of Israel I make known what is sure."** Speaking on the Lord's behalf, Hosea is announcing that judgement is sure—not just a possibility or probability. God's mind is fixed and even the people know what is coming their way.

Similarly, if God's New Covenant people willingly persevere in unrepentant sin, we can be absolutely sure chastening is on its way. It won't be just a mere possibility, but as certain as the sunrise. The Lord's flock must abide in the sphere of daily confession and repentance, leaving what is ungodly and cleaving to righteousness. Neither should the commemoration of the Lord's Supper be the sole occasion of introspection as every day yields forth the opportunity. The more self-examination is indulged, the more successful God's people will be. Anyone who takes a bath only once a month, or brushes his teeth weekly would distress countless people in more ways than one. Hence, none who are born of God should reckon that "once-a-month" heart cleansing is tolerable.

Waywardness Continues

Hosea reveals in verse 10 that **"The princes of Judah have become like those who move the landmark."** These "princes of Judah" are the administrative officials. Although the terminology does not address the king, it probably includes those who serve under the king's authority. Wickedly, they moved the landmarks—ropes or lines used to mark property boundaries. The landmarks designated who owned respective plots of land, so, in reality, these officials were stealing property and infringing upon the possessions of others by moving people's landmarks while blatantly violating the Mosaic Law.

Deuteronomy 19:14,

"You shall not move your neighbor's landmark which the men of old have set in the inheritance that you will hold in the land that the LORD your God is giving you to possess."

Deuteronomy 27:17,

"Cursed be anyone who moves his neighbor's landmark. And all the people shall say 'Amen'."

Moving landmarks was a form of stealing—cruelty to the eighth commandment. Theft is an aggressive sin and none of the converted should breach this rule that God has set in place. If we have stolen, recompense should be made.

The result is that **"upon them I will pour out my wrath like water,"** stressing God's angry passion and indignation. Whenever a simile or illustration is disclosed in Scripture, thought should be given towards what portrait it paints. Wrath poured out like water is an intimidating sight. Imagine one of your own kindred seizing a full bucket of water and pouring it down upon your head. The liquid will not merely touch you; it will soak into your outfit. The coming judement is uncontained like the bursting of a dam that is torrential moving far and wide. All this is brought about because they steal from their neighbours.

"Ephraim is oppressed, crushed in judgment, because he was determined to go after filth," says verse 11. "Oppressed" and "crushed" are the significant words in this verse. Both terms appear in a similar passage of Scripture that remarks about the curses of being disobedient to the covenant.

Deuteronomy 28:33,

"A nation that you have not known shall eat up the fruit of your ground and of all your labors, and you shall be only oppressed and crushed continually."

It can be deduced from the aforementioned that their disobedience brings problems for their agricultural and farming industry. God uses whatever means necessary to get His message across to Israel and the verse advises that the purpose of Him bringing oppression and crushing is because they have gone after filth. Vanity, emptiness, and worthlessness is what they pursued.

Keenly, we should be aware that God can perform identical deeds today. Even though the Old Testament dispensation is in the rear-view mirror, God can still put His wrathful hand upon a people because of overwhelming sin and wickedness.

During the 17th century, in colonial, pre-independent Jamaica, there was a city located on its southern shore known as Port Royal. In the 1700's, Port Royal was known as "the wickedest city on Earth".

Journalist Mark Oliver penned that the metropolis was "so overrun with liquor, slavers, and prostitution that one in every four buildings was either a bar or a brothel."[iv] On a crucial day in June, "the ground beneath the city of sin began to shuffle causing the prostitution houses to collapse while a tidal wave overshot the city walls. Thousands died and their bodies polluted the water. But in the eyes of many around the world, the destruction of Port Royal was no tragedy. It was nothing short of divine retribution; the hand of God coming down to smite a modern-day Sodom and Gomorrah."[v]

Christ's bride must abide in piercing this dark world with the light of righteousness. In reality, it is the people of God who hold back God's hand of judgement upon so much of His domain. Remember that God promised to not destroy Sodom if only ten righteous people could be found there (Genesis 18:32).

Never be discouraged by those who attempt to give the impression that Christians are the cause of the world's hardships. Rather, it is the followers of Jesus Christ who bear the solution to the problem because we carry the message of the Gospel—the only message that can transform the heart of sinful man.

A Wound is Opened

In verse 12, God reveals **"But I am like a moth to Ephraim, and like dry rot to the house of Judah."** Interestingly, both the moth and dry rot are mentioned together in Job 13:28, which states "Man wastes away like a rotten thing, like a garment that is moth-eaten." The commonality between these two objects is that they both make things decay and unfit for use. While moths spoil garments, dry rot destroys wood. In Israel's case, the outright source of their decay and lack of success as a kingdom will be God Himself. Not only will He allow it, He will be the solitary cause of it.

The truth of this text cuts squarely against the false teaching in many churches today. There are enough unbiblical lies being broadcasted from modern-day pulpits to make even the devil blush.

"God won't ever hurt you."

"Anything negative that happens in your life can never be from the hand of God."

Such proclamations are absolutely false because not only does God allow hurtful situations, sometimes He is the sole cause of them. He is not haphazard but intentional in His judgement.

Verse 13 opens with **"When Ephraim saw his sickness, and Judah his wound."** Here, "sickness" and "wound" are alike. Wound implies a sore that is infected and flowing with bodily fluids, like pus, to the point that it must be compressed and bandaged up. This is not a small abrasion; the flesh is in a horrid state. However, Ephraim (Israel) and Judah did not have actual wounds on their bodies. The metaphors were used to show the sinful state of each individual nation. These are the results of their sin.

Regrettably, the response was that **"Ephraim went to Assyria, and sent to the great king."** The Assyrian king was sought by Israel. It cannot be presumed what the matter was about, but for whatever it was, Israel drew near to Assyria instead of her Master. So distant were they from God that He was not even considered in the process.

Who do you seek first when you encounter tribulations? Where do you run when you're in a jam? Whose help do you summon when the money gets low and bills get high and frustrations rise? Family, friends, social media, and newspapers should not be our first sources of solace. The first person we should seek is our God.

Hosea sets the record straight by divulging that **"he is not able to cure you or heal your wound."** Assyria's king had not the power to correct the situation; only Israel's (heavenly) King had the power to do so. Equally, all breath-filled humans are wretched sinners possessing incurable wounds that cannot be self-medicated. Only "Dr. Jesus" can fix our wounds. Isaiah 53:5 affirms such by stating,

"But He was pierced for our transgressions; He was crushed for our iniquities; upon Him was the chastisement that brought us peace, and with His wounds we are healed."

Jesus' precious blood was shed on Calvary's cross as the only antiseptic that could heal our spiritual sores. His sacrificial work must be personally received by faith in order to prove effective to the individual sin-sick offender.

The prophetic word continues with (vs. 14) **"For I will be like a lion to Ephraim, and like a young lion to the house of Judah."** Lions are powerful, ferocious, fearless, and deadly creatures. The average lion weighs around 226 kilograms (500 pounds) and is about 8 feet long. Its roar can be heard up to five miles away from its source. When God uses a lion as a metaphor for Himself, He is not bidding to be friendly or amiable. He intends to grab His people's attention by invoking fear and trembling because Israel and Judah have persisted in rebellious vices for centuries. No longer does He desire to be the "God of Wonders"; instead, He will be the "Lion from Zion".

The result is that **"I, even I, will tear and go away; I will carry off, and no one shall**

rescue." God, as a fierce lion, reveals His method of attack. He will capture them, carnage them, and haul them away. What a frightening depiction!

Yahweh must never be treated frivolously. Young and old, wise and unwise, believers and unbelievers alike must treat God in earnest since not doing so may spell doom. Hebrews 10:31 warns that *"It is a fearful thing to fall into the hands of the living God."*

Waiting Takes Place

On God's behalf, verse **15** submits **"I will return again to my place."** The lion metaphor is still in view and he has killed his prey and now returns to his lair. He does this **"until they acknowledge their guilt and seek my face, and in their distress earnestly seek me."** The Lord patiently waits for both kingdoms to do two things— acknowledge their guilt and seek His face. This is all anyone who is out of step with God ever needs to do, whether he be sinner or saint. If you read this as an outlaw who has never turned from your wicked ways and trusted in Christ the only Saviour, I urge you to do so even now. Acknowledge your guilt and utter hopelessness. Then, seek God's face by fleeing to Christ and fully placing your full confidence in His atoning sacrificial work to receive eternal forgiveness.

If you read this as a converted saint who is not walking in fellowship with God, this still applies to you. Acknowledge and confess your sin and rebellion, and seek His face by pleading to Him for cleansing and renewal. In whatever condition you may find yourself, if you humbly come, He will humbly receive.

> Discuss

1. What does it mean to keep a short account of sin?

2. What actions today serve as modern-day equivalents of "moving landmarks"?

3. Why is spiritual healing to be preferred above physical healing?

4. Many pastors/ministers today shy away from preaching Old Testament passages. Is there a danger in this? If so, what is that danger?

5. Is the lion metaphor appropriate to use when speaking of God? Are there other parts of the Bible that compare God to a lion? List some.

9

RUNNING IN REBELLION

6:1-10

¹ *"Come, let us return to the* LORD; *for he has torn us, that he may heal us; he has struck us down, and he will bind us up.* ² *After two days he will revive us; on the third day he will raise us up, that we may live before him.* ³ *Let us know; let us press on to know the* LORD; *his going out is sure as the dawn; he will come to us as the showers, as the spring rains that water the earth."* ⁴ *What shall I do with you, O Ephraim? What shall I do with you, O Judah? Your love is like a morning cloud like the dew that goes early away.* ⁵ *Therefore I have hewn them by the prophets; I have slain them by the words of my mouth, and my judgment goes forth as the light.* ⁶ *For I desire steadfast love and not sacrifice, the knowledge of God rather than burnt offerings.* ⁷ *But like Adam they transgressed the covenant; there they dealt faithlessly with me.* ⁸ *Gilead is a city of evildoers, tracked with blood.* ⁹ *As robbers lie in wait for a man, so the priests band together; they murder on the way to Shechem; they commit villainy.* ¹⁰ *In the house of Israel I have seen a horrible thing; Ephraim's whoredom is there; Israel is defiled.*

In Ireland, greyhound racing is an organized, competitive sport in which greyhounds sprint around a dirt track. They run because they are chasing a "lure". The lure is a toy-like object that moves rapidly along the trajectory in front of the galloping hounds. Thus, the greyhounds follow in hot pursuit. This image of a greyhound chasing a lure is similar to how God pursues His people Israel. Constantly and faithfully, He is after them, urging them to turn in repentance. Nevertheless, they ignore His beckoning call.

A Desired Response

Hosea begins this chapter by urging in verse 1, **"Come let us return to the LORD."** God's prophet concedes that both North and South have veered away from their foundation and rejected the covenant that God made with them. Having rejected God's map, they lay drifting off course. As God's mouthpiece, Hosea calls them back to their foundation and to the correct course of travel.

Likewise, maybe you have deviated off course spiritually and have lost your footing. The Word of God is blowing the trumpet; it sends out a clarion call. Turn back to the God who saved you! Turn back to a vibrant relationship with Him! The prophet further explains that **"he has torn us, that he may heal us"**. "Torn" here implies pulling something to pieces strip by strip like tearing a sheet of paper to shreds.

Often, God does this in our lives to get our attention. He tears us to pieces, strip by strip, because of our refusal to obey. Note, however, the purpose. It is so that He may "heal us". "Heal", in this verse, conveys the idea of mending or stitching up an infected wound. Possibly, you have encountered a situation in your own life where you have obtained a deep flesh cut and obtained stitches as a result. That is the portrait Hosea paints. Indeed, God does rip us to pieces on occasion, but it is never for trivial purposes, because He tears us to pieces with the intention of stitching us back up again once we turn to Him. If you feel torn to shreds, the good news is that the same God has the skill and power to stitch you back up and He not only has the ability to do so, He finds pleasurable delight in said action.

The positive news remains with **"he has struck us down, and he will bind us up."** Being struck down is like participating in a boxing match and being punched to bits. After executing the TKO (Technical Knockout), God's opponent lies flat on the canvas unconscious.

Yet, despite knocking us lifeless, He is willing to get down and pick us up bandaging all our wounds. He locates our breaks and bruises and wraps them securely.

The cry of verse 2 is that **"After two days he will revive us; on the third day he will raise us up."** Figuratively speaking, Israel and Judah have died a thousand deaths because of their rebellion. Nevertheless, if they repent, He will bring them back to life. When they turn to Him in deep sorrow, seek His mercy, and commit themselves to Him, He will raise them up from the grave. God punishes in order to give peace. He destroys in order to deliver. In this life, His acts of retribution are always to produce a turning to Him.

Also, observe the insinuation in this verse. "After two days" and "on the third day" hints briefly at the future resurrection of the coming risen Messiah, the Lord Jesus. At times, in the Old Testament, Jesus Christ is set forth overtly in the text—clearly, obviously, and plainly. At other times, in the Old Testament, Jesus is set forth covertly and you may have to read between the lines or observe the fine print.

Later, 1st century Jews should not have misconstrued Jesus' true identity because His fingerprints were all over the Old Testament Scriptures—both concealed and revealed.

Nevertheless, there are people alive today to whom both the Old and New Testaments are accessible, yet they miss the significance of Jesus' divine identity and purpose. Are you a guilty party? Do you understand fully who Jesus Christ is? Have you committed yourself to the kingship of Jesus the Promised Messiah?

There remains a lesson for Christians as well. Often, we study the Bible as if through a telescope. It's reckoned to be some ginormous entity and we are only concerned with observing its larger parts—we only scan and survey. Rather, we must study the Bible as if through a microscope. Smallest details must be intensely examined and investigated. Proverbs 30:5 reminds us that "every word of God proves true" and we may bypass truckloads of data by not taking precaution to observe and examine the Bible closely.

The sentence ends **"that we may live before him."** The word translated "before" here in the Hebrew language literally means "face". Therefore, it literally reads, "that we may live in His face". God's eyes are always upon us and no deed or thought is hidden from His sight.

There's an old Gospel chorus that goes...

"*My God is writing,*

My God is writing,

My God is writing,

He's writing all the time.

He sees all you do,

He hears all you say,

My God is writing all the time."

What a difference it would make in our lives if we constantly remembered that everything we do is before the face of God and nothing is beyond His vision.

Hosea urges the people with (vs. 3) **"Let us know; let us press on to know the LORD."** That they should acquire knowledge and be thoroughly acquainted with their God is the prophet's desire. His attributes and how He sovereignly manages both the world and their lives should be meticulously studied. But not only were they encouraged to have this knowledge, they were encouraged to "press on" in this knowledge. The phrase "press on" here literally means "to run after" or "to pursue". The word can even be translated as "to persecute". Israel should not lazily settle for meager knowledge about God, but persist in knowing more about His person and character.

This should be the desire of every Christian as well as the opportunities for growth and education regarding God are unending. Significant effort must be devoted to increasing our understanding of godliness. All Christians, without exception, must press on in this matter because none of us have attained a full knowledge of our great God and Saviour. Before salvation, it was God who ran after us. After salvation, it is we who should be running after God. Charles Spurgeon, The Prince of Preachers, correctly asserted about biblical education that *"No one ever outgrows Scripture; it widens and broadens with our years."*

They should press on because **"his going out is sure as the dawn."** With absolute certainty, if someone continues to press on in knowing God, He will show up and show out as sure as the sun rises at daybreak every morning. God responds to those who respond to Him. James 4:8 declares "Draw near to God and He will draw near to you." If you are a believer who feels that God has been distant, it is not He who is the problem. You are the problem. More than likely you are not pressing on to know the Lord, because if you did His going forth in your life would be as sure as the daybreak. The remainder of the verse further confirms this fact by saying **"he will come to us as the showers, as the spring rains that water the earth."** The spring rains—or "latter rains" as they are sometimes termed—fall in Palestine around March or April right before the harvest and the maturation of certain crops.

In The Bahamas, the mango is a popular fruit. Interestingly, almost yearly our people surmise that mango trees will not bear abundantly because of a lack of rain. However, one single day of torrential downpours about two weeks before the official start of mango season can produce a substantial harvest. So many mangoes are procured from trees that they quickly become scornful to the point where people are determined to give them away.

Latter rains in Palestine operate in a similar way. Immediately before harvest, there is a dense soaking of rain into the soil so that the crops grow and ripen in a flash. Hosea is illustrating that if Israel and Judah return to the Lord, pressing on in knowing Him, there will be a pouring out and showing out of His blessings upon them.

Thus, if you are willing to turn to God and persist in your relationship with Him, there will be a pouring out of spiritual blessings upon your life as well. I cannot legitimately confirm that there will be material blessings as there would be for Israel and Judah since they operated under a different covenant. However, I can confirm, on the authority of the New Testament, that there will be spiritual blessings (Romans 5:27; Ephesians 1:3). Be reminded, though, that thus far this is only a hypothetical proposition. This is what they *should* do and not what they *did* do.

A Disappointing Reality

The prophet then blurts out **"What shall I do with you, O Ephraim? What shall I do with you, O Judah?"** He interrogates these nations the way a parent does a wayward child. Essentially, He's saying "What in the world am I going to do with you?" Because nothing seems to make a difference in them, He is extremely frustrated; it's as if all His efforts cannot bring them to repentance.

If you struggle with the hard-heartedness of non-Christian kindred, God empathizes with you and understands that frustration. He knows the agony and anger that you endure because He has dealt with it since the beginning of time. Your vexations of just a few years have been His from time immemorial. His complaint is that **"Your love is like a morning cloud, like the dew that goes early away."** The imagery is that their love and loyalty for God is transient and fleeting and does not permanently remain. May the same not be said of God's people today. An "on and off" relationship with God is a travesty. These are the folks that attend church faithfully half the year, and cannot be found within a mile of a church the other half. Decline to be inconsistent in your devotional life because your love for God should endure throughout varying circumstances.

Consequences come into the fold with (vs. **5**) **"Therefore, I have hewn them by the prophets."** To "hew" is to cut or carve wood or stone into pieces. God's prophets will cut these people to pieces with the Word of God because their divine assignment was to expose immorality, pronounce judgement, and call for repentance. Similarly, God has called men today to stand in Christian pulpits around the world and imitate their example. They are to bravely swing the sword of the Word of God and allow it to slice whenever, however, and whomever it wishes.

Hebrews 4:12-13,

> *¹² For the word of God is alive and active. Sharper than any double-edged sword, it penetrates even to dividing soul and spirit, joints and marrow; it judges the thoughts and attitudes of the heart. ¹³ Nothing in all creation is hidden from God's sight. Everything is uncovered and laid bare before the eyes of him to whom we must give account.*

As with the prophets, this should be the primary task of every preacher in every church in every crevice of the Earth.

He continues to divulge that **"I have slain them by the words of my mouth."** Again, God affirms the power of His Word. Israel was unfaithful and the only appropriate response was for them to hear God's Word through His prophets.

Jeremiah 23: 29,

> *"Is not my word like fire," declares the Lord, "and like a hammer that breaks a rock in pieces?*

What is needed in this generation is for the words of God to ring loud once again. Politics, social media, and non-profit organizations cannot and will not transform the world into a more upright state. Only the very words of God from Holy Scripture have the power to usher in such a result.

Furthermore, **"my judgement goes forth as the light."** Just as light pierces darkness, God's judgement will pierce these nations. It will passage through swiftly and surely. The reason is that (vs. **6**) **"I desire steadfast love and not sacrifice, the knowledge of God rather than burnt offerings."** Steadfast love is synonymous with loyalty and loving-kindness. The Hebrew word *hesed* symbolizes an inner quality of the soul that has a passion and zeal for God. This verse does not imply that they were forbidden to sacrifice; it only means that steadfast love was to be valued above sacrifice. Similarly, the text does not imply that God did not accept burnt offerings. Instead, the knowledge of God was to be treasured beyond burnt offerings. Principally, God stresses that they keep the main thing the main thing. For both kingdoms, love and intimacy with God was to be of chief importance. To the contrary, they were enamoured with empty practices of sacrifices and burnt offerings. The New Testament paraphrases the same idea in Matthew 15:8 with *"This people honours me with their lips, but their heart is far from me."*

Surely, the same thing that happened to Israel can happen to us. It is frightening how easily Christians can get caught up in performing duties for God while our hearts remain far from Him. The redeemed must keep the main thing the main thing—cultivating loyalty and love for the God who saved us and growing in intimacy with Him. Such is the river from which all tributaries flow. It is the foundation upon which the house of our spirituality is built. Outward service to the Lord is important, but it is secondary to that which is primary.

A Determined Rebellion

Verse 7 reveals **"But like Adam they transgressed the covenant; there they dealt faithlessly with me."** Normally, one would think "Adam" refers to the first created man. However, the word "there" in the text challenges that logic. "There" refers to a place, not a person. So, is there a place called Adam named in Scripture? The answer is yes. Joshua 3:16 speaks of Adam, a city on the east bank of the Jordan River that was located along the course between Ephraim and Gilead. This line of reasoning is supported by Gilead being mentioned in the next verse. Strong evidence suggests that this is the "Adam" referred to in verse 7. Unfortunately, Scripture nowhere uncovers how the covenant was transgressed but it is certain the term "transgression" indicates they were unfaithful to God.

The cry of verse 8 is **"Gilead is a city of evildoers, tracked with blood."** Gilead, which probably refers to Jabesh-Gilead, is a city overrun with so much violence that it said to "be tracked with blood." It literally means bloody footprints. Since residents are tracking blood with their sandals all over the city, the imagery shows that there is no respect for the sanctity of life. Sadly, this attitude is typical of the times in which we live. It seems that most jurisdictions globally are grappling with an escalation of violence. Bloodshed. Murder. Mass shootings. This seems to have become normality. Added to that, localities that do not struggle with outward violence still seem to fail in the realm of inward violence—violence in the wombs. Millions of babies are slaughtered around the world on a yearly basis. I wonder how God feels as He surveys much of the planet today. It is highly unlikely that He would reckon it to be much different from Hosea's time.

Verse 9 adds to the list of problems with **"As robbers lie in wait for a man, so the priests band together; they murder on the way to Shechem; they commit villainy."** Just when you thought things could not get any worse, they do. The situation is that clans of priests—the same priests whose duty it was to serve God in the Temple—were lying in wait to rob and murder citizens on the way to Shechem. While having the responsibility of serving God, they were guilty of the most heinous crimes. No wonder why God was moved to pour out His judgement on these nations. To say they were determined in their rebellion is an underestimation. This was not falling into sin or a moment of weakness; "devilish wickedness" better defines their actions. Those who were to be the godliest became the most evil. May the Lord keep those who profess to know Him from committing such atrocities.

Hosea explains that (vs. 10) **"In the house of Israel I have seen a horrible thing; Ephraim's whoredom is there; Israel is defiled."** There's an adage that goes "the more things change, the more they remain the same." Israel is at that point right now. Situations may seem different at first glance, but beneath the surface, nothing much has improved. Israel retained an addiction to committing adultery and are yet unfaithful to the covenant—embracing sin and declining to change their minds.

Are you still running away from God? Do you still neglect repentance? This very moment I implore you to run no longer and submit to Him wholeheartedly. Graciously, Jesus revealed in John 6:37b that *"whoever comes to me, I will never cast out."*

> Discuss

1. "God punishes in order to give peace. He destroys in order to deliver." Where else is this principle taught in Scripture?

2. Why is an "on and off" relationship with God not the ideal?

3. How is God's Word like a fire? How is God's Word like a hammer? (Jeremiah 23:29)

4. In what ways was Gilead no different from cities today?

5. Is the problem of Matthew 15:8 still prevalent today? Why or why not?

10

HARD-HEADED HEBREWS
6:11-7:7

¹¹ For you also, O Judah, a harvest is appointed. When I restore the fortunes of my people, ¹when I would heal Israel, the iniquity of Ephraim is revealed, and the evil deeds of Samaria, for they deal falsely; the thief breaks in, and the bandits raid outside. ² But they do not consider that I remember all their evil. Now their deeds surround them; they are before my face. ³ By their evil they make the king glad, and the princes by their treachery. ⁴ They are all adulterers; they are like a heated oven whose baker ceases to stir the fire, from the kneading of the dough until it is leavened. ⁵ On the day of our king, the princes became sick with the heat of wine; he stretched out his hand with mockers. ⁶ For with hearts like an oven they approach their intrigue; all night their anger smolders; in the morning it blazes like a flaming fire. ⁷ All of them are hot as an oven, and they devour their rulers. All their kings have fallen, and none of them calls upon me.

Oswald Chambers, in his classic devotional *My Utmost for His Highest*, stated "The essence of sin is the refusal to recognize that we are accountable to God at all." I believe that statement hits the nail on the head. As human beings, we are accountable to God who made us for His glory; yet, often we shove that principle to the rear of our minds. Certainly, this was the case with those to whom Hosea preached and, unfortunately, for the most part, his efforts fell on deaf ears. God is profusely opposed to those who revel in sin.

Hope Erased

In verse 11, Hosea prophesies, **"For you also, O Judah, a harvest is appointed."** Although the lion's share of Hosea's ministry focused upon the Northern Kingdom of Israel, he occasionally made prophetic remarks toward the Southern Kingdom of Judah. In this example, he informs that "a harvest is appointed." Typically, the term harvest is used favourably, suggesting the reaping of God's blessings especially through physical provision. However, Scripture uses "harvest" with a derogatory tone as well, characterized as a reaping of God's judgement, which is its meaning here (Jeremiah 51:31-33; Joel 3:11-13; Revelation 14: 14-16, 19-20).Therefore, Judah awaits a harvest of retribution.

It continues with **"When I restore the fortunes of my people."** "Fortunes" may be more appropriately rendered in English as "captivity". God looks forward to a time when the people would be restored from their captivity. The Babylonian Captivity is believed to be the centre of attention in this clause and Judah, like Israel, will be taken captive by Babylon due to their sin. Yet, God will not abandon His remnant in Babylon and after seventy years will provide them the opportunity to return to the Promised Land.

How amazing that even while threatening judgement, Yahweh is already promising a time of release and reprieve from the same! When examining the Old Testament—especially the prophetic writings—so easy can one become overwhelmed by God's holiness and the execution of His wrath. Still, we must not permit ourselves to be persuaded that He is devoid of mercy. Here, God foretells His mercy even before His judgement becomes a reality. Again, all God's attributes must be held in balance and never should one of His perfections be preeminent above others. God is, indeed, holy; but He is also merciful.

Chapter 7 begins with the clause **"when I would heal Israel."** "Heal" in the Hebrew text is *rapha*. Most believers at some point have heard the term "Jehovah Rapha" which means "the God who heals". *Rapha* means "to mend by stitching" or "to sew together" just as a surgeon does to the deep wound of his patient. God's desire is to stitch Israel up. Notice God's heart never rejoices in punishment and He never revels in destruction. Nonetheless, He must act in accordance with His holiness; but His heart is always to heal and mend the wound He has inflicted.

Dear reader, these may be your thoughts toward God. Maybe His hand of discipline has ran through your life like a freight train. Understand that He performs such actions so that you can turn to Him and He can stitch you up. God's desire is to correct us, the same way a loving Father punishes to correct his son.

Sadly, as soon as the glimmer of hope appears, it vanishes. Hosea says that **"the iniquity of Ephraim is revealed."** Instead of Israel's healing, more sin comes into the picture. The root of the word translated "iniquity" in this verse literally means "to bend" or "twist" accurately explaining how perverted and crooked sin is. The Heavenly Father gives us straight commands and righteous laws to follow that are without flaws and errors. Sinfully, though, we bend and twist these commands out of their original shape. What God has entrusted to us, we corrupt to suit our own desires. The next phrase points to **"the evil deeds of Samaria."** At this juncture, be reminded that "Ephraim" denotes the entire Northern Kingdom because the tribe of Ephraim was the largest tribe located there, and Samaria is the capital city and metropolis of the North. Unsurprisingly, a concentration of evil flourishes in the capital city of Samaria since more often than not, capital cities have larger populations which generally leads to more frequent occurrences of sin.

Heathen Express Themselves

The verse also informs that **"they deal falsely."** "Falsely" here implies a hoax or a scam. These people were professionals at producing falsehoods. Today, falsehoods are as prevalent as ever. With the increase in technology has come a myriad of devious schemes designed to swindle the unsuspecting out of their money. The number of scams in circulation today are as numerous as the grains of sand on any given seashore. Although this is the status quo for hell-bound sinners, God's people must have no part in such systems of wickedness—trickery and deception—for base gain being an abhorrence to the servants of Christ.

In these falsehoods that Hosea denounces, **"the thief breaks in, and the bandits raid outside."** Citizens' homes were burglarized and outside possessions were pilfered—these possibly being beasts of burden and ripened fruits. This description is not far removed from the reality of our day. Goods have become more advanced, but the problem remains the same. Clearly, there is nothing new under the sun as Ecclesiastes 1:9 confirms.

"What has been is what will be, and what has been done is what will be done, and there is nothing new under the sun." Often we agonize and get bent out of shape over the happenings of our time while the Scriptures teach that nothing is unfolding now that has not already done so. Moreover, God remains sovereign and no occurrence is outside of His jurisdiction. Spurgeon once admirably articulated that "the sovereignty of God is a soft pillow for the anxious head." During the entire rollercoaster of life, we can rest confidently in who God is.

Verse 2 informs that **"they do not consider that I remember all their evil."** They neglected to ponder in their hearts that God could recall every single evil deed they performed. The same applies to us, as our Creator can recollect every rebelliously naughty action done whether it is known to others or not. No one and nothing escapes His memory. Hosea adds **"Now their deeds surround them; they are before my face."** He uses imagery of people encompassed by their deeds. There are no exits and there is no escape because the omnipresent God observes them all. Therefore, no one can stand in his own righteousness on the final Day of Judgement because as much as we may attempt to perform good, the Lord always knows our evil and even one immoral act is enough to catapult us into everlasting fire. We are in need of a righteousness that comes from another—an alien righteousness—a foreign righteousness. Thankfully, God has provided an avenue for mankind to obtain this righteousness. It is acquired only through trusting in His perfect, sinless Son, Jesus Christ.

Romans 10:1-4 summarizes the thought well.

> ^{1}*"Brothers, my heart's desire and prayer to God for them (Israel) is that they may be saved. ^{2} For I bear them witness that they have a zeal for God, but not according to knowledge. ^{3} For, being ignorant of the righteousness of God, and seeking to establish their own, they did not submit to God's righteousness. ^{4} For Christ is the end of the law for righteousness to everyone who believes."*

Sir/Madam, whose righteousness are you trusting in for access to Heaven? The question can be worded another way. Why should you be allowed to enter God's heavenly presence? If your answer has anything to do with your personal character, you are depending upon your own righteousness. Sadly, you've been duped. You must submit your incorrect opinions to the truth of the Bible: only the righteousness of Christ is sufficient to make you right with God.

Verse 3 of this chapter says **"By their evil they make the king glad, and the princes** by their treachery." It can be deduced from other portions of Scripture like Romans 13 that God established government and earthly rulers to discourage wrong behaviour and encourage right behaviour in society. This verse inverts that expectation as the heads of state rejoiced over evil and wrong-doing, a disgraceful incident. Criminal activity and lawlessness should never elate any governing administration. This is a sure-fire sign of judgement since civilization is flipped on its head. Correspondingly, John Calvin argued that "When God wants to judge a nation, He gives them wicked rulers."

Holiness Eradicated

Hosea charges that (vs. 4) **"They are all adulterers."** More often than not in Hosea's prophecy, the expression "adultery" had been used to show the unfaithfulness of Israel toward her God—spiritual adultery. However, one must question whether actual physical adultery is implied in this accusation as well. I reckon it is fitting to draw that conclusion because the book of Hosea commences with an adulterous affair. Gomer, Hosea's wife, was routinely unfaithful to him. Still, God demanded that Hosea marry Gomer in order to demonstrate Israel's disloyalty to its Founder. Thus, physical adultery was used to illustrate spiritual adultery. With verse 4 under the microscope, if there is spiritual adultery, we can conclude that physical adultery is already commonplace. The *Targum*, an ancient Jewish writing, seems to support this interpretation. Commenting on Hosea 7:4, the *Targum* emphasizes "they all desire to lie with their neighbour's wives." God's unbending standard is that all who have taken part in the solemn oath of marriage be faithful to their spouse in every possible way. Failure to do so meets with dreadful, merciless penalties. Proverbs 7:21-27 gives vivid depictions while strongly warning against this iniquity.

> [21] With much seductive speech she persuades him; with her smooth talk she compels him. [22] All at once he follows her, as an goes to the slaughter, or as a stag is caught fast[e] [23] till an arrow pierces its liver; as a bird rushes into a snare; he does not know that it will cost him his life. [24] And now, O sons, listen to me, and be attentive to the words of my mouth. [25] Let not your heart turn aside to her ways; do not stray into her paths, [26] for many a victim has she laid low, and all her slain are a mighty throng. [27] Her house is the way to Sheol, going down to the chambers of death.

In addition, **"they are like a heated oven whose baker ceases to stir the fire, from the kneading of the dough until it is leavened."** The baker's task in the Old Testament era was to refrain from stirring the fire for a certain time so a proper level of heat could be maintained in the oven. Both heat and energy were sustained until it was time to bake the dough. It is not certain how this illustration connects to physical or spiritual adultery, but it appears that these people were always "cooking up something in the kitchen" lying in wait for a plan to hatch. Planning and deception were involved and their sins were pre-determined and then executed.

Verse **5** reveals that **"On the day of our king the princes became sick with the heat of wine."** "The day of our king" was a special event that involved the king and could have been a birthday or coronation when the king was formally inaugurated. The rest of the verse concerns how the leaders and officials submerged themselves in so much intoxicating drink that they became sick to their stomachs—a "hangover" of sorts. Restraint and moderation lie nowhere near their dwelling. "Heat" emphasizes that they have a passion for this activity; it is their way of life. Today, as well, people are addicted to this sad way of living. Being washed and wasted is their reason for living. They think they have control of the bottle, but really the bottle has control of them and their undeniable addiction can only be broken through the power of the Gospel of Jesus Christ.

Next, he **"stretched out his hand with mockers."** The king, who should be setting the standard for holiness and professionalism in the nation, is befriending scornful people and they are obviously having a momentous impact on him for evil rather than for good. Choose the company of your inner circle wisely and carefully. 1 Corinthians 15:33 warns "Be not deceived: bad company ruins good morals." As the saying goes, "birds of a feather, flock together."

Hierarchy Exterminated

Verse **6** begins **"For with hearts like an oven they approach their intrigue"** and, again, the illustration of an oven speaks to passion and desire. At first glance, this English translation of the verse may not seem comprehensible. The word "intrigue" does not appear to fit well in the logical flow of this sentence. However, the word has more than one meaning in English. The most familiar meaning is to arouse the interest, desire, or curiosity. An alternative meaning, though, fits with this sentence—the practice of engaging in secret schemes. This group was plotting a secret ambush of those in authority. Supplementary to that, **"all night their anger smolders; in the morning it blazes like a flaming fire."** Although their anger remains hidden and quiet for some time, subsequently it is released and blazes like a forest fire.

As a result, verse 7 acknowledges that **"All them are hot as an oven, and they devour their rulers."** Leaders of the land are wiped out by these uncommitted traitors. One might enquire as to when this literally came to fruition. It seems that it occured in 2 Kings 15: 10,14,25,30.

> [10] *Shallum the son of Jabesh conspired against him and struck him down at Ibleam and put him to death and reigned in his place.* [14] *Then Menahem the son of Gadi came up from Tirzah and came to Samaria, and he struck down Shallum the son of Jabesh in Samaria and put him to death and reigned in his place.* [25] *And Pekah the son of Remaliah, his captain, conspired against him with fifty men of the people of Gilead, and struck him down in Samaria, in the citadel of the king's house with Argob and Arieh; he put him to death and reigned in his place.* [30] *Then Hoshea the son of Elah made a conspiracy against Pekah the son of Remaliah and struck him down and put him to death and reigned in his place, in the twentieth year of Jotham the son of Uzziah.*

Four kings are consecutively slaughtered in the 15th chapter of 2 Kings. More than likely, this is what the prophet is referencing.

Finally, God admits that **"All their kings have fallen, and none of them calls upon me."** Despite the tragedies of their kings being assassinated, they refuse, still, to turn to the Lord of Israel. They are head strong, stony-hearted and unashamed. Friend, are you head-strong? Are you hard-hearted? Are you unrepentant? Do you refuse shift your direction? What is it in your life that you refuse to agree with God on? What are you in denial about? God's people must humble themselves and submit to His will in every area of their lives. Ignore the gamble to imitate those hard-headed Hebrews.

> Discuss

1. In Jeremiah 51:31-33, which nation reaps a harvest?

2. "Yet, God will not abandon His remnant in Babylon and after seventy years will give them the opportunity to return to the Promised Land." What does this imply about God's character?

3. Are you surprised to know that scams of some variation existed in the Old Testament period? What does this say about the heart of man?

4. Fill in the blank. Christian salvation is faith-based. Every other religion's salvation is _____-based. Do you agree with that statement? Why or why not?

5. List 5 things Christians/churches should do when governments institutionalize sin.

11

THE SILLY SEASON

7:8-16

⁸ Ephraim mixes himself with the peoples; Ephraim is a cake not turned. ⁹ Strangers devour his strength, and he knows it not gray hairs are sprinkled upon him, and he knows it not. ¹⁰ The pride of Israel testifies to his face; yet they do not return to the LORD their God, nor seek him, for all this. ¹¹ Ephraim is like a dove, silly and without sense, calling to Egypt, going to Assyria. ¹² As they go, I will spread over them my net; I will bring them down like birds of the heavens; I will discipline them according to the report made to their congregation. ¹³ Woe to them, for they have strayed from me! Destruction to them, for they have rebelled against me! I would redeem them, but they speak lies against me. ¹⁴ They do not cry to me from the heart, but they wail upon their beds; for grain and wine they gash themselves; they rebel against me. ¹⁵ Although I trained and strengthened their arms, yet they devise evil against me. ¹⁶ They return, but not upward; they are like a treacherous bow; their princes shall fall by the sword because of the insolence of their tongue. This shall be their derision in the land of Egypt.

Your interpretation of the term "silly season" probably depends on where you reside. If you're from Europe, "silly season" is a reference to the summer period where frivolous, giddy news stories are largely reported in the absence of major news stories. However, if you're from The Bahamas, "silly season" can refer to the season of political posturing and campaigning in the months leading up to a long-awaited general election. Usually people and politician alike get into an excited frenzy to the point where the most foolish and outlandish things are said and done simply to garner votes. People temporarily lose their "marbles" during this time. The latter is an example of what takes place in this text. Although not politically motivated, it is the nation of Israel who is being senseless.

Clueless

Verse 8 begins this section by stating **"Ephraim mixes himself with the peoples."** This verse continues the imagery that commenced earlier in the chapter of a baker baking (vs. 4,6,7). Ephraim amalgamates itself with the peoples of heathen nations, just as a baker mixes dough before placing it in the oven. Usually, mixing and mingling with others is seen through positive lenses, but in Hosea's context, mixing is one of the most outrageous actions Israel could be involved in because God had given them strict orders to remain separated from the influences of pagan nations. Intermarrying and close associations were explicitly forbidden. Psalm 106:34-39 gives eye-opening insight into this absurdity.

> *34 They did not destroy the peoples as the Lord had commanded them, 35 but they mingled with the nations and adopted their customs. 36 They worshiped their idols, which became a snare to them. 37 They sacrificed their sons and their daughters to false gods. 38 They shed innocent blood, the blood of their sons and daughters, whom they sacrificed to the idols of Canaan, and the land was desecrated by their blood. 39 They defiled themselves by what they did; by their deeds they prostituted themselves.*

This is a detailed account of the problems that arose as a result of Israel mixing with these evil lands.

The Christian must be aware of how he interacts with unbelievers. God has not called New Testament Christians to be totally separated from unbelievers as was the case with Israel, because the believer is to shine the light of the Gospel and impact others toward godliness. However, the Christian's default is to be in the world (in order to witness to unbelievers) but not of the world. Unfortunately, some who tag themselves as followers of Christ are influenced by the world's system more than they influence the world's system. God's wisdom must be sought in order to properly navigate this difficult dynamic in our lives, both individually and in the church of Jesus Christ corporately.

The baking analogy continues with **"Ephraim is a cake not turned."** By observing ancient Jewish customs, it is believed by some scholars that the "cake" mentioned here was similar to a thin pancake which was fervently heated on one side, baked on hot stones. This cake was only half-done. A half-done cake is mostly inedible. Israel mixing with rebel nations made them ineffective and useless in God's eyes.

If deep caution is not exercised, Christians will encounter a similar fate because of sin. Centuries gone by are pregnant with countless lives that have been wrecked, testimonies that have been tarnished, and ministries that have been demolished and left near death because of human depravity. Even God's people are liable to falling into the most shameful atrocities if care is not taken to avoid enticements to evil. As an aside, none who name the name of Christ should ever rejoicingly find satisfaction in the faltering of another believer since Scripture admonishes to "take heed" lest you also slip and indulge in humiliating sin (1 Corinthians 10:12).

Furthermore, (vs. 9) **"Strangers devour his strength."** "Strangers" are the non-Jews, and since Egypt and Assyria are named in the context a few verses later, it is, perhaps, safe to assume that those nations are the "strangers". "Strength" is believed to describe their material gain like crops and agricultural resources. "Devour" is used in several instances in Hosea's prophecy in association with grains and crops. So, Egypt and Assyria will weaken Ephraim economically.

The comment goes further, **"and he knows it not."** Ephraim cannot understand or discern what is happening because the nation is clueless. Proverbs 9:10 asserts that, *"The fear of the Lord is the beginning of wisdom"*. The utter vacuum of wisdom in the nation is due to their lack of fear for God and the binding and blinding nature of sin.

Identical are its effects upon the people of God and it can blind us to the things that are manifestly obvious. Let us recall the narrative in 2 Samuel 12:1-15 when the prophet Nathan went to King David and told a short parable concerning two men—one rich and the other poor. The only item the poor man possessed was a lamb. The wealthy man confiscated the poor man's lamb and prepared it for his guest who was arriving in town.

David, upon hearing the parable, was infuriated and declared that the wealthier man deserved to die, but should first restore the lamb four-fold because he had no mercy on the poor man. Nathan revealed to the king that he (David) was the rich man being illustrated in the parable. David was so far down in the mines of sin that he could not perceive that Nathan was demonstrating the events of his own life. Iniquity stupefies us and renders us clueless.

The verse includes that **"gray hairs are sprinkled upon him."** Gray hairs typify advancement in years. It is always interesting to compare pictures of current world leaders before they take office to pictures of the same politicians after demitting office—especially if they are black-haired. In most instances, the number of grey hairs drastically increase during their tenure. Clearly, it portrays just how much the weight of leadership has aged the individual. The Northern Kingdom's disobedience has aged it prematurely. They are becoming old, senile, and weak as a nation.

The verse concludes **"and he knows it not."** Clueless! They cannot comprehend the gravity of what is happening to them spiritually. At this juncture, one cannot help but recall what happened to Samson after Delilah shaved his head. She shouted, "Get up, the Philistines are upon you!" Indeed, he did stand to his feet, but the Scriptures inform that he did not know that his strength had departed from him.

Sin has the capacity to age us spiritually, and (depending on the kind of sin) even age us physically. As a matter of fact, in many cases, the more a person sins the less healthy they look. The deeper we go, the harder it is to emerge at the surface. Daily self-examination, confession, and repentance is compulsory to living a victorious Christian life.

According to verse 10, **"the pride of Israel testifies to his face."** This declaration is an exact replica of Hosea 5:5 verbatim, and, as it did in that setting, here it paints the picture of a court room situation. Pride has taken the stand as witness, and the defendant being prosecuted is the Northern Kingdom, while Pride gives evidence of its arrogance, self-centeredness, and haughtiness. It is impossible for Israel to deny its conceit before God—Him being judge, jury, and executioner.

Disappointingly, Hosea discloses that **"yet they do not return to the LORD their God, nor seek him, for all this."** Remaining as stubborn as a mule, they refuse to turn His direction and search Him out despite all God has said and done for them. Maybe you, dear friend, are ignoring God—ignoring what He has said, what He has done, what He wants, or who He is. The time is now to shift your thinking before it is too late.

Senseless

The Lord adds that (vs. 11) **"Ephraim is like a dove."** Doves were not uncommon creatures in the land of Palestine and served as a dependable source of food. The subsequent simile is that they are **"silly and without sense"** because the doves of the land were always laser-focused in their pursuit of food, a quality that does not deserve complaint. Nevertheless, they were often so fixated that they neglected to consider the suspicious activity within their immediate locality resulting in them, ironically, becoming food even while they were hunting food. Having gained a reputation of being easy to hunt and trap, they were regarded as silly and lacking common sense. "Silly," in the Hebrew text, carries the idea of being "open-minded". This kind of individual is easily influenced and is the antithesis of how God's children should conduct their lives. Every thought, ideology, opinion, agenda, and doctrine should not be given the green light to influence our thinking. That is the precise meaning of "silly" in our text. Postmodernism and pluralism demand that people always leave their mind open to influence. With God, this is not always advisable and can sometimes prove to be destructive. Ephesians 4:11-14 makes this clear.

> ^{11} And he gave the apostles, the prophets, the evangelists, the shepherds and teachers, ^{12} to equip the saints for the work of ministry, for building up the body of Christ, ^{13} until we all attain to the unity of the faith and of the knowledge of the Son of God, to mature manhood, to the measure of the stature of the fullness of Christ, ^{14} so that we may no longer be children, tossed to and fro by the waves and carried about by every wind of doctrine, by human cunning, by craftiness in deceitful schemes.

2 Corinthians 10:5 agrees as well.

> ^{5} We destroy arguments and every lofty opinion raised against the knowledge of God, and take every thought captive to obey Christ.

Thus, Christians should not give liberty to thoughts that defy Christ or His Written Word, because the Lord reckons those who do so as "silly".

It further announces, **"Calling to Egypt, going to Assyria."** Israel's dependence and hopes have been set on pagan people who do not know God. The present-day equivalent of this would be Bible-believing Christians seeking the help of Muslims and/or Hindus in spiritual matters. As for Jewish monotheism, this should have been an abomination. Also, Egypt, of all places, is mentioned! Why would Israel want any help from Egypt? Their ancestors were slaves in Egypt for 430 years and were treated like dogs—or maybe less than dogs when you evaluate the care with which some dogs are treated in today's world. Moses was probably turning in his grave. Again, however, sin is blinding and makes us clueless regarding reality. It hinders us from seeing the gigantic mountain standing so close to our faces that, if we blinked, we would scratch it with our eyelashes.

The effect is that (vs. 12) **"As they go, I will spread over them my net."** God portrays himself as a hunter—and, particularly, a dove hunter. He has plans to pursue these Israelite "doves" and promises that **"I will bring them down like birds of the heavens"**. Though doves usually fly high, He has enacted a scheme to bring them down to the ground; great humiliation is on the horizon. Biblically and historically, this has frequently been God's reaction to overwhelming, widespread sin. Citizens of the Earth should wisely take note and take heed.

He explains that **"I will discipline them according to the report made to their congregation."** This report recalls the promise the Lord swore to His people in Deuteronomy on several occasions.

Deuteronomy 28:1-2 says,

> ¹ "And if you faithfully obey the voice of the Lord your God, being careful to do all his commandments that I command you today, the Lord your God will set you high above all the nations of the earth. ² And all these blessings shall come upon you and overtake you, if you obey the voice of the Lord your God.

Vs. 15-16 says,

> ¹⁵ "But if you will not obey the voice of the Lord your God or be careful to do all his commandments and his statutes that I command you today, then all these curses shall come upon you and overtake you. ¹⁶ Cursed shall you be in the city, and cursed shall you be in the field.

The long and short of the oath was that if they obeyed, they would be blessed, but if they disobeyed they would be cursed. As simple as that was to comprehend and execute, they still disobeyed God. As a matter of fact, over the span of the Old Testament, they defied God more often than they submitted.

Still, let us not be too hard on Israel because Christians sometimes resist God as well. A primary purpose of the Old Testament was to demonstrate that mankind does not have the capacity within himself to keep the law of God and please Him. His own chosen nation could not do it and neither will anyone outside that jurisdiction be able to. This is the motive behind Jesus Christ invading Earth and living a sinlessly perfect life with the result that only those who change their minds and receive Him into their lives as Saviour and King could be reckoned as perfectly sinless before God the Father. The biblical term for this is justification. It means to "declare righteous". Have you been justified? God's only acceptable standard is outright moral perfection. You must score 100%. You must achieve an A+. You must obtain full marks on His examinations. Regrettably, that standard is impossible for us sin-stained earthlings to attain. Only the Lord Jesus Christ can accomplish that on our behalf. Christians, indeed, *are* saved by works—but only by the works of the Lord Jesus.

Hosea continues his prophecy with (vs. 13) **"Woe to them, for they have strayed from me! Destruction to them, for they have rebelled against me! I would redeem them, but they speak lies against me."** "Woe" is an exclamation used to express grief, regret, distress, calamity, or affliction. Israel is oblivious to the colossal sum of affliction rushing toward them because they have strayed, rebelled, and spoken lies. They have not succeeded in shaking off their silliness and senselessness.

Heartless

Another dilemma was that (vs. **14**) **"They do not cry to me from the heart."** Observe that the problem was not that they were not crying; it was that they were not crying from their hearts. Their sadness—insincere and superficial—lacked true commitment. The same can happen in the lifecycle of God's people since easy lays the ability to pretend there is outward repentance when there is no accompanying inward repentance. Tears do not confirm repentance and neither does a sad face. Repentance is verified by the turning of one's heart in an opposite direction. To be clear, at times that turning of heart will express itself outwardly in the emotions, but that is not a fail-proof test.

Echoes of Joel 2:12-13a ring aloud in this setting.

[12] *"Yet even now," declares the Lord, "return to me with all your heart, with fasting, with weeping, and with mourning;* [13] *and rend your hearts and not your garments."*

In ancient times, the rending of garments was a customary act done in situations of utter sadness and calamity where clothes would literally be ripped to pieces. Joel, a minor prophet like Hosea, understood that at times the rending of garments was only mere smoke while the heart remained unbothered. God's children should never be guilty of engaging in fraudulent or superficial repentance. Only true, heartfelt, and genuine repentance is suitable for the believer.

The verse also indicates that **"they wail upon their beds."** To "wail" is to yell or howl with a loud voice. The text has earlier attested to them not wailing in repentance, so what was the purpose of their wailing? As alluded to earlier in the chapter, God's judgement has overtaken them, and they are under discipline. Recall to memory the Ten Plagues in Exodus and that during the last plague death passed over the Egyptian homes and slaughtered every firstborn. Consequently, Scripture pronounced that there was "a great cry in Egypt" which was akin to a howling. Nevertheless, after a short time span, they changed their minds and pursued the Israelites into the Red Sea with the goal of re-enslaving them. They wailed, but they did not repent! They were saddened by their judgement, but not saddened by their sin.

"For grain and wine they gash themselves; they rebel against me" concludes that verse. The Jews cut and slice their flesh in an effort to gain favour with the pagan gods. No longer do they seek Yahweh, the only true and living God, for their blessings. This is a replay of Israel's actions when Elijah faced the prophets of Baal on Mount Carmel (1 Kings 18:28).

Verse **15** says **"Although I trained and strengthened their arms, yet they devise evil against me."** God provided parental guidance for the nation for centuries; He was the father and Israel was the child. Yet, they concocted evil plans against Him. In our day, parents experience the same heartache when a child turns on them despite all the love and support that child has absorbed over the years. God is intimately familiar with that pain and can strongly identify with the struggle of those who raise children in contemporary society. Such trials do not mean you are an unfaithful parent. God was the perfect parent and was still treated with scorn by His offspring.

Verse **16** adds **"They return, but not upward."** Having sought ungodly societies like Egypt and Assyria, they indulge in perverse activities and return to their homeland without seeking God. They neglect to look "upward" to seek His face. His existence has no bearing upon their souls. This is as ridiculous as a husband vanishing from home without notice for a week, and then returning home and immediately going to bed without giving anyone in the household an explanation for his absence.

Metaphorically, **"they are like a treacherous bow."** A treacherous bow is a faulty bow that malfunctions because it is undependable and unreliable. It fails to complete the task for which it was created. Consequently, **"their princes shall fall by the sword because of the insolence of their tongue."** The Northern Kingdom's leaders will be slain in battle and it is their tongues that lead them to their graves. The book of James calls the tongue "a fire" and "a world of iniquity". This minute bodily member will be the origin of their demise. Well would God's children do to take stock of the words that are issued out of our mouths. Words are so powerful they can set wars into motion. The Bible urges that the conversations of the mouth be always with grace and seasoned with salt. How are your words toward those in your home? How are they toward those in your church or school or workplace? Mankind, throughout the millennia, has been injured more by the tongue than by the gun. God's people should fervently seek to distance themselves from verbal transgressions that have the potential to scar other's souls for life.

Hosea's final statement is that **"this shall be their derision in the land of Egypt."** In the book of Exodus, Israel watched as God judged Egypt. In the book of Hosea, Egypt will witness God judging Israel. That nation, once the pride and joy of Jehovah, because of its defiance, will become the laughing stock of ancient civilization as ridicule becomes its motto.

Discuss

1. Christians are called to be "in the world but not of the world." How can this dynamic be navigated without neglecting our responsibility to be salt and light on the one hand and not compromising our godly testimony on the other?

2. Give an example of someone in Scripture who expressed outward grief but was not truly repentant inwardly. Give a present-day example of how this same dishonesty may look.

3. What practical steps can be taken to guarantee our tongues are not used as "a fire" and "a world of iniquity"? How might James 1:19 fit into this equation?

4. "It is better to repent without weeping, than weep without repenting." Do you agree or disagree. Why?

5. Should Christians seek out the help of other religions in spiritual matters? Why or why not?

12

REAPING THE WHIRLWIND

8:1-7

¹*Set the trumpet to your lips! One like a vulture is over the house of the* LORD, *because they have transgressed my covenant and rebelled against my law.* ² *To me they cry, "My God, we—Israel—know you."* ³ *Israel has spurned the good; the enemy shall pursue him.* ⁴ *They made kings, but not through me. They set up princes, but I knew it not. With their silver and gold they made idols for their own destruction.* ⁵ *I have spurned your calf, O Samaria. My anger burns against them. How long will they be incapable of innocence?* ⁶ *For it is from Israel; a craftsman made it; it is not God. The calf of Samaria shall be broken to pieces.* ⁷ *For they sow the wind, and they shall reap the whirlwind. The standing grain has no heads; it shall yield no flour; if it were to yield, strangers would devour it.*

Few events cause anxiety and trepidation in people's souls like the report of someone going missing. In 2002, a teenager by the name of Elizabeth Smart was abducted from her home at knifepoint in the early hours of the morning on June 5th. The residents of Salt Lake City, Utah activated an immediate search once the sun rose. She could not be found anywhere. However, after nine arduous months, Elizabeth and her abductor were located. What is most shocking about this narrative is that Elizabeth Smart had made public appearances in the same urban area with her abductor during that time. They visited a library, grocery stores, and even a restaurant together in the Salt Lake City area, but no one recognized her. How could this happen? She was forced to wear a full-length robe and veil that concealed most of her face. Someone even unknowingly filmed her and her captor in a park together, but no one realized who she was. Though many saw her, they paid her no mind—she was overlooked on many occasions. Thankfully, God is not like man. He sees and knows everything. Furthermore, if there is one thing He cannot and will not overlook, it is sin.

A Disturbance

Hosea begins this eighth chapter (vs. 1) with **"Set the trumpet to your lips."** This instrument, the equivalent of a ram's horn, sometimes called a shofar had a loud, piercing sound to forewarn the people of impending danger. For example, if an army approached, this horn would signal the people to mobilise themselves for battle. Hosea desires to impose that same mood on those listening to his prophecy. In other words, there is danger on the horizon. And what is that danger? It is that **"One like a vulture is over the house of the LORD."**

"Vulture" comes from a Hebrew word which means "to lacerate". To lacerate something is to tear it to pieces or to wound it by stabbing it. The emphasis is that vultures are birds of prey. These creatures rarely attack healthy animals. Alternatively, they pursue animals that are wounded or sick, and pick them to pieces and, upon death, the entire corpse is consumed. Hosea paints a vivid picture of the threat upon the nation of Israel. Wounded and sick because of its evil, a vulture encircles it waiting to gobble it up. What or who is this vulture? Although the text does not reveal the identity, it is highly probable that Assyria is waiting to ravage them. More than a few times in Holy Writ, God uses metaphors of a bird of prey such as a vulture or an eagle to portray His judgement upon Israel by inviting other nations into the land to wreak havoc.

Deuteronomy 28:49-51 follows this pattern.

> *[49] The Lord will bring a nation against you from far away, from the ends of the earth, like an eagle swooping down, a nation whose language you will not understand, [50] a fierce-looking nation without respect for the old or pity for the young. [51] They will devour the young of your livestock and the crops of your land until you are destroyed. They will leave you no grain, new wine or olive oil, nor any calves of your herds or lambs of your flocks until you are ruined.*

Discern that these verses in Deuteronomy make clear that God even judges His own chosen nation. Many take issue with certain portions of Scripture like passages in the book of Judges where the Jews overrun the Promised Land executing masses of its inhabitants with the edge of the sword. Understandably, these actions do not sit well with the average person. Conversely, however, it can be observed from passages like the one under scrutiny that God uses pagan empires as devices to pulverize His own people. The crux of the matter is that God is a flawless and fair judge who uses whatever means He pleases to bring doom. Therefore, occasionally He utilizes Israel to discipline other nations—as in Judges—and at other intervals He uses pagan nations to break Israel—as in Hosea. The point is that God never penalizes anyone undeserving of it.

Why the impending danger? It is **"because they have trangressed my covenant and rebelled against my law."** Recalling the covenant that God ratified with His people in the *Torah*, succinctly stated, the covenant is this: "if you obey my words, I will bless you and if you disobey my words I will curse you."

At this stage, it is responsible to make a pertinent enquiry. Can New Testament Christians claim this covenant for themselves? Will God always bless believers for obedience and curse them for disobedience? The answer is a resounding no. It would be hazardous to translate that particular promise from the Old Testament directly into the New Testament era.

Why?

1. We are not living in Old Testament times. The word "testament" is equivalent to the term "covenant", so we live not under the old covenant, but under the new covenant. For this, we should burst forth with thankfulness having access to great blessings under the new covenant that those who once lived under the old covenant did not enjoy—the indwelling Holy Spirit being a chief example.

2. Most Christians today are not citizens of the nation of Israel. God initiated this covenant with a specific group of individuals living on a precise piece of land and because the majority of Christians today are not citizens of that country, we cannot claim promises made directly to them.

This distinction is important to highlight because a misinterpretation of it leads to an indulgence of some form of "prosperity gospel". The hazardous dogma of the prosperity gospel is not a concept that is snatched out of thin air, but, rather, has its foundations in the misapplication of the Old Testament. It reckons the Old

Testament Jew as equal to the New Testament Christian—a colossal blunder since New Testament believers are not entitled to this promise directly. To be clear, God *does* love and demand obedience. Even so, the modern Christian cannot always expect to be blessed materially as a result of obedience. John Piper made a similar observation when he spoke the following: "If God's love for His children is to be measured by our health, wealth, and comfort in this life, then God hated the Apostle Paul." Yes, God does sometimes bestow material blessings, but such assurances cannot be directly claimed from the Old Testament Scriptures.

The Lord admits that it is (vs. **2**) **"To me they cry, 'My God, we Israel know you'."** In their opinion, they understand who God is. Now that the vulture is hovering over them, suddenly they have time to dialogue with God, and the Jews give the impression that their bond with God is vivacious. Regrettably, their actions drown out their words. They are talking the talk, but not walking the walk. The same is true of many today. They profess to know God, but with their works, lifestyle, and actions, they deny Him.

Titus 1:15-16,

> *15To the pure all things are pure, but to the defiled and unbelieving, nothing is pure; but both their minds and their consciences are defiled. 16They profess to know God, but they deny him by their works. They are detestable, disobedient, unfit for any good work.*

Do you truly know God?

Is it the walk of your life or is it just the talk of your lips?

Progressing further in the passage (vs. **3**), **"Israel has spurned the good; the enemy shall pursue him."** If you've watched a rugby game, you've probably seen one player "stiff arm" another. The word "spurned" here carts that notion. It's the act of pushing something to the side or casting something off. Observe, however, that they are pushing to the side "the good". The moral compass should lead them to embrace good and stiff arm wrong. Again, "the good" here is submitting to the covenant. Unwisely, they are stiff-arming that which pleases and honours God.

That's not only the Jewish default nature, but the default nature of all human beings. We give a stiff-arm to the good and instead embrace the evil. It's who we all are without exception. Sin is the only character quality that all people under the sun have in common. Romans 3 declares that *"there is none righteous, no not one."*

Personally, I believe there are levels of spiritual blindness when it comes to non-Christians. However, the one who is most blinded is the person who does not consider himself a sinner. That goes beyond being blind; it's having your eyeballs plucked out of their sockets.

The first step to receiving salvation is admitting that it is necessary and those who refuse to admit their need of a Saviour are elevating themselves to the same level as God, since only He is sinlessly perfect. To uphold that mindset is to draw nigh to blasphemy.

Returning to the text, because the good has been rejected, God will remove His protection and sanction their enemies to swallow them whole. God is also disappointed that (vs. 4) **"They made kings, but not through me. They set up princes, but I knew it not."** The Lord was not involved with and, therefore, does not consent to the appointment of these executives. In the Old Testament, the coronation of kings was a sacred act. That sovereign was anointed by having oil poured on his forehead in order to authorize his position as the Head of State. It was repulsive for someone to be anointed king without the prophets and priests first seeking God, but this was precisely what was happening.

According to Psalms 127:1a, *"Unless the Lord builds the house those who build it labor in vain."*

It is imperative that we seek God's face over the major decisions of our lives. Believers often make hasty decisions over serious matters without seriously praying, fasting, and pondering them thoroughly. Thus we make moves that we later come to regret or that impede our spiritual progress. Who should I date? Who should I marry? What career path should I pursue? Where should I attend university? Which job opportunity should I take? How much money should I give to God's work? Should I sell my house? Should I further my education? God's face should be sought over such decisions and failure to do so often leaves us frustrated.

To be clear, there are certain decisions in which God need not be sought because they go squarely against His will. For example, a child of God does not need to pray about whether or not God wants him/her to marry a non-Christian, since that violates clear scriptural teaching. Christians are not to be unequally yoked with unbelievers (2 Corinthians 6:14). You do not need to pray about whether God wants you to work in an establishment that exists primarily to promote sin. However, for other major decisions that are legitimate options, we must be seeking God.

Disloyalty

The remainder of the verse tells that **"With their silver and gold they made idols."** What makes this offense so egregious is that the silver and gold used to construct idols was provided for them by God, as His blessings upon them resulted in the ownership of these precious metals (Hosea 2:8).

How do we use the tangible blessings that God has given us? Where do we go with the car that we drive? What do we watch with the television that we have? Who do we text with the cellphones that we have been entrusted with? How do we spend the money that we make? It would be just as egregious an offense for us to take the blessings that God provided us and use them for committing sin. The conclusion of the verse is **"for their own destruction."** These idols will bring about Israel's downfall because they have removed their focus from the true and living God to worthless, dead statues. We all need to be on guard against the worship of idols in our own lives. Our hearts steadily produce one idol after the next after the next. What is an idol? An idol is anything in our lives, besides God, that is foremost in standing. If God is not holding the principal place right now in your life, whatever is at that position is the idol.

A car can be idolized.

A television can be idolized.

The cellphone can be idolized.

Money can be idolized.

A job can be idolized.

Our loved ones can be idolized.

Really, anything and everything can be idolized. Are we currently paying homage to any idols? If we are, we need to demote that idol and promote God back to the highest position. Also, the prophet reveals (vs. **5**) **"I have spurned your calf, O Samaria.** Notice, earlier he declared that they "spurned"—they stiff-armed the good. Currently, God returns with a stiff-arm of His own. He rejects their calf—the idol they worshipped. Furthermore, **"My anger burns against them."**

The word translated "anger", in Hebrew, plainly denotes "a nose" presenting the idea of someone breathing rapidly with fury to the extent that their nose begins to flare up. God is beyond upset. His fury is burning because of their idolatry.

When did this take place? The account is given in I Kings 12:25-30.

> [25] Then Jeroboam built Shechem in the hill country of Ephraim and lived there. And he went out from there and built Penuel. [26] And Jeroboam said in his heart, "Now the kingdom will turn back to the house of David. [27] If this people go up to offer sacrifices in the temple of the Lord at Jerusalem, then the heart of this people will turn again to their lord, to Rehoboam king of Judah, and they will kill me and return to Rehoboam king of Judah." [28] So the king took counsel and made two calves of gold. And he said to the people, "You have gone up to Jerusalem long enough. Behold your gods, O Israel, who brought you up out of the land of Egypt." [29] And he set one in Bethel, and the other he put in Dan. [30] Then this thing became a sin, for the people went as far as Dan to be before one.

In summary, Jeroboam was fearful that the citizens of the Northern Kingdom would eventually give their allegiance to the king of the Southern Kingdom through worshipping at the Jewish Temple. Therefore, he constructed two golden calves in the North, commanding his people to worship there instead to avoid any travel and possible defecting. Israel commits traitorous idolatry all because of one man's insecurity.

Insecure people leave a bloody trail of destruction wherever they go. All God requires is your best effort consistently. Give your full energy, trust in the Lord, and leave the outcome to His divine sovereignty.

The Lord wants to know, **"How long will they be incapable of innocence?"** He desires one innocence firstly and chiefly. Purity and cleanliness is obligatory for God's people.

Equally, He wants the same from us today. He demands purity, cleanliness, and holiness. The fulfillment of that standard can be challenging because we retain carnality in our flesh even as converted people. Yet, holiness must be tenaciously pursued. Thank God for the great comfort of I John 1:9, *"If we confess our sins, He is faithful and just to forgive us our sins and to cleanse us from all unrighteousness."* Our calling is to be laundromat Christians, routinely submitting ourselves to a wash whenever soiled with dirt.

Verse 6 reveals more insight about the idol by saying **"For it is from Israel; a craftsman made it; it is not God."**

Foolish and futile is the veneration of golden calves since they are merely the works of men's hands that are void of God's presence, and neither symbolize Him.

All peoples worldwide must come to grips with this truth about the idols and shrines that are erected globally. Kneeling before images and praying to them bring you no closer to God. Paul told the men of Mars Hill that *"the God who made the world and everything in it, being Lord of heaven and earth, does not live in temples made by man nor is He served by human hands as though He needed anything since He himself gives to all mankind life and breath and everything."* (Acts 17:24-25)

The worship of images and objects as though they are God is nothing short of idolatry.

Exodus 20:4-5 says,

> *4 "You shall not make for yourself a carved image, or any likeness of anything that is in heaven above, or that is in the earth beneath, or that is in the water under the earth. 5 You shall not bow down to them or serve them, for I the Lord your God am a jealous God, visiting the iniquity of the fathers on the children to the third and the fourth generation of those who hate me,*

Verse 6 ends with **"The calf of Samaria shall be broken to pieces."** The approaching Assyrian army will desecrate this idol. It will be the end of idolatry, but only the beginning of their mutilation.

Idol worship always lends itself to destruction one way or the other.

The Disaster

Verse 7, the climax of the passage, proclaims **"For they sow the wind, and they shall reap the whirlwind."**

Israel will encounter much more than they bargained for. The modern phrase "shoot the breeze" is somewhat similar to what is meant here by "sow the wind" and as the saying goes they will reap what they have sown.

There are 3 laws of sow and reaping:

1. You will always reap exactly what you sow. (If you sow corn, you will reap corn

not tomatoes.)

2. You will always reap after you sow. (It may take some time for you to reap, but you will reap.)

3. You will always reap more than you sow. (Whatever you sow will be multiplied. One corn seed produces several ears of corn.)

The same three laws apply spiritually, and because Israel has sown a wind, they will reap a storm. What seeds are we sowing in our own lives? We must unswervingly keep watch on ourselves. How easy is it to set the microscope over other people's lives and bypass our own. We must monitor what we plant because we will harvest that same fruit.

In addition, **"The standing grain has no heads it shall yield no flour."** God's judgement extends to their farming industry. Their crops will not yield abundantly as they once did. Even so, **"if it were to yield strangers would devour it."** Even if their crops were to produce fruit, God would not allow them to enjoy the fruits of their labour. In lieu, the strangers and foreigners will enter and reap. God's retribution is serious, intentional, and direct. It is impossible for Him to overlook the deep sin that Israel finds itself drowning in.

> Discuss

1. Is God a fair and flawless judge? Why or why not?

2. Give two examples of the dangerous outcome of assuming all Old Testament principles should be applied directly into the New Testament era.

3. Is the weakening of a nation's material success a form of judgement from God? Why or why not?

4. Do you agree that the natural laws of sowing and reaping apply spiritually as well? Use Scripture to support your answer.

5. Is it wrong for professed Christians to bow down and pray to images that represent Christianity?

13

GIVE ME THE REAL THING

8:8-14

⁸ Israel is swallowed up; already they are among the nations as a useless vessel. ⁹ For they have gone up to Assyria, a wild donkey wandering alone; Ephraim has hired lovers. ¹⁰ Though they hire allies among the nations, I will soon gather them up. And the king and princes shall soon writhe because of the tribute. ¹¹ Because Ephraim has multiplied altars for sinning, they have become to him altars for sinning. ¹² Were I to write for him my laws by the ten thousands, they would be regarded as a strange thing. ¹³ As for my sacrificial offerings, they sacrifice meat and eat it, but the LORD does not accept them. Now he will remember their iniquity and punish their sins; they shall return to Egypt. ¹⁴ For Israel has forgotten his Maker and built palaces, and Judah has multiplied fortified cities; so I will send a fire upon his cities, and it shall devour her strongholds.

The Eiffel Tower in Paris, France is one of the most sought after tourist destinations in the entire world—and for good reason. It is a masterful, massive, and magnificent structure that must be seen in real life to absorb its full grandeur.

No picture, painting, replica, or movie can capture the full scope of the Eiffel Tower. Those things may give you a snippet of the shape and structure of the landmark, but once you visit the location in person, all other images will be wiped from the hard drive of your mind. It is likely that your first encounter with the tower will be imprinted on your brain for the remainder of your life. No picture does it justice. The real thing is to be preferred.

In the current text, Israel engages in much religious activity. There is show, but no substance. There is form, but no faithfulness. True, authentic worship of their God is desperately lacking. Israel does not possess the real thing.

Unholy Alliances

In verse 8 Hosea proclaims **"Israel is swallowed up."** "Swallowed", in this verse, is the same Hebrew word translated as "devoured" at the end of verse 7, portraying that the nation will be utterly consumed and gobbled up by its enemies. Israel is both the farmer whose crops will be destroyed as well as the actual crop which encounters destruction. It further presses that **"already they are among the nations as a useless vessel."** "Among the nations" speaks to the fact that other nationalities in close proximity are watching Israel. Unfortunately, "useless vessel" indicates a broken or shattered pot that was ineffectual for any purpose. At this point in Israel's history, their existence held no value because they were not working in the purpose that God preordained for them. Therefore, they were of no use.

Are you walking in God's purposes for your life? Are you seeking to know and execute His plans? Every Christian should be seeking to both know and fulfill God's will because He has not saved anyone to sit idly by fiddling their thumbs. All believers are saved on purpose for a purpose. Even if you are unsure of that calling, you must be actively searching it out. **"For they have gone up to Assyria"** begins verse 9. Stupidly, Israel has sought out unholy alliances with unholy nations, the chief of these being the Assyrian kingdom. Recall that in chapter 5:13, Hosea reported that Israel already went to Assyria to inquire of their king. Verse 9 refers to one of two potential scenarios. The first option is that Menahem, King of Israel, gave Pul, who is Tiglath-Pileser, funding to help maintain his grip on his Assyrian throne. 2 Kings 5:19-20 records this.

> *[19]* Pul the king of Assyria came against the land, and Menahem gave Pul a thousand talents of silver, that he might help him to confirm his hold on the royal power. *[20]* Menahem exacted the money from Israel, that is, from all the wealthy men, fifty shekels of silver from every man, to give to the king of Assyria. So the king of Assyria turned back and did not stay there in the land.

The second option is when Hoshea paid money to Shalmsneser the King of Assyria.

2 Kings 17:3 chronicles the account by saying "Against him came up Shalmaneser king of Assyria. And Hoshea became his vassal and paid him tribute."

Whichever situation verse 9 refers to, the attention of the matter is that Israel has become subservient to the Assyrians and only maintain the status of a slave nation. The stanza continues **"a wild donkey wandering alone."** Israel is compared to a lonely, wild donkey in the wilderness existing all by itself. What's telling about this metaphor is that naturally the wild donkey is not a creature that lives alone; instead, it travels in herds. Israel is entirely out of its comfort zone and has no true friendships. Ordinarily, God would be Israel's truest and closest companion, but He has pulled away because of her unfaithfulness, leaving her in a solitary state.

Perhaps you feel God is no longer your closest companion. Maybe His friendship with you has felt distant as of late. If that is your current condition, it's not God who has abandoned you, it is you who have abandoned God. James 4:8 implores Christians to *"Draw near to God, and he will draw near to you."* That's a promise in Scripture that can be claimed directly by all of God's sheep. If you were once nearer to God than you presently are, I invite you to begin drawing near again. Begin communing again. Begin fellow-shipping again. God's nearness to the believer is like two magnets pushed toward each other at opposite poles. The closer they get to one another the greater the magnetic pull between them. Moving closer and closer to each other, eventually they fasten together in a tight bond.

Also, **"Ephraim has hired lovers."** Israel, the lonely wandering donkey that has no friends, is forced to pay for affection—an apt illustration of someone who engages prostitutes. Their unholy alliance with heathen nations will cost them, not only metaphorically, but literally; their pockets being squeezed. When Israel loved her first husband, there was no cost. As a matter of fact, their love relationship with Yahweh fattened their pockets and made their cups overflow significantly. That love relationship was free of charge, but these lovers will cost them money. Their love does not come without a payment.

What a blessing it is to know that, even today in a world where almost everything requires a charge, the greatest love relationship of all is still free. You do not need finances to be saved. You do not need credit cards to receive forgiveness. Eternal life does not require writing a cheque. Soul conversion is not reliant on money. The only thing you need is change—a change of mind and heart. You must relinquish sin and cling fully and simply to the finished work of Jesus Christ on Calvary's cross; thereby commencing a love relationship with your Creator. Thus, even though we are paying more and more for the most rudimentary items of this life, we can rest assure that salvation, forgiveness, and eternal life will always be free of charge. It always has been, and it always will be.

The writing moves on with (vs. 10) **"Though they hire allies among the nations."** "Hire allies" in this verse is synonymous with "hired lovers" in verse 9. These are the godless nations with whom Israel prostitutes itself, and even though they appear to be allies now, Israel will eventually come to realize, in due course, that they are their adversaries.

Similarly, none who entice the believer to live rebelliously against God is a true friend. Not one who encourages unfaithfulness is an ally of God's child. These promptings come only from the foes of God. It is imperative for every Christian to carefully scrutinize who is in their inner circle, because ultimately your closest associations will influence your spiritual life for better or for worse. Many today can testify to having been tricked and beguiled by those whom they falsely believed were their allies.

Hosea reveals **"I will soon gather them up."** The gathering that takes place here may seem to be a positive action at first thought, but, it is negative. This is a gathering and assembling of Israel for judgement. Other minor prophets use "gather" in the same way.

Joel 3:2,

"I will gather all the nations and bring them down to the Valley of Jehoshaphat. And I will enter into judgment with them there, on behalf of my people and my heritage Israel, because they have scattered them among the nations and have divided up my land."

Zephaniah 3:8,

"Therefore wait for me," declares the Lord, "for the day when I rise up to seize the prey. For my decision is to gather nations, to assemble kingdoms, to pour out upon them my indignation, all my burning anger; for in the fire of my jealousy all the earth shall be consumed.

Typically, in the Minor Prophets, gathering is done to mobilize for judgement.

Furthermore, **"the king and princes shall soon writhe because of the tribute."** "Writhe" translated here is a word which literally means "to become small" or "be diminished". As a result of an imposed taxation by the Assyrian Empire, the Jewish monarchy will become weak and subject to a submissive governance. "Tribute" is a burden of taxation that will degrade them to an almost slave-like level. Prestige and power will be snuffed out of the Jewish monarchy. When even the highest office in the land is not exempt from yielding to the authority of another, things must be in a dreadful state. Ungodly alliances will strip them of every sense of pride and self-worth and Israel will suffer in humiliation.

Certainly, ungodly alliances have a way of stripping Christians as well. It can strip us of our good testimony, time, treasures and our effectiveness for God's Kingdom. Because we are called to live in the world, but not be of the world, those who are God's chosen must always be on the lookout for unholy alliances and seek to detach ourselves from them. A magnifying glass must be set over the friends we keep, the past-times we share, the organizations we support, and even the churches we join, to discern if we are caught up in unholy alliances because they will prove corrosive to our spiritual lives sooner rather than later.

Ungodly Actions

The 11th verse says that **"because Ephraim has multiplied altars for sinning they have become to him altars for sinning."** An increase in worship sites cloaked the nation. Normally, this would be looked at favorably, but this is abominable. Either of two options were achieved in this verse. First, they could have been offering a number of sacrifices to various gods instituting a pluralistic culture. Since heathen realms worshipped voluminous gods, it makes logical sense that the altars were multiplied to accommodate their quantity. Perchance, they no longer trusted the one, true God so they invoked others to ensure all avenues of help were sourced. Another option is that Ephraim was mixing Jewish worship with Baal worship. This syncretistic practice of bringing pagan rituals to Jewish altars would have been equally repulsive in the eyes of God. Although it is not certain what truly took place, it cannot be ruled out that verse 11 includes a blending of both notions. With judgement on the horizon, it is conceivable that God was at His wits end with a combination of these offences. Yet, let not the aim of the verse go unnoticed. There was a marked increase in religious practices which the Israelites probably enacted to appease their guilt for unfaithfulness to God. Working hard at the altar, they wished to gain a covering for their trespasses. Miserably though, no amount of sacrifice could wash away the guilt of their idolatry. Even their acts of seeking forgiveness were acts of disobedience because they did not seek the Lord in the way set forth by Him.

Empty, outward worship is no substitute for a heart that is right with God. No amount of teaching, giving, dancing, singing, or liturgy can remove the stain of a disobedient conscience. God's divine order has always been internal first and external second. Giving the external precedence over the internal results in deficiency and possibly destruction. The Northern Kingdom was only concerned with the externals of empty worship and it will cost them exceedingly. If God's people follow suit in these days, it will cost us dearly as well.

Hosea prophesies (vs. 12) **"were I to write for him my laws by the ten thousands, they would be regarded as a strange thing."** The Lord puts forward a hypothetical situation stating that if He were to present to His people, Israel, His laws by the thousands they would not even be remotely familiar with them. "Strange" carries with it the impression of being a foreigner. The tenets of God's law is foreign to the people of Israel, so there is no wonder they are light-years away from Him. Unholy alliances and ungodly activities are unpreventable if they do not know the law of God.

Hosea's time sounds similar to our time in history. Among the many difficulties with Christendom, the biggest issue we face today is that Christianity is becoming more and more detached from the Word of God, the Bible. The most empty, impotent, and deceptive doctrines and values are being seized by the Christian Church while the Word of God remains on a derelict shelf somewhere collecting dust. People are irrationally seeking visions and dreams as if God has not spoken clearly and sufficiently through the men who penned Holy Scripture. All this has left Christianity—even evangelical Christianity—in a state of disarray and confusion. Most believers get their theology from worship music rather than biblical expositors and theologians. If Christianity is to be rescued from this deadly, spiritual pandemic, what must be unashamedly demanded is a return to the Bible. What we must have is a revival of teaching, preaching, and living the Scriptures—not just some of it, but all of it. The roving ship of the Church must be brought back to shore and anchored permanently in the unchanging Word of God. If not, the atrocities the Jews committed in Hosea's era will seem like a meager, trivial matter in comparison to the horrendous future of Christianity.

To begin verse 13, Hosea asserts **"As for my sacrificial offerings, they sacrificed meat and eat it."** This verse is linked to verse 11. When offerings were obediently sacrificed on altars, the opportunity to eat the meat was a natural byproduct. The lawgiver expressly allows His priests to eat meat from the sacrifices as a means of sustenance (Leviticus 6:26; 7:31-35). Eating meat was not an infraction. However, the end of the verse notes that **"the Lord does not accept them."** The reason He does not is because they are offered in an idolatrous fashion as alluded to in the 11th verse.

Unfavorable Adversity

The prophetic script continues **"now he will remember their iniquity and punish their sins."** The North's sins have not been correctly atoned for. Sacrifices were not conducted in the manner that God ordained; therefore, they were not acceptable to Him. As a result, their sins are uncovered and lay bare before the Almighty God and He will punish.

Every human being is a sinner and each one is guilty of iniquity repeatedly. If you desire your sins to be atoned for, they must be covered God's way. Under the Old Covenant, God provided specific instructions concerning how iniquity was to be purged. Now, under His New Covenant, He has presented a new set of instructions concerning the same. The only mode in which sin can be dismissed is by individually taking hold of the sacrifice made by the Lamb of God on Golgotha's Hill. You must put yourself under His covering. You must be purged by His blood. You must personally seize the gift that is offered you by Jesus Christ and His atoning work. Apart from that, my friend, your sins lie exposed and God will remember your iniquity, and will punish your sins by casting you into the Lake of fire to be tormented for all eternity. If you want your sins forgiven, they must be forgiven God's way and not your own. All your righteous efforts are like polluted garments to Him (Isaiah 64:6). You must enter by way of the cross. You must pass through the blood. Unless you call upon the name of Jesus for rescue, you will not escape the unquenchable fire.

Also, **"they shall return to Egypt."** What does this mean? Will they literally return to their previous scene of slavery? More than likely that is not what Hosea desires to communicate. What it does mean is they will return to the same kind of condition they endured in Egypt. In Egypt, they were out of place. In Egypt, they were slaves. In Egypt, they were treated like dogs. In Egypt, they were whipped and beaten. The Jews were in bondage in Egypt and to "Egypt" they will return. They shall encounter the opposite of the exodus. Just as they were taken out of oppression into the Promised Land, they will be taken out of the Promised Land back into oppression. Egypt is a metaphor for the Assyrian invasion and the exile they will endure.

Sin has consequences. Repetitive, habitual sin has even worse consequences. Dangerous it is for any people to become engrossed in waywardness since they will inevitably have to face a day of terrible reckoning. Fellow Christians, stand firm in holiness and righteousness, because we are the dams who hold the tsunami of God's awful judgement at bay.

Added to that is **"for Israel has forgotten his Maker and built palaces."** When verse **14** identifies God as Israel's "Maker", it not merely insinuates that He is Israel's Creator. Included in that euphemism are the ideas that He called them as a nation, made a covenant with them, gave them the law, and provided for and protected them.[vi] He should have meant everything to Israel because He was everything for Israel. Unfortunately, though, the Lord has been removed from their memory and instead "palaces" were being constructed. These were major building projects which gave them a false sense of security as a nation. Surprisingly—or not— Judah plays copycat.

It is discovered that **"Judah has multiplied fortified cities."** Attempting to strengthen their towns in order to protect against their rivals, they put sizable sweat into security and safety. It will all be to no avail. The trust they had in the structures they built was egregiously misplaced. They were not principled under the precepts of Psalm 20:7, *"Some trust in chariots and some in horses, but we trust in the name of the Lord our God."* The Jews, who were far-off from the spiritual state of the Psalmist's description, were performing the contrary. Their version would be "we trust in palaces and in fortified cities; therefore we will not trust in the name of the Lord our God."

What is your trust in? Is it in your intelligence or money? Is it in your family name or the stability of your government? Is it in your own abilities or talents? If your confidence is not chiefly in the Lord, the ground beneath your feet is as soft as a spider's web. Trusting God is foundational to the victorious Christian life. We are not only saved from sin by faith in Jesus Christ, we must also live daily by faith in Jesus Christ. This is the essence of what it means to be a victorious Christian.

Because of their lack of trust and rebellion, God cautions that **"so I will send fire upon his cities."** The remark of "fire" portrays the idea that utter obliteration will occur because of war, and, more specifically, uncovers how cities were set ablaze after being conquered by the enemy. Hosea's contemporary, Amos, uses the image of fire several times in his writings also (Amos 1:4,7,10). Finally, **"it shall devour her strongholds."** Fortified, protected citadels will be consumed and swallowed whole as the whale did with Jonah. Both Israel and Judah will be forever changed because of God's judgement.

> Discuss

1. Why is syncretism wrong? Use Scripture apart from the verses quoted in this chapter to support your answer.

2. "More and more Christianity is becoming detached from the Word of God, the Bible." Do you agree or disagree? Give reasons to support your answer.

3. Give an example of something that has happened in the Church (locally or globally) to support the reality of Question 2.

4. What are the dangers of believers receiving their theology from worship music instead of Bible preachers and theologians?

5. Why was the shedding of Jesus' physical blood important? Use Scripture not cited in this chapter to support your answer.

14

FLOODS OF FURY

9: 1-6

¹*Rejoice not, O Israel! Exult not like the peoples; for you have played the whore, forsaking your God. You have loved a prostitute's wages on all threshing floors.* ² *Threshing floor and wine vat shall not feed them, and the new wine shall fail them.* ³ *They shall not remain in the land of the* LORD, *but Ephraim shall return to Egypt, and they shall eat unclean food in Assyria.* ⁴ *They shall not pour drink offerings of wine to the* LORD, *and their sacrifices shall not please him. It shall be like mourners' bread to them; all who eat of it shall be defiled; for their bread shall be for their hunger only; it shall not come to the house of the* LORD. ⁵ *What will you do on the day of the appointed festival, and on the day of the feast of the* LORD? ⁶ *For behold, they are going away from destruction; but Egypt shall gather them; Memphis shall bury them. Nettles shall possess their precious things of silver; thorns shall be in their tents.*

Church history is chockfull of classic sermons. High on the popularity scale is "Sinners in the Hand of an Angry God", a message preached by the scholar Jonathan Edwards to his own church in Northampton, Massachusetts in 1741. God used this sermon as a linchpin in what would eventually be termed "The Great Awakening". The Great Awakening was a mighty, spiritual revival that overtook the American colonies between 1730 and 1755. A sermon replete with imagery, this excerpt tells of the imminent wrath of God upon sinners.

"The wrath of God is like great waters that are damned for the present; they increase more and more, and rise higher and higher till an outlet is given; and the longer the stream is stopped, the more rapid and mighty is its course, when once it is let loose.

It is true that judgement against your evil works has not been executed hitherto; the floods of God's vengeance have been withheld; but your guilt in the meantime is constantly increasing and you are everyday treasuring up more wrath; the waters are constantly rising and waxing more and more mighty; and there is nothing but the mere pleasure of God, that holds the waters back, that are unwilling to be stopped and press hard to go forward.

If God should only withdraw His hand from the flood-gate, it would immediately fly open and the fiery floods of the fierceness of and wrath of God would rush forth with inconceivable fury, and would come upon you with omnipotent power. If your strength were ten thousand times greater than it is, yea ten thousand times greater than the strength of the stoutest, sturdiest devil in hell, it would be nothing to withstand or endure it."

Jonathan Edwards paints a vivid picture of the imminence of the judgement of God.

The text of Scripture at hand gives the same idea—although, perhaps, not as dreadfully—that a refusal to repent of sin leaves the imminent door to judgement wide open.

"**Rejoice not, O Israel!**" (vs. 1) is how the ninth chapter commences. God forbids His people from being merry about the season at hand. There is no place for joy or gladness so Israel should not even begin to beam at this time. They should "**exult not like the people.**" Even though heathen lands may be happy, Israel ought not be. Egypt and Assyria may be glowing but Israel cannot. The reason being that "**you have played the whore, forsaking your God.**" Naturally, "whorish" language returns to Hosea's vocabulary. Israel is still unfaithful to her spouse and exists as a two-timing traitor yet fornicating with other lovers. By and large, the nation is unfaithful and uncommitted to their love relationship with God. God birthed that nation. God first called Abraham. God gave them the law. God made a covenant with them. God brought them out of slavery to Egypt. God gave them victory in the Promised Land. Nevertheless, in spite of all this, they have abandoned their God.

Have you abandoned God? Have you spat in the face of His saving grace? Have you removed yourself from pursuing a relationship with Him? Are you living a life of sin and transgression? Have you thrown your Bible to the curb and taken up worldly philosophies? Then you, my friend, are also playing the whore just as the state of Israel was. You are being loose with your body. You are being unfaithful to your spouse. You are a two-timing renegade. God will tolerate none of it.

He further scolds with **"you have loved a prostitute's wages."** "Prostitute's wages" is translated as two words in English, but it comes from a single word in the Hebrew language that, quite frankly, means the price someone would pay a prostitute for the services she performs. Israel is the grammatical subject of this clause, so this suggests they collect some benefit for their immorality as a nation. As a result of prostituting themselves, they reaped profit.

They reaped it **"on all threshing floors."** A threshing floor was an essential space in Jewish farming society. It was an outside area where newly-picked grain was spread over a surface of stone. Next, an animal, such as an ox or horse, would be brought onto the threshing floor and walked over the grain so as to crack the kernels. The outside, unwanted shell of the grain was separated from the inside, edible part during this activity. Israel was receiving her reward for prostitution by way of grain supply. Having compromised spiritually, its lovers provide it with grain as a reward for her adulterous escapades.

Is there any area in your life in which you are currently compromising spiritually? Are you sliding biblical principles to the side so you can reap better benefits or more money? The willingness to compromise is the Achilles heel of the modern Church. Unfortunately, the further the Church compromises, the more God perceives it as an institution of prostitution. Many who profess to follow Jesus in our day seem more concerned with what is traditional, political, or fashionable, over what is biblical. Spiritual compromise never strengthens the church, it only weakens it.

The 2nd verse informs that **"threshing floor and wine vat shall not feed them."** Having already discussed the threshing floor, the wine vat was an instrument used to compress and crush grapes, extracting its juice. A winepress is a similar object. Usually, there were two levels to the wine vat: the top level where crushing took place and the bottom level where the juice was collected.[vii] Furthermore, **"the new wine shall fail them."** Both the grain and the wine will be cut off from Israel—their most precious resources failing because of God's judgement for their adultery.

Sometimes God does that in individual lives as well. He may strip us of our progress in courtship, making love relationships fail. Social standing may be ripped from our bosom. He may stop us dead in our tracks, all to get us to return to Him. Occasionally, God turns off the tap of our lives so the waters of blessing cease to flow, because when they do, we find ourselves straying from the mark He has set. Has God turned off the tap in your life? It is time to inspect whether or not you are gone astray.

The Consequences

It is also revealed that (vs. 3) **"they shall not remain in the land of the LORD."** Observe to whom the land belongs. It's not Israel's land; it's God's land. From early in Israel's history, God established this truth.

Leviticus 25:23,

"The land shall not be sold in perpetuity, for the land is mine. For you are strangers and sojourners with me."

The land beneath their feet was still the territory of Jehovah. He only loaned it to them for as long as they remained faithful to His covenant. The right to take the land back when He pleased was never surrendered by the Lord.

Likewise, the tiniest atom and molecule belongs to God. All—without exception—is His; none of it belongs to us. Psalm 24:1-2 utters that *"The earth is the Lord's and the fullness thereof, the world and those who dwell therein, for he has founded it upon the seas and established it upon the rivers."*

Human beings own nothing. He owns it all, from the smallest atom to the largest galaxy and everything between.

Believers struggle with giving money to the Lord's work because they are ill-informed about their own possessions. In reality, they have no possessions. Everything is a loan from Heaven that the Lord can recall according to His sovereign will. The better we apprehend that biblical principle, the easier it is to be a cheerful giver.

Since the people do not want to conduct themselves according to God's will, there could be only one result. It is that **"Ephraim shall return to Egypt."** This verse is the identical idea to Hosea 3:13b. Returning to Egypt is the reversal of their liberation from Egypt. The God who took them out of captivity will deliver them back to captivity. Again, the land was Yahweh's merciful provision for them, but since they drenched themselves in debased debauchery, God would not continuously reward them by giving them access to the land of Palestine. Hosea further explains that **"they shall eat unclean food in Assyria."** "Unclean food" proposes that they will not have opportunity to obey the dietary laws given them in the Torah. Not many options will be available and they will be forced to eat whatever they can. Since they want to live in sin, God will give them over to sin entirely. "You want sin? Fine! You can have it". Assyria, obviously, is the territory they will be forcibly taken into against their wishes.

What's interesting about Egypt and Assyria is that these are the two nations they are in bed with politically. They were their primary lovers in prostitution. Glancing at the rearview mirror, we can recall Hosea 7:11,

Ephraim is like a dove, silly and without sense, calling to Egypt, going to Assyria.

Peering forward we will encounter Hosea 12:1,

Ephraim feeds on the wind and pursues the east wind all day long; they multiply falsehood and violence; they make a covenant with Assyria, and oil is carried to Egypt.

Ironically, both realms will be the barrels from which the bullets of Israel's judgement is shot—the clouds from which the rain of their judgement falls. Often in life, it's possible for the very people who have partnered with us in sin to turn against us and become our opponents. It's possible for the selfsame deeds of our rebellion to be put in reverse and mow us down. Never assume those you sin with will perpetually have your best interest in mind—nothing could be further from the truth. Sin is loyal to no one but itself. The more speedily we arrive at that reality, the safer we will be. Next, it is publicized (vs. 11) that **"they shall not pour drink offerings of wine to the LORD."** God's spokesman continues to elaborate on what the livelihood of the Jews will be outside of the land. The drink offering was a small component of their sacrificial system and would cease when they entered exile. In addition, **"their sacrifices shall not please him."** This is a reference to the Old Testament sacrificial system and probably shines a spotlight on the particular animals that were duly sacrificed. Remember, however, that syncretism was in full effect and the Israelites intermingled devotion to the Lord with devotion to Baal. It is no wonder they could not please God. To Him, their behaviour was detestable. Sacrificing to the Lord when they enter exile will be a titanic waste of time, it having as much affect upon God as a falling feather has upon an earthquake.

Moreover, "it shall be like mourner's bread to them; all who eat of it shall be defiled." According to the Levitical law, anything and anyone that had contact with the dead was reckoned unclean (Leviticus 21:11). Bread handled by those who lamented dead loved ones fell into that category. This is how God views Israel's attempt at sacrificing animals while in exile. It resembles an unclean substance. He is building a metaphor—sacrificial offerings equal defiled bread. It is worthless to God and is refused by Him. Pursuing further, the prophet reveals that **"their bread shall be for their hunger only."** Such bread will be exclusively used to fill their stomachs and serve a natural purpose instead of a spiritual purpose after their deportment. Efforts at sacrificing are as productive as a hamster on a wheel. Thus, **"it shall not come to the house of the LORD."** "House of the LORD" is not an allusion to the Temple. In the present context, it is a reference to the Lord's land as specified in verse 3. Therefore, the bread that this generation eats will not enter the Lord's territory and will remain outcast. Just as the people go, so goes their provisions. God will drive the children of Israel, and everything they own, into banishment and will erect a "no trespassing" sign over His property.

The Catastrophe

According to verse 5, Hosea queries **"what will you do on the day of the appointed festival, on the day of the feast of the LORD?"** This question is rhetorical so He does not anticipate a response. Really, He is making a statement. Helpless they will lay on this day and all their efforts will flop. "Day of the appointed festival" and "day of the feast of the Lord" are synonymous with one another. They both refer to the same season. Among Bible commentators, there are minor differences of opinion on which festival/feast this verse discusses. However, I reckon it is most wise to conclude that both of these terms refer to the annual Feast of Booths also called the Feast of Tabernacles. It was a festival instituted by God to commemorate the wilderness journey of the Israelites. There are two reasons why it is fitting to determine this verse has the Feast of Booths as its subject.

Firstly, the best commentary on Scripture is Scripture itself. Hosea 12:9 reads, "*I am the Lord your God from the land of Egypt; I will again make you dwell in tents, as in the days of the appointed feast.*"

The verse finishes with "appointed feast". That exact term is used in Hosea 9:5. Also, in this specific feast it is revealed that they "dwell in tents". Dwelling in tents is exactly what took place at the Feast of Booths. The booths located there could also be classified as "tents".

Secondly, the Feast of Booths is addressed in Deuteronomy 16:13.

*"You shall keep the Feast of Booths seven days, when you have gathered in the produce from your **threshing floor** and your **winepress**."* Our present text has two items in common with Deuteronomy 16:13. These are the threshing floor and the winepress. The Feast of Booths was the occasion there and is most likely the occasion here in Hosea. In my opinion, both of these examples serve as sufficient evidence that the feast under question is the Feast of Booths.

Hosea says (vs. 6) **"behold they are going away from destruction."** Seemingly, some Israelites would try to escape the coming ambush by fleeing to Egypt, believing they were their allies. In other words, they bolt to Egypt in order to escape the Assyrian onslaught. However, **"Egypt shall gather them; Memphis shall bury them."** This segment of the population will be received in Egypt, but the ultimate goal will be their demise. Precious lives will be lost there. Memphis is where their bodies will be entombed. The city was a popular metropolis located on the River Nile and was notorious for having a gigantic graveyard. Memphis would[viii] not lack the room to accommodate their lifeless bodies. Egypt, the same people they had unholy alliances with, will coup their fake friendship.

Once more, those who sin with you will sin against you. Those who gossip with you will gossip about you. Foolish is the adulterous husband who determines his mistress will never break their confidence. The worker who participates in theft or fraud must not assume complicit co-workers will unceasingly keep their mouths shut. Trust no sinful alliance because, in the end, it will strike back like a cobra. Sin has no allegiances.

Next, **"nettles shall possess their precious things of silver; thorns shall be in their tents."** "Nettles" are wild weeds that grow up because Israel is shipped away and there is none to tend to the land. Plausibly "their precious things" are the idols made of silver they commit whoredom with, forsaking their Master. "Thorns" further submits a homeland that is abandoned and left wanting. God's judgement will leave the territory overgrown while the people are slaves to the kingdom of Assyria.

> Discuss

1. Why was Israel forbidden to be involved with the affairs of nations like Egypt and Assyria?

2. Give an example of a Christian "playing the whore" today?

3. "Occasionally, God turns off the tap of our lives so the waters of blessing cease to flow, because when they do, we find ourselves straying from the mark He has set." Has this ever occurred in your life? If so, when?

4. "The best commentary on Scripture is Scripture itself." In what ways can this fact benefit personal Bible study? What significance do cross-references have?

5. What was the significance of the Feast of Booths/Feast of Tabernacles to Israel?

15

GUARDIANS OF THE TRUTH
9:7-9

⁷ The days of punishment have come; the days of recompense have come; Israel shall know it. The prophet is a fool; the man of the spirit is mad, because of your great iniquity and great hatred. ⁸ The prophet is the watchman of Ephraim with my God yet a fowler's snare is on all his ways, and hatred in the house of his God. ⁹ They have deeply corrupted themselves as in the days of Gibeah: he will remember their iniquity; he will punish their sins.

Church historian, T. H. L. Parker, once authored a book on the preaching of the Genevan reformer John Calvin in which he listed several qualifications of a biblical preacher. The third qualification listed was that of courage. Parker wrote, "The preacher needs courage—not courage to believe but courage to proclaim the truth, however unpalatable, and to rebuke wherever rebukes are necessary. It is inevitable that he will arouse opposition."[ix]

Parker then proceeded to quote John Calvin himself who said, "They that intend to serve God faithfully and to proclaim His Word will never lack enemies to make war against them…Insomuch that the man who serves God in bearing his word faithfully will never have peace nor go without stings and unmolested, nor be without many enemies."[x]

I believe both statements well represent the situation of the ministry of the prophet Hosea. Hosea was not called to an easy task as there would be much opposition headed his direction. Nevertheless, as God's mouthpiece, he was to stand firm and unashamedly proclaim all that God revealed to him.

Stand For the Truth

In verse **7,** Hosea announces **"the days of punishment have come; the days of recompense have come."** "Punishment", in this verse, conveys the idea of being visited with judgement while "recompense" speaks to a reward for one's actions. Here, the reward is undesirable so it is a retribution. Israel will pay the price for its sin. Notice that both verbs are past tense and declare "have come" rather than the more expected "shall come". Most times in Hosea's prophecy thus far, the judgement was looked at as being future. Just observe earlier in chapter 9 where verse 3 says *"Ephraim shall return to Egypt and they shall eat unclean food in Assyria".* Also, verse 6 informs that *"Egypt shall gather them; Memphis shall bury them."*

For most of Hosea's prophecy thus far, the word "shall" was used, but here "have come" is employed suggesting that the action is already passed. Has the exile already happened? More than likely it has not. Yet, what Hosea is emphasizing is that the judgement predicted is so sure to take place that he declares it in the past tense speaking as if the situation has already occurred. Hosea's mandate is to stand firm and unashamedly articulate the truth to this rebellious generation.

Present-day preachers and proclaimers of God's Word must do exactly the same. Christian ministry is not for softies. The sacred desk does not summon men with no backbone or conviction. Those whose only interest is to pander to people's innate desires should steer clear of God's pulpit. Why? The Lord's messengers are called to orate the truth, and more often than not, the truth hurts. People don't like the truth. People, even Christians, don't want the truth. Truth makes people uncomfortable. Truth gets under people's skin. Truth punctures people's souls. God's truth must be proclaimed even through adversity, otherwise we qualify only as disloyal, defiant servants—suns that don't shine—alarms that don't sound—salt that doesn't savour—swords that don't slice. The masses must know that God judges sin and that Hell is real and eternal. People must know that abortion is murder and that homosexuality is still an abomination. That there is only one way to Heaven is a Scriptural truth that must not be abandoned. Any man who seeks only to tell people what they want to hear should tender his resignation straightaway, because he does not have what it takes to be God's agent. Untold thousands stand in pulpits globally whose only concern is to be cool and trendy. Give us men again whose faces are set as a flint toward the truth.

Furthermore, Hosea informs that **"Israel shall know it."** Interestingly the word "it" in this clause is not in the original Hebrew text. "It" was only added in some English versions to give flow to the expression. Therefore, some other Bible translators render this clause as "let Israel know". The key idea is that Israel needs to know the truth, and Hosea will be the one to dispatch it to them. As an Old Testament prophet, after he had received revelation from God, he was to dispense that knowledge to his Jewish audience. The message was not exclusively for himself; the message was to be proclaimed. Even so, everything written in Scripture is fair game for the preacher. Nothing is off limits—not one chapter or verse or even one word. All of God's Word is free to be expounded clearly and unashamedly. The Bible is not only a private study tool; everything was written to be declared from the highest mountaintop. Christ's Church needs all of the Bible—the entire entity—and not merely the sections that sit well with us. We must ingest the fragments we don't relish because all of it flows from God's throne—from Genesis to Revelation—every single verse. Spurgeon's suggested remedy is "if there is any verse that you would like left out of the Bible, that is the verse that ought to stick to you like a blister, until you really attend to its teaching."

Stand in Spite of Ridicule

The script further adds **"the prophet is a fool; the man of the spirit is mad."** "Fool" is used to describe someone who despises wisdom and is a silly individual. "Mad" describes somebody who is outright insane. Hosea allows a sneak peek into what the people are saying about him. They insist that this prophet has lost his marbles and belongs in a mental asylum. The utter disrespect boils over for this man of the spirit. "Man of the spirit" means man of God's Spirit which inspires and speaks through him. Israelis are furious with Hosea and regard him as an outcast.

Equally, every preacher who remains truthful to God's Word will be considered senseless and/or treated like a castaway from time to time. High is the cost of what it means to be God's spokesperson. It comes with penalties. Never envy men who are called to lead the church of God because it can be a difficult road. You step into a room and people turn their heads. Others avoid you after the service. Observing the parking lot one can see different "meetings" when church is ended. We ministers call that the "preacher roast"! It's not a bed of roses by any stretch of the imagination; and if it is a bed of roses for anyone, that is a good indication that such preacher needs to vacate his post. Persons—even professed Christians—will call you stupid for proclaiming the truth of Holy Scripture. Men of God, are you flowing with the tide or against it? Are you a sellout or are you sold out for the truth?

The text presses forward to tell us Hosea is treated as such **"because of your great iniquity."** The term "iniquity" at its root means that which is "twisted" or "bent". In other words, something has been distorted and made crooked. In this context, the people are crooked. That exemplifies sin—taking that which God has perfectly given us and twisting it to suit our desires. The prophet is treated this way because the people are twisted inside and what's located within will inevitably manifest itself in their actions. So plentiful is their love for sin that they are totally opposed to Hosea's message. They also treat him this way because of their ***"great hatred"***. Toward the things of God, they are hostile and bitter. They hate anything godly. They hate anyone godly. Paul describes a similar breed of people in Philippians 3:18-19 when he says,

> [18] *For many, of whom I have often told you and now tell you even with tears, walk as enemies of the cross of Christ.* [19] *Their end is destruction, their god is their belly, and they glory in their shame, with minds set on earthly things.*

Because these people don't want to acknowledge their guilt and renounce their sin, they respond to Hosea with anger.

The same thing happens now. When folks should repent upon hearing the message, they instead react to the message. Rather than seeking cleansing from the Lord, they choose to clash with His servant. All called by God to preach holy writ must be prepared to undergo Hosea's experience. People will get angry with you, reject you, and slander your character. As Socrates said "when the debate is lost, slander becomes the tool of the loser."

Nevertheless, this should be your rock of refuge during those times. Here is where you should take comfort. Those who reject you when you do proclaim the truth are not ultimately rejecting you; they are rejecting God. If you're preaching the Bible, the message did not originate with you. God is its author, therefore they are rejecting Him. This is precisely the message God gave Samuel when Israel pronounced they wanted a king to be like all the other nations.

1 Samuel 8:4-7

> ⁴*Then all the elders of Israel gathered together and came to Samuel at Ramah* ⁵ *and said to him, "Behold, you are old and your sons do not walk in your ways. Now appoint for us a king to judge us like all the nations."* ⁶ *But the thing displeased Samuel when they said, "Give us a king to judge us." And Samuel prayed to the Lord.* ⁷ *And the Lord said to Samuel, "Obey the voice of the people in all that they say to you, for they have not rejected you, but they have rejected me from being king over them.*

Rather than being frustrated with those who reject what we teach from the Scriptures, we should pity them. If what we have taught flows from the biblical fountain, they are essentially rejecting God. Please note, however, that the caveat is that your teaching must be firmly grounded in God's book because if it is not, your flock only rejects you since you are not standing but falling into filth. If you are not carefully, accurately, and faithfully expounding Scripture you are not speaking on God's behalf.

Stand with a Purpose
"The prophet is the watchman of Ephraim" is the next expression. Hosea marks himself as the watchman of the nation. Who was a watchman? It was an individual who looked out for a city, especially at night, in order to warn them in case they came under attack from an enemy. If the watchman spotted danger during his "watch", he would blow the trumpet to alert the city to prepare themselves for battle. Hosea's role, however, was not to be a physical watchman but a spiritual watchman. God divinely revealed to him that danger was imminent, and he warned God's people of that danger.

"With my God" emphasizes that this duty was fulfilled with God's help through divine revelation and Hosea did not fulfill this task on his own. He was under the influence of a divine Spirit.

The watchman metaphor is not unique to Hosea. Jeremiah and Ezekiel also employ the same image (Jeremiah 6:17; Ezekiel 3:17).

All who are God's ministers today are called to be watchmen. We ought to be alert and awake, always blowing the trumpet to warn people of approaching spiritual dangers.

The unbeliever is always in danger of being cast into the lake of fire for all eternity. He must be warned of the coming peril. The believer, likewise, is always in danger of many things. False doctrine, laziness, prayerlessness, temptation, besetting sins, jealousy and envy, pride, and bitterness names just a few. All of these must be watched and warned against as they have dreadful spiritual consequences. God's ambassadors are also watchmen and a watchman who never blows the trumpet is no watchman at all. Unfortunately, the text informs that **"yet a fowler's snare is on all his ways."** A "fowler" is a type of bird and a "snare" is a trap. Because of his preaching, Hosea is perceived by the nation as a turncoat–a betrayer of sorts. Therefore, he is a wanted man whom the nation tries to imperil by means not revealed in the text. The word "snare" suggests they tried to revenge his faithfulness to God and God's message.

As strange as it sounds, in many cases, a man's faithfulness to God may be determined by how many people hate him more than by how many people love him. Anyone who has the applause of the majority, including unbelievers, can never be faithful to God's message. Only those who are full of compromise will ever acquire such appreciation. These are those who are departed from God's Word. They have created their own religion. They serve as counterfeits. The world loves them because they are of the world and not of God. The fowler's snare has been evaded because they have rejected the Scriptures. They are prostitutes, not prophets.

Also, there is **"hatred in the house of his God."** Although earlier in verse 4 "the house of the Lord" referred to the physical land of God, here it probably refers to the Jewish Temple itself. The reason is that the prophet himself is the topic of discussion in this context and the prefix "his" is used–house of "his" God–showing Hosea's relationship to God. The Temple was the one site where Hosea should have readily received support for the words he spoke, but instead it seems to be the exact location where he was opposed.

At times, even in God's church, God's man will be opposed as he stands upon the Word of God. Consequently, ministers must seek God's face for aid to stand firm because when the tidal wave of opposition comes, only the sustaining hand of God will keep us from being pummeled to the ground and overrun. Only God's grace will keep you from going the direction of the current.

Stand in Spite of Disobedience
"They have deeply corrupted themselves as in the days of Gibeah" is the claim of verse 9. The prophet explains that their ruin and decay is unsearchable. Corruption is bad all by itself but the addition of the term "deep" means their actions go beyond what is normally deemed bad or degraded. They are at an all-time low that cannot be put into words. How deep in sin are they? The text explains that it is "as in the days of Gibeah". These events are described in Judges 19:22-26.

> ^{22} As they were making their hearts merry, behold, the men of the city, worthless fellows, surrounded the house, beating on the door. And they said to the old man, the master of the house, "Bring out the man who came into your house, that we may know him." ^{23} And the man, the master of the house, went out to them and said to them, "No, my brothers, do not act so wickedly; since this man has come into my house, do not do this vile thing. ^{24} Behold, here are my virgin daughter and his concubine. Let me bring them out now. Violate them and do with them what seems good to you, but against this man do not do this outrageous thing." ^{25} But the men would not listen to him. So the man seized his concubine and made her go out to them. And they knew her and abused her all night until the morning. And as the dawn began to break, they let her go. ^{26} And as morning appeared, the woman came and fell down at the door of the man's house where her master was, until it was light.

Worthless, awful, and horrific are appropriate labels to describe the men of Gibeah. Several sins rise to the surface in that chapter including homosexuality, parental abandonment, rape, and murder. It must be assumed that some of the sins that took place in Gibeah are also mimicked in the Israel of Hosea's day, otherwise the comparison would be useless. Hosea called these sins "deep corruption".

God's opinion regarding sin, especially these sins, is that they are not only representative of corruption they epitomize "deep corruption". Homosexuality/lesbianism, murder, and rape disgusts the God of the Bible. Under no circumstances, does He accept such evil behaviour. While the world celebrates many who commit such atrocities, the Lord sees these as activities of worthless, corrupt, and degenerate men. Unless the gospel of Jesus Christ is wholeheartedly embraced, those who violate God's standard in these ways will beg the judgement of God upon their very existence—temporarily and eternally.

As it is written in 1 Corinthians 6:9-11,

> ^{9} Or do you not know that the unrighteous will not inherit the kingdom of God? Do not be deceived: neither the sexually immoral, nor idolaters, nor adulterers, nor men who practice homosexuality, ^{10} nor thieves, nor the greedy, nor drunkards, nor revilers, nor swindlers will inherit the kingdom of God. ^{11} And such were some of you. But you were washed, you were sanctified, you were justified in the name of the Lord Jesus Christ and by the Spirit of our God.

If you are caught up in any one of these lifestyles, please know that there is hope of forgiveness—a forgiveness that is found only in the sacrificial work of the Lord Jesus Christ. Turn to the Lord today and be cleansed by the fountain of His blood.

Furthermore, retribution is confirmed by the last half of the verse which states **"he will remember their iniquity he will punish their sin."** Because of the bull-headed nature of these people and their penchant for detestable sin, God will direct to them exactly what they have warranted. The refusal of the people to repent in no way nullifies the prophet's message. God has spoken. The people have rejected His warnings. Thus, they will reap what they have sown.

Discuss

1. "The sacred desk does not summon men with no backbone or conviction." What is a "sacred desk"? Why have some Christians historically given it this nickname? Do you agree or disagree with this statement? Why or why not?

2. Why have so many preachers surrendered to the pressures of postmodernity?

3. Why can a pastor also be considered a watchman?

4. Should men who preach the truth as written in the Scriptures expect opposition? Why or why not?

5. What impact does a man's calling have on his willingness to endure the challenges of ministry?

16

A DRIED-UP ROOT

9: 10-17

¹⁰ *Like grapes in the wilderness, I found Israel. Like the first fruit on the fig tree in its first season, I saw your fathers. But they came to Baal-peor and consecrated themselves to the thing of shame, and became detestable like the thing they loved.* ¹¹ *Ephraim's glory shall fly away like a bird—no birth, no pregnancy, no conception!* ¹² *Even if they bring up children, I will bereave them till none is left. Woe to them when I depart from them!* ¹³ *Ephraim, as I have seen, was like a young palm planted in a meadow; but Ephraim must lead his children out to slaughter.* ¹⁴ *Give them, O LORD—what will you give? Give them a miscarrying womb and dry breasts.* ¹⁵ *Every evil of theirs is in Gilgal; there I began to hate them. Because of the wickedness of their deeds I will drive them out of my house. I will love them no more; all their princes are rebels.* ¹⁶ *Ephraim is stricken; their root is dried up; they shall bear no fruit. Even though they give birth, I will put their beloved children to death.* ¹⁷ *My God will reject them because they have not listened to him; they shall be wanderers among the nations.*

One year, as an anniversary celebration, my wife and I took a cruise. The first two days passed without a hitch. However, on the third day, the seas became bumpy and the boat rocked so much that, at times, we were forced to grab ahold of the railings.

That afternoon, after leaving port, we headed toward the dining hall for a meal. Upon entering the dining hall, to the left a teenage lad was exiting the dining hall on the right with his head hanging toward the ground.

We eventually passed each other, but about two seconds after, we were startled by what sounded like water splashing behind us. Being alarmed, we immediately spun around and realized the young man had brought up all of his food as he regurgitated onto the tile floor. Unfortunately, he did not make it to the restroom in time.

It is easy to imagine that God feels the same way about Israel, His people, when we take this passage of Scripture into examination. It's almost as if they have repulsed him so deeply that His only recourse is to spew them out of His mouth.

Nostalgia

God informs in verse 10 that **"like grapes in the wilderness I found Israel."** He describes His relationship with Israel in its infancy using a simile. Grapes are a juicy, sweet, and refreshing fruit, and since they can be used in copious ways like for making raisins and wine, they are also a treasured fruit. However, take careful note that they are located "in the wilderness". A wilderness is a place that is routinely dry and hot most of the year. Hence, not much vegetation is found in such regions. Although a wilderness is not identical to a desert, it would be relatively similar. Just as a wary traveler would be thrilled to find grapes in a wilderness, God was thrilled with the nation of Israel at its inception and He loved and found joy in His flock, gushing over them with happiness. The verse adds **"like the first fruit on the fig tree in its first season."** In ancient Eastern cultures, of which Israel is a specimen, figs were a delicacy and what was most prized was the first set of figs that grew on the tree annually. The first yielding of figs was an honoured possession in Old Testament times, the desirableness of which Scripture clearly records.

Isaiah 28:4,

and the fading flower of its glorious beauty, which is on the head of the rich valley, will be like a first-ripe fig before the summer: when someone sees it, he swallows it as soon as it is in his hand.

Micah 7:1,

Woe is me! For I have become as when the summer fruit has been gathered, as when the grapes have been gleaned: there is no cluster to eat, no first-ripe fig that my soul desires.

There was great yearning for the first group of figs.

Take note, however, that the text not only asserts that Israel was like the first fruit on the fig tree; it compares it to the first fruit on the fig tree in its *first* season. Certainly, the Jews must have been zealous after getting the first ever bearing of figs on the tree. God explains that this is how **"I saw your fathers"** and, again, He speaks of Israel at its initial stage as a nation. "Fathers" is probably a reference to the patriarchs Abraham, Isaac, Jacob, and their generations. How precious they were in God's sight! He was jealous for them and yearned after them. **"But"**, unfortunately, **"they came to Baal-peor and consecrated themselves to the thing of shame."** The expression "but" shows contrast in that there is going to come a shift in His feelings toward His people; the apple of His eye will unreservedly disappoint their Master. "Consecrated" means they devoted or committed themselves to something, but the million-dollar question is what shameful thing did the Jews commit themselves to at Baal-peor? The answer can be sited in Numbers 25:1-9.

> "While Israel lived in Shittim, the people began to whore with the daughters of Moab. ² These invited the people to the sacrifices of their gods, and the people ate and bowed down to their gods. ³ So Israel yoked himself to Baal of Peor. And the anger of the LORD was kindled against Israel. ⁴ And the LORD said to Moses, "Take all the chiefs of the people and hang them in the sun before the LORD, that the fierce anger of the LORD may turn away from Israel." ⁵ And Moses said to the judges of Israel, "Each of you kill those of his men who have yoked themselves to Baal of Peor." ⁶ And behold, one of the people of Israel came and brought a Midianite woman to his family, in the sight of Moses and in the sight of the whole congregation of the people of Israel, while they were weeping in the entrance of the tent of meeting. ⁷ When Phinehas the son of Eleazar, son of Aaron the priest, saw it, he rose and left the congregation and took a spear in his hand ⁸ and went after the man of Israel into the chamber and pierced both of them, the man of Israel and the woman through her belly. Thus the plague on the people of Israel was stopped. ⁹ Nevertheless, those who died by the plague were twenty-four thousand."

Israel worshipped the false god, Baal, at the place called Peor; hence the location is called Baal-peor in Hosea's prophecy. First, they transgressed by participating in idolatry. Verse 3 articulates that they "yoked" themselves to Baal, the term being a synonym for the word "consecrated" in verse 1 of this chapter. Secondly, the men were sexually promiscuous with the women of Moab. These verses record that even while Moses and the people profusely wept before the God-endowed tabernacle because of their transgression, one man was so audacious that he postured a

Moabite woman before all the congregation and took her into the chamber—an act that was anathema because God's population was not to engage in sexual relations or marry Gentile people (Deuteronomy 7:3-4). In addition, they **"became detestable like the thing they loved"** meaning Israel became just as wicked and shameful as the idols they betrothed themselves to. The incident made them repulsive in God's sight.

Neither is God content with the idolatry and sexual perversion of modernity. Quite frankly, sex has become an idol unto itself and billions of people prostrate themselves before it daily. Today's world is entirely engrained in the "do as you feel" attitude when it comes to sexual conduct. Nothing is off limits anymore. Not only is fornication and adultery commonplace, but homosexuality and lesbianism is proliferating. Some have exchanged the biblical standard of two genders for a never-ending, never-satisfied onslaught of counterfeit genders with a side order of a ball of confusion. The God of the Bible gapes at it all with disgusted eyes and He abhors it. The contemporary world imagines that it is ushering in a new era of intelligence, advancement, and sophistication when even brute beasts have a healthier moral compass than some segments of humanity.

What's more dismal is that those who are indulgent of such lifestyles will only reap the judgement of God—judgement in this life and judgement in the life to come. Eternal Hell awaits those that live sexually immoral lifestyles not in accordance with the standard set in God's Word.

Again, 1 Corinthians 6:9-10 is the standard text that supports this position.

> *⁹ Or do you not know that the unrighteous will not inherit the kingdom of God? Do not be deceived: neither the sexually immoral, nor idolaters, nor adulterers, nor men who practice homosexuality, ¹⁰ nor thieves, nor the greedy, nor drunkards, nor revilers, nor swindlers will inherit the kingdom of God.*

Yet, hope always peeps over the horizon.

Those who turn from such paths of sinfulness and accept the glorious gift of forgiveness through what Jesus Christ ensured on Calvary's cross can have eternal life and escape the coming wrath of God on the day of judgement. Christ's blood is sufficient to wash any sinner and purge him wholly. There is no sin that He cannot and will not forgive. Verse 11 of 1 Corinthians 6 goes on to say *"And such* were some of you. But you were washed, you were sanctified, you were justified in the name of the Lord Jesus Christ, and by the Spirit of our God."

No matter how deeply fixed you are in a fallen nature, if you humbly seek pardon at the foot of Jesus' cross, He will certainly grant you the desires of your heart and clothe you in His own spotless righteousness—a permanent and perfect righteousness.

Right now, I urgently implore you to wholeheartedly seize the gift of eternal life and eternal peace that is offered by the sinless Lamb of God by speaking to Him and pleading before Him.

Desertion

The 11th verse testifies that **"Ephraim's glory shall fly away like a bird"** because the Northern Kingdom's glory was not intrinsic. Its glory was derived completely from God. Therefore, the mention of Ephraim's glory in this verse is identical to God's glory, and that glory will depart from the nation and soar into an unreachable stratosphere. This is not the first time the theme of God's departing glory appears in Scripture. A similar concept can be found in 1 Samuel 4:21-22.

In that setting, the Ark of the Covenant which represented the presence of the Lord was taken by the Philistines into their territory.

> [21] And she named the child Ichabod, saying, "The glory has departed from Israel!" because the ark of God had been captured and because of her father-in-law and her husband. [22] And she said, "The glory has departed from Israel, for the ark of God has been captured."

Here in Hosea, no ark has been captured but the effect is the same. God's glory and presence has left His people.

When I ponder this ordeal, I cannot help but be delighted that Christians reside under the New Covenant rather than the Old. Under the Old Covenant, the presence and power of God, which is His Holy Spirit, was not guaranteed to remain with the individual or group of individuals unceasingly. Although it was not a frequent occurrence, as has already been discussed, God's presence left His people Israel. Similarly, the Holy Spirit was not a permanent fixture for Old Testament saints. The Holy Spirit came upon individuals to help them fulfil specific tasks and then left.

However, when it comes to the New Testament believer, God's presence and power indwells perpetually by way of His Spirit who never leaves His post of residence. Dear believer, you can rest assured that you have God's presence and power residing in you permanently. He is not nomadic or sporadic in His dealings with God's transformed people, and our hearts should abound with elation at the magnificent blessing we have in the form of the New Covenant.

Then, Hosea avows that there will be **"no birth, no pregnancy, no conception"** because God has departed and will cease Israel's production of offspring. No longer will they produce children for future generations. Note the progression of the clause—it flows from that which is most obvious to the human eye to that which is least obvious.

"Birth" is the process through which the child exits the mother's womb. "Pregnancy" refers to the growth process of the child in the mother's womb. "Conception" is accomplished by a male sperm fertilising a female egg which becomes a zygote and matures into a human being.

If conceptions are no longer achieved, then undoubtedly births will stop. God brings a judgement upon the Jews so disheartening that if a nation experienced the same occurrence today even unbelievers would view it as a form of retribution from the Almighty. A populace that does not produce offspring will soon become extinct. Also, recall that Jewish culture in the Old Testament era diverged significantly from modern Western society in that a barren woman was often scorned and perceived as cursed. To put all the women in the country under the same banner of judgement would produce wide-scale misery for both genders, mothers and fathers. This ranks as one of the worse judgements they will bear.

Even more dreadful is that (vs. 12) **"Even if they bring up children, I will bereave them until none is left."** If their children survived the ordeal, God would still pursue them bringing their souls down to the grave. None of the Kingdom's offspring will escape God's wrath. If this is not legitimate judgement from God, then the entire biblical concept of retribution is mere daydreaming.

This thought process goes counter to the modern "Christian" mind. Many presume God's only desire in life is to bless and heal His people. Those who believe such do not know God or His Word. In this text, God actively and doggedly pursues depriving Israel of one of their most precious blessings—the ability to yield children. God is no less willing to replicate the same today when those who profess to be

Christians support and promote agendas that are overtly anti-God and anti-Bible. The God of the New Testament and Old Testament are one and the same, and Christ's bride must beware lest we come to encounter the God who is a "consuming fire".

"Woe to them when I depart from them!" is the rest of the verse. "Woe" is an interjection that cries out because of grief or despair. There will be inconsolable lamenting because Yahweh has removed His presence from their midst as a nation.

When the God of the Bible is wilfully removed from any setting "woe" will always be the result. Any society that removes God and His authority will become degenerate, moving backward rather than forward. They will imitate monsters more than rational human beings. Left to himself mankind will be given over to his reprobate and reprehensible pangs which spiral forcefully downward into the deep darkness of Hell. It's only through embracing God and obeying God that a people will be brought back to life, health, and sanity.

Desolation

According to verse **13, "Ephraim, as I have seen, was like a young palm planted in a meadow."** Hosea goes back to using imagery as in verse 10. A palm tree planted in a meadow is picturesque and shows that God cared for and loved the nation as something that was special to Him and admired by Him. However, there is a contrast with **"but Ephraim must lead his children out to slaughter."** The word for "slaughter" in the Hebrew indicates someone who is a slayer/murder. It is the same word used to describe what Cain did to Abel in Genesis 4:8. Israel will go out to someone who will murder them and this explains what will happen at the hands of the Assyrian army. God is persistent in warning them of the threat of judgement which involves the lives of their precious children. He has already informed them of an approaching epidemic of barrenness and the young children who already live will be massacred.

The cry of verse **14** is **"Give them, O LORD—what will you give?"** Hosea proceeds to offer up his own imprecatory prayer, the definition of which is one that invokes judgement or calamity on a particular individual or group of individuals. Most often in Scripture, the psalmist David, is known to offer up imprecatory prayers to God against his enemies. The prophet affirms what God has already declared and calls on God to apply the judgement that they are most worthy of because of their lack of response to his preaching.

He begs for God to **"Give them a miscarrying womb and dry breasts"** reinforcing the judgement that God has already promised. "Miscarrying womb" suggests the inability to have children and "dry breasts" indicates the inability to feed children. The dry breasts are added insurance to the dilemma. It's ironic that this judgement seems to be a play on Israel's engaging in Baal worship, which included indulgence in sexual rites and rituals that were promised to guarantee fertility and the ability to produce many children. God uses this judgement to "hit them where it hurts" since they had abandoned Him to pursue false gods. He was and is the giver of life and since they dishonoured Him, He would snatch away the blessings they so deeply desired.

The saints of God must always remember from whom our blessings flow because incorrect worship puts us in danger of having our most prized favours withdrawn. We should tremble at the very thought of giving to another the glory that ultimately belongs to Him. As Isaiah 42:8 confirms, *"I am the Lord; that is my name; my glory I give to no other, nor my praise to carved idols."*

Frustration

The prophet further announces that (vs. **15**) **"Every evil of theirs is in Gilgal."** Some Scriptural interpreters believe that the reference to Gilgal here recalls the time when Saul was inaugurated as king of Israel in spite of God not wanting Israel to have an earthly sovereign like its generational colleagues. It was God's intention for Him to be their king. However, this interpretation does not suit the current reference to Gilgal best because although Saul was inaugurated at Gilgal (1 Samuel 11:12-15) the conflict—and thus the sin—essentially took place at Ramah (1 Samuel 8:4-9). It is preferable to interpret the reference to Gilgal within the context of Hosea's prophecy. In Hosea 4:15, the cry was for Judah to "enter not into Gilgal" nor go up to "Beth-aven".

Thus, it is believed that altars or shrines to false gods were set up at both of these locations as Bethel (which means "house of God") was called Beth-aven, meaning "house of iniquity". If Gilgal is coupled with Beth-aven, then something wicked took place there, which violated Israel's covenant to worship Yahweh alone.

The statement also reveals that **"there I began to hate them."** "Hate", the term of note, describes one's feelings toward his foe and the activities that took place in Gilgal angered God, bringing about a fierce emotion toward them.

Those who persist in downright disobedience could never be on God's side. We live in a world where almost everyone claims that God supports their cause, and He must be horror-struck as He sits in Heaven on His throne observing those who declare to have His aid. In spite of this glaring inconsistency, it must be unashamedly proclaimed that God is never in support of those who promote sin, even if immorality is strategically redefined or repackaged. God hates it with burning fury. In order to determine the causes that God supports, the Scriptures must be examined—not political parties, civil organizations, or their affiliates. "Hate" is a forceful term, but an appropriate one to explain God's sentiment toward evil especially when it is institutionalized as it was at Gilgal.

Furthermore, **"Because of the wickedness of their deeds I will drive them out of my house."** Evil had reached such awful heights that the only step left to take was for God to expel them out of the land that He had given them. "My house" here is not an allusion to the Temple but to the physical land the Lord provided Israel, which is consistent with the term's meaning in Hosea 9:4. Also, it is interesting that the expression "drive them out" is used to describe what the Lord promised to do for the Israelites before they arrived into the Promise Land by committing to driving the Canaanite people groups out of said land so that Israel could enjoy it.

Exodus 23:29-31

> [29] *I will not drive them out from before you in one year, lest the land become desolate and the wild beasts multiply against you.* [30] *Little by little I will drive them out from before you, until you have increased and possess the land.* [31] *And I will set your border from the Red Sea to the Sea of the Philistines, and from the wilderness to the Euphrates, for I will give the inhabitants of the land into your hand, and you shall drive them out before you.*

In the present context, however, He threatens to drive His own people out of His land because they immersed themselves in the same Canaanite practices that God hated.

God's Old Testament citizens were not immune to judgement by the hand of God, and His New Testament citizens should not expect to escape such either. Our covenant may have changed, but God's character has not.

God asserts that **"I will love them no more"**, promising to remove His affection, benevolence, and devotion from a marriage that has gone awry. This marriage is on the rocks. God is at His wits end with Israel and His frustration boils over.

The reason is that **"all their princes are rebels"**. "Princes" refers to the political and civil leaders of the nation who had morally turned away from God as well. Notice that although they were not the religious leaders, God still expected obedience from them; they were not let off the hook because spiritual matters were not their main business. God holds them accountable for their actions as He did the prophet and priest.

Truthfully, everyone without exception is called to submit to God's authority because He is the supreme ruler of the universe. Anyone reading who may be a politician or civil leader must understand that you are called to submit to God as well. You are called to obedience. If you neglect to arrange yourself under the exercise of His reign, you too will face the retribution of God, both now and in eternity. Submission is not just a mindless hobby for religious folks. The Bible tells us that one day every knee will bow and every tongue will confess that Jesus is Lord to the glory of God the Father (Phil 2:10-11).

Eviction

It is verse **16**'s charge that **"Ephraim is stricken."** "Stricken" means to be literally struck down by receiving a debilitating blow. Also, **"their root is dried up; they shall bear no fruit."** Hosea ends this section the way he began, using the language of trees that produce fruit. Because God has given the deathblow to Israel, the roots no longer adequately function, and it dries up becoming lifeless and barren. The nation's blessings come to a halt as they are now dying.

Sadly, **"Even though they give birth, I will put their beloved children to death."** The fruit spoken of in the prior clause is likely the fruit of the womb—precious children—so this judgement is the opposite of what they expected to obtain from Baal worship. God's judgement is not haphazard but deliberate and tactical. "Beloved" in the original Hebrew suggests something that is delightful and that one takes pleasure in. Unhappily, this judgement of God will pierce deep into the soul and the nation will be in anguish for their children.

How foolish it is for anyone to presume they are beyond the reach of God's judgement. Popularity and strength are of no consequence before the Father. The God of Heaven who sits high as Sovereign knows unerringly what buttons of vengeance to push in order to bring knees buckling swiftly to the floor. Now is the time to exchange a haughty and rebellious attitude for a humbly submissive one. Now is the time to seek God's mercy through His Son Jesus Christ.

The problem is that (vs. **17**) **"My God will reject them because they have not listened to him."** Notice Hosea does not only call Him God, but calls Him "my God" acknowledging their personal relationship even if the rest of the nation is as irreligious as ever. That Yahweh was the God of Israel in an official sense, did not mean that all citizens knew Him intimately.

Likewise, just because God is the Creator of every man does not mean that He is the father of every man. He may be God, but the question is "Is He your God personally?" Do you know Him personally? Does His Holy Spirit indwell you? Do you have intimate communion and fellowship with Him?

Scripture warns in Matthew 7:21-23 by saying

> [21] *"Not everyone who says to me, 'Lord, Lord,' will enter the kingdom of heaven, but the one who does the will of my Father who is in heaven.* [22] *On that day many will say to me, 'Lord, Lord, did we not prophesy in your name, and cast out demons in your name, and do many mighty works in your name?'* [23] *And then will I declare to them, 'I never knew you; depart from me, you workers of lawlessness.'*

Even though the aforementioned crowd performed outward expressions of worship, they did not truly know God. They did not possess the new heart and new spirit that Ezekiel prophesied concerning (36:26-27). A true believer does not have only a head knowledge of God but a heart knowledge as well. Nevertheless, the reason God will disdain them is because they have already disdained Him by not obeying His laws or heeding the voice of His man-servant Hosea.

The result is that **"they shall be wanderers among the nations."** Israel will be exiled from its homeland and sent out as nomads moving from place to place because of their deep-seated rebellion against the will and word of God.

> Discuss

1. Why is today's attitude of sexual freedom dangerous, not just to Christianity, but to all of humanity?

2. "It must be unashamedly proclaimed that God is never in support of those who promote sin, even if immorality is strategically redefined or repackaged". Give an example of immorality being redefined or repackaged in today's world.

3. What does Matthew 7:21-23 reveal about many today who claim to know God?

4. What are some dangers that may accompany the merging of politics with Christianity?

5. Every human being is accountable to Yahweh. Do you agree with the aforesaid statement? Why or why not?

17

THE DARK SIDE OF SUCCESS

10:1-6

¹Israel is a luxuriant vine that yields its fruit. The more his fruit increased, the more altars he built; as his country improved, he improved his pillars. ²Their heart is false; now they must bear their guilt. The LORD will break down their altars and destroy their pillars. ³For now they will say: "We have no king for we do not fear the LORD; and a king—what could he do for us?" ⁴They utter mere words; with empty oaths they make covenants; so judgment springs up like poisonous weeds in the furrows of the field. ⁵The inhabitants of Samaria tremble for the calf of Beth-aven. Its people mourn for it, and so do its idolatrous priests—those who rejoiced over it and over its glory—for it has departed from them. ⁶The thing itself shall be carried to Assyria as tribute to the great king. Ephraim shall be put to shame, and Israel shall be ashamed of his idol.

As a young lad, one of my favourite items to enjoy on a playground was the see-saw. The see-saw operated best when two individuals sat on opposing ends. As one person went up, the other came down and then the reverse action would take place.

The unshakable and unbreakable rule of the see-saw is that when one side is at the highest of heights, the other side is at the lowest of lows.

The image of a see-saw succinctly illustrates what is sometimes the relationship between material prosperity and spiritual fervency. In many cases, the more someone encounters material prosperity the less spiritual fervency he will have. From this portion of Hosea's prophecy, we glean that this was certainly a flaw of the nation of Israel. Although, they prospered materially in Hosea's era, they were spiritually deficient: material success extinguished their spiritual flame.

God Blesses

Verse 1 commences proclaiming that **"Israel is a luxuriant vine"** comparing the North Kingdom to a vine that is prosperous and produces fruit. The Authorized Version uses the word "empty" in the place of "luxurious" here because that is one of the primary meanings of the Hebrew word *baqaq*. However, the word can also mean "to spread out" and that is the nuance here painting the picture of something that is fruitful or lively.

What further confirms that the translation should be interpreted as "luxuriant" instead of "empty" is the remainder of the verse—**"that yields much fruit."** None would refer to a vine that yields favourably as "empty", but "luxuriant" or "fruitful" would accurately describe such. The text adds more to the description with **"the more his fruit increased."** Initially, it was revealed that the vine has already produced fruit; now added to that picture is an increase in fruitfulness. Let's remember that Israel is the vine, so Hosea is referring to the condition of the nation and God has blessed Israel in such a way that it abounds in material and physical success. This would include anything and everything they considered beneficial to them as a country like agricultural resources, political stability, gold and silver etc.

The downside, though, is that **"the more his fruit increased the more altars he built."** Why would God be displeased with the building of altars? As was observed earlier, there are two options available.

1. These altars were built to foreign false gods which Israel worshiped. God's expectancy was that they worship Him alone because He was/is the one and only true God and the worship of other gods was the equivalent of spiritual whoredom. God saw them as an unfaithful spouse in their marriage to Him.

2. These altars were originally built to Yahweh, but Israel also sacrificed to false deities on those same altars in order to "cover their bases". In other

words, the veneration of other gods took place because the God of the Jews was not powerful enough to be everything they needed–impotent rather than omnipotent. Heathen gods were invoked in case Yahweh needed assistance.

No matter which option is historically accurate, God was appalled with their actions. Syncretism, the mixing of different religions, has always been disgraceful in the eyes of the God of the Bible.

That emotion has not changed even to this very day.

Anyone who truly receives Jesus Christ as His Saviour and embraces Biblical Christianity will also reject every other religion as erring and false. Biblical Christianity and Islam, Buddhism, Hinduism, or the New Age movement cannot merge because you are either a follower of Jesus Christ or a follower of darkness. Acts 4:12 declares *"and there is salvation in no one else, for there is no other name under heaven given among men by which we must be saved"*. The Lord Jesus can never share His glory with another.

If your personal habit is to set other religions alongside the worship of Jesus Christ, it is time to make a choice. Either you embrace Jesus Christ wholeheartedly and commit your life fully to Him, or you leave Him alone completely, but do not blaspheme the name of Almighty God by clinging to Him in unison with other cheap, impotent imitations.

The verse continues to affirm that **"as his country improved, he improved pillars."** Success as a nation brought about the proliferation of pillars, which are the same objects referenced in Hosea 3:4 saying, *"For the children of Israel shall dwell many days without king or prince, without sacrifice or pillar, without ephod or household gods."* Such were columns of stone built to heathen gods. From the time the Jews first entered the Promised Land, they were commanded by God to obliterate these very objects.

Exodus 23:24,

*You shall not bow down to their god nor serve them, nor do as they do, but you shall utterly overthrow them and break their **pillars** in pieces.*

Exodus 34:13,

*You shall tear down their altars and break their **pillars** and cut down their Asherim.*

Instead of breaking down pillars, they were improving them.

Prosperity should draw us closer to God, but often for humanity—even God's people—it has the opposite effect. Frequently prosperity makes us forget God and makes us mirror the world. Sometimes the more we obtain, the more carnal we get, and the less we have, the more godly we are. Israel should have been prepared for this occurrence because God had already warned of the challenge that prosperity could bring upon them as a nation.

Deuteronomy 8:11-14,

> [11] *"Take care lest you forget the* LORD *your God by not keeping his commandments and his rules and his statutes, which I command you today,* [12] *lest, when you have eaten and are full and have built good houses and live in them,* [13] *and when your herds and flocks multiply and your silver and gold is multiplied and all that you have is multiplied,* [14] *then your heart be lifted up, and you forget the* LORD *your God, who brought you out of the land of Egypt, out of the house of slavery,*

It should come as no surprise that the average saint would love the prospect to enhance his or her quality of life, but the reality is that for many of us—if that were to happen—our hearts would draw us away from God, and if truth be told, we are spiritually healthier being given daily bread than a full harvest of blessings. Tim Challies saw the danger of success when he stated that "Prosperity knits a man's heart to the world. He thinks he is finding his place in it, but in reality it is finding its place in him."

Maybe you are a follower of Christ who has recently encountered great blessings. Have they drawn you closer to Him or away from Him? Are you still pursuing God's purposes or are you now panting after a life of luxury? If success has led you off course, now is that time to reassess and realign your heart with God's.

"Their heart is false" is the first phrase of verse 2. The Hebrew word translated "false" literally means "smooth" and we should envision someone who is a "smooth talker". He is deceiving and duplicitous. Because of this defect in them, **"now they must bear their guilt."** In other words, they have been declared guilty and now they deserve punishment.

So let's recap. The nation of Israel increased altars and pillars—an action which demonstrated that their heart is deceiving and duplicitous. Because their hearts are of such condition, they deserve penalty and God, who is impeccably just, will never punish anyone ill-deserving of punishment. However, the fact of the matter is that all of humanity does evil and the reason we do evil is because it originates from our hearts.

Consequently, we all deserve punishment and the only way it can be escaped is through accepting and embracing the Saviour who was punished as a substitute on behalf of sinful men. No other avenue exists to elude God's wrath; purgatory is as real as the tooth fairy. Anyone who does not trust in the substitute will one day be punished.

Next, **"The Lord will break down their altars and destroy their pillars"**. *Araph*, the Hebrew word translated as "break down", is most often used in the context of breaking the necks of animals to be sacrificed in the Old Testament. What they should have done of their own volition to the altars and pillars, the Lord will do for them. Regrettably, the Lord will do it through judgement when the Assyrians arrive to ravage the land, annihilating all their spaces of false worship.

It is always wise for earthly subjects to yield to the Lord, because, in the end, He will have His way no matter what. He will do that which His faultless heart desires with or without us. God's sovereign purposes can never be thwarted, and it should be preferred to find ourselves on the right side of history like Hosea rather than the wrong side like the Northern Kingdom.

The People Rebel

In the **third** verse Hosea prophesies, **"For now they will say: 'We have no king, for we do not fear the LORD; and a king—what could he do for us?'"** Difficulty exists in determining the thrust of this verse and there is little agreement among Bible scholars regarding the same. It does seem clear, though, that Hosea is representing the people in what he says here.

In my opinion, the reference "we have no king" refers to a time in the nation's history when there was a chain of assassinations in the North. In 2 Kings 15, which is believed to coincide with the season of Hosea's ministry, Zechariah, Shallum, Pekahiah, and Pekah were all executed after adversaries conspired to wipe them out. It is certainly believable that Hosea could be referring to an intermission between the monarchies when the citizens were kingless. Another possibility is that it refers to the time when the Northern king Hoshea was captured and put in prison by Shalmaneser, the king of Assyria (2 Kings 17:1-5).

In any event, Israel did not presently have a king and the situation weighed upon its citizens heavily. "Fear" here means "to morally revere" to the point where one may even be frightened. It is no surprise, then, that their lack of fear for God also produced a lack of ethics.

Certainly, modern humanity suffers from the same malady. The reason moral conviction is being eroded at record levels today is because people no longer fear God as they did in decades and generations gone by. Healthy fear of God is advantageous for all societies—even when non-Christians are taken into consideration. Lack of fear only produces moral decay, degradation, and recklessness. Outside of God's own sovereign acts like natural disasters and the like, the only way the fear of God will be restored back to humanity is through the witness of the church of Jesus Christ—through its preaching and through its living. Christian preachers must return to unabashedly bellowing forth the Holy Scriptures in its totality, and Christians must return to effectively living the Holy Scriptures in its totality. Fellow preachers, are you faithful to your business to preach all of God's Word? Fellow saints, are you faithful to your mission to live all of God's Word? Without this, there will be no fear of God as it was in Hosea's time and the moral decay will continue.

In addition, the people will cry **"and a king—what could he do for us?"** In essence, they are saying "we have no king now, but even if we had a king what would he be able to do?" The people are absolutely right in their analysis of this hypothetical conversation. Remember, it has been foreseen that God has "broken down their altars" and "destroyed their pillars". Accordingly, the judgement of the Assyrians Empire has already engulfed them, there is nothing any king can do to assist them.

This is similar to how things work when it comes to life and death and the message of the Gospel. Now is the time to repent of your sins. Now is the time to trust in Christ. Now is the time to change your mind and receive the Good News of the Gospel.

If you pass into eternity without the robe of Jesus' righteousness, there is nothing any king, pope, politician, saint, angel, or demon can do for you when God pours out His eternal wrath on a lost soul, and relegates him to the unquenchable fire.

Fortunately, however, you can do something for yourself right now by responding to the Gospel message and turning to the Lord Jesus Christ in faith to escape the coming deluge of fire.

It is verse 4's claim that **"they utter mere words; with empty oaths they make covenants."** "They" here probably continues the notion established at the end of verse 3 and refers to the behaviour of northern kings who make covenants either with their citizens or with other nations, without intending to keep them. Their word is not their bond and it carries no weight. In the Bible, covenant making was a solemn matter. The word translated as "covenant" in the Hebrew text comes from a root word that means "to cut down" or "a cutting".

In Old Testament times, the ancient custom was to make a covenant by, first, slicing an animal in half. Once accomplished, both halves were placed on the ground on opposite sides of one another, and the two parties making the covenant would walk down through the middle of the two halves signifying their bond to the solemn oath.

This is similar to what took place when God made a covenant with Abraham in Genesis 15:7-18, with the exception that God ratified the covenant by Himself (vs. 17). The purpose of the slaughtered animal was to imply that it would be better for the two parties to be slaughtered as well, rather than break the solemn they made with each other. It was no small matter for kings to break covenants.

It is no small matter, either, when kings break covenants today. Word-honouring national leaders have always been scarce. Most political leaders today seem to be as familiar with lying as they are with breathing. Still God's standard has not changed and He demands that civil authorities be people of their word. Whether you are one who hopes to run for political office one day or one who currently works in the political sphere, please recognize that the God of heaven will hold you responsible for how you execute your public duties. The eternal Sovereign under whose authority you govern—or will govern—is observant as to whether or not you will do so in an ethical manner. Psalm 22:28 warns "For kingship belongs to the Lord and he rules over the nations." None will be exempt from the Day of Judgement including earthly governors.

Moreover, not only kings make covenants, we members of the masses do the same in daily living. We make business covenants. We make marriage covenants. We make family covenants. It is incumbent upon us to hold fast to the earthly covenants that we have made because our word should be as good as gold. Our yes should be yes and our no should be no (James 5:12) as Christians hold fast to what they have promised since Christ held fast to what He promised. Never can anyone rightfully accuse Him of broken promises and we must strive for the same unblemished testimony. Are your promises unalterable? Do you keep your word?

The text continues **"so judgment springs up like poisonous weeds in the furrows on the field"** explaining that God will judge these covenant breaking kings in ways they do not anticipate. Poisonous weeds are obviously detrimental to one's health and "furrows of the field" continues the agricultural metaphor that begins the chapter. Usually in fields where organized crops are planted, small trenches are dug in rows. Seeds are planted in these small trenches and covered with topsoil. The small trench, only several centimeters deep, is what this verse labels as a furrow. The furrows is the location from which the new plant germinates and sprouts through the topsoil. Instead of fruitful vines growing from these furrows, weeds will grow and not just any kind of weeds but poisonous weeds, being totally opposite to the farmers desire. Because of their covenant breaking, a terrible result is on the way.

The Idols are Seized

Then, verse five states that **"the inhabitants of Samaria tremble."** The focus shifts to the capital city of the Northern Kingdom, Samaria, where the residents tremble. "Tremble" here comes from a root word that means "to turn aside in fear" and it is equivalent to how a parent feels when their child goes missing. The parent is in tremendous fear of what may have happened to their precious little one.

Still, the reason the city people tremble in the text is not because of a missing child. The text goes on to assert that it is **"for the calf of a Beth-aven."** Yet again, an idolatrous calf is revered in Beth-aven, Moses' name of spite for the town of Bethel. Take note that this is what they were trembling in great fear for. They had such affection and trust in this calf that when it deserted them they quivered, showing the unlimited nature of their heathenism. One would have expected them to just move on, but they quaked in anguish and agony after the idol—the monotheistic children of Jacob who were to worship none but Yahweh.

How did they plummet to such unfathomable depths? When did this all begin? I believe it commenced at the time their ancestors entered the Promised Land. From the first day God ordered Israel to banish all the occupants of Canaan, otherwise they would ensnare them. Israel expelled a majority of the vile people groups, but not all to the will of their Creator.

Judges 1 informs us that many of the tribes of Israel did not drive out the Canaanites that dwelt near them, but instead committed them to forced labor (Joshua 1: 27-36).

The second chapter of Judges begins by saying,

> *¹Now the angel of the LORD went up from Gilgal to Bochim. And he said, "I brought you up from Egypt and brought you into the land that I swore to give to your fathers. I said, 'I will never break my covenant with you, ² and you shall make no covenant with the inhabitants of this land; you shall break down their altars.' But you have not obeyed my voice. What is this you have done? ³ So now I say, I will not drive them out before you, but they shall become thorns in your sides, and their gods shall be a snare to you." ⁴ As soon as the angel of the LORD spoke these words to all the people of Israel, the people lifted up their voices and wept.*

It all began with just a slight bit of compromise. Not all the tribes of Israel permitted the Canaanites to remain on their property—only a few of them did. Yet, from that time to Hosea's day, idolatry was an unrelenting stumbling block for Israel.

Compromise is analogous to a fire. Unless you extinguish it entirely, it will find a way to burn. Countless denominations and their churches lay flatly on the ash heap of ruin because the seeds of compromise, planted long ago, have grown to large, thick trees and produced voluminous fruit. Once the dogmas of Scripture have been compromised and the Bible is regarded as an advice manuscript rather than a binding constitution to believe and obey, Satan will have a picnic and convert churches into nothing more than superficial social clubs.

This principle applies personally as well. As the Bible says "a little leaven leavens the whole lump", so do little acts of sin balloon into big sin quite rapidly (1 Corinthians 5:9). God's elect must unswervingly perform surgery on our own souls using the Bible as the scalpel, the needle, and the stitching thread. We must continue to judge our own selves so that we may not be judged of the Lord (1 Corinthians 11: 31). Other people's lives should be viewed through a telescope while our own should be examined through a microscope, because individual compromise—although often quiet—expands quickly.

The text progresses by saying **"its people mourn for it and so do its idolatrous priests."** Surprisingly, Samaria's dwellers are distraught over the situation as they possessed a passionate affection to these idols. You know you are devoted to something if its removal distresses you. However, the idolatrous priests who are employed to serve in the worship of this calf mourn as well. These are not Levitical priests who serve in the Jewish Temple. Let's recall that Samaria is the capital city of Israel and not only did they permit false gods, they permitted the priests to facilitate the worship of these gods as well.

The equivalent of this today would be a Muslim imam stepping into Bible-believing church, standing behind the pulpit, opening a Koran, and preaching from the Koran to the saints of that church. For the people of God, this was deplorable, displaying abysmal iniquity and the reason God has already pronounced judgement. Israel was not just having a few issues, they were lost down the dark hole of sin.

Furthermore, **"those who rejoiced over it and over its glory"** is the next expression. Hosea expresses no remorse for the emotional pain they endure while reminding his audience that these are the same folks who were thrilled to worship filth. He uses the term "glory" sarcastically because this was the object of their glorying when they should have gloried in the true God.

Thus, it is no surprise that **"it has departed from them."** The calf will be booked into exile and will lead the way for the people who are soon to follow. Where is the calf going? The next verse tells us. Verse 6 says **"the thing itself shall be carried to Assyria."** Assyria will be the destination of the calf just as Assyria will be the destination of God's rebellious people and it will be used **"as a tribute to the great king."** This is the second occasion of the term "great king" in Hosea, the first time being Hosea 5:13.

"When Ephraim saw his sickness, and Judah his wound, then Ephraim went to Assyria, and sent to the great king. But he is not able to cure you or heal your wound."

The "great king" is the reigning monarch of the Assyrian empire who will accept this idolatrous calf as a present from those who invade the land of Israel. The term appears more than honourable and it is puzzling that the prophet would use such a label for a pagan king when he does not even use such for the God of Israel. More than likely, however, he uses it jeeringly since Israel had chucked its King aside and it revealed that, for them, the Assyrian ruler was "the great king" and the King of Heaven was not.

Also, **"Ephraim shall be put to shame and Israel shall be ashamed of his idol."** The result of all this will be a flooding torrent of embarrassment for the nation that was to be God's bride. Likewise, the wayward Christian always risks embarrassing himself when he falls headlong into sin without restraint.

> Discuss

1. Give an example of how syncretism may occur today?

2. What practical steps can a Christian take to show love to people of other religions without compromising their Christian faith?

3. List three verses from three separate books of the Bible that affirm Jesus Christ as a substitute for sinners.

4. Why would Hosea, God's prophet, refer to the pagan Assyrian monarch as, the "great king"?

5. "Other people's lives should be viewed through a telescope while our own should be examined through a microscope." How can this mindset benefit God's child?

18

WHEN THE HAMMER FALLS

10:7-10

⁷Samaria's king shall perish like a twig on the face of the waters. ⁸The high places of Aven, the sin of Israel, shall be destroyed. Thorn and thistle shall grow up on their altars, and they shall say to the mountains, "Cover us," and to the hills, "Fall on us." ⁹From the days of Gibeah, you have sinned, O Israel; there they have continued. Shall not the war against the unjust[a] overtake them in Gibeah? ¹⁰When I please, I will discipline them, and nations shall be gathered against them when they are bound up for their double iniquity.

Natural disasters seem to be a way of life for most of the modern world. From blizzards to mudslides; volcano eruptions to hurricanes; earthquakes to floods, natural disasters significantly devastate perspective regions of the earth.

Perhaps, however, the most feared disaster is the tsunami.

Tsunamis strike fear in the hearts of many due to the exorbitant amount of damage that can be accomplished to people and property alike in such a short space of time.

In some realms where tsunamis regularly occur, alarms sound off whenever the threat is evident. Immediately, the masses begin making their way to higher ground for refuge. None would dare play spectator sport as high ocean waters converge on their communities.

Only strong buildings are able to withstand the overwhelming blow. Almost everything else is whisked away by the incoming ocean. The tsunami pushes forward quickly, powerfully, and comprehensively with little hindrance to its devastating progress.

Sometimes the effect of God's judgement is like a tsunami—speedy, strong, and sure. Unfortunately, in the present set of verses, the Northern Kingdom is on the receiving end of such judgement and no one is able to hinder God's heavy hand.

He Judges the Powerful

Verse **7** sets out with **"Samaria's king shall perish."** This is the capital city of the Northern Kingdom and the label "Samaria's king" is perhaps utilized to bring attention to the national throne. However, Samaria's king is essentially all of Israel's king and he is on the verge of perishing. The underlying word for "perish" means "to become silent" or "to cease" and in effect, it means to make an end of something. Thus, the northern king's reign and life will come to an end simultaneously. The king mentioned here is likely the same king cited in Hosea 10:3 when Hosea says,

For now they will say: "We have no king, for we do not fear the LORD; *and a king—what could he do for us?"*

Then it offers a metaphor for how he will perish by stating it will be **"like a twig on the face of waters."** "Twig" here can convey the idea of either a branch broken off or a piece of wood that is chipped off. The simile presents a picture of Israel as a twig which will be tossed to and fro in the waters of God's terrible wrath, swallowed up and vanishing from sight. Once the king dies, his power and influence will be hastily drowned and forgotten.

Multitudinous are the heads of state throughout the millennia who have terrified and coerced populations for decades—some of them alive today. Rest assured, though, that when God determines to act in contradiction to unjust leaders, none will stop him from swallowing them whole as the whale swallowed Jonah. Saints that reside in regions oppressed by evil dictatorial renegades must keep their eyes firmly fixed on both God's sovereignty and power. His sovereignty reminds us that He is at the controls of every single situation, not only in our personal lives, but throughout the entire Earth and He will make a move when He determines it is right to do so. God's power convinces us that nothing can halt His hand from forcefully annihilating ungodly, vile rulers no matter how robust their arm of power may be at the time. The God who executed Samaria's king is the same God who can decapitate any king anywhere.

He Judges Places

"The high places of Aven" is the first phrase of verse 8. "Aven" is an abbreviated form of Beth-aven meaning "house of wickedness", a vindictive term for Bethel, whose name really meant "house of God". The progression throughout this prophetic book is noteworthy. Hosea moves from calling Bethel "house of God" to "house of wickedness". Then he takes a step further, and moves from Beth-aven to just "Aven" alone meaning "wickedness". Basically, the prophet says "Just forget the term 'house'. This city should just be called 'wickedness' altogether!" It is vital to recall that Hosea was only God's spokesperson, so Hosea's proclamation was truly God's proclamation. The more Bethel advanced into iniquity, the more Bethel exasperated its Maker, to the point that He could only call it "wickedness".

Indeed, all have sinned and fallen short of God's glory (Romans 3:23). However, after conversion, the believer's desire should be to extract as much sin from his life as possible. We will never be sinless in this carnal flesh, but we will desire to sin less, and the less defiled we are, the more pleasing we are to our heavenly Father. Bethel had never been a faultless city, but in times previous they were more delightful to God. Nevertheless, the state of affairs, by this period in Hosea's ministry, had become so grim that they could only be called "Aven".

Additionally, the principle applies to nations. Undoubtedly, iniquity will be extant in all lands until God ushers in the eternal state. Nevertheless, in this present age, God is most satisfied with lands where there is less depravity—evidenced at the time by Northern rebuke being more common than Southern rebuke. The more sin is present the more God is angered and it is the duty of God's flock to counteract the tide of godlessness in their country of residence. We must engage society and speak up for what is right while blamelessly forestalling against what is wrong. Proverbs 14:34 urges that "Righteousness exalts a nation, but sin is a reproach to any people." The identity of the "high places" must be determined as well. These were shrines of Canaanite origin located on mountaintops and hilltops where non-Jewish deities were worshipped, and they were the scene of much sexually immoral activity done in esteem to those gods.

Next, the text threatens that **"the sin of Israel shall be destroyed."** We must interrogate the term "sin of Israel". Does it reference the high places as objects or does it reference Bethel/Beth-aven, the location? Although it is challenging to decipher, it's perhaps superior to interpret it as a reference to Beth-aven. The reason being that a few verses earlier, it is discovered that one of the idolatrous calves is also at Beth-aven along with its priests. That city did not only have the ungodly high places, but an idolatrous calf too. Thus, they boiled over in sin surpassing other citadels of Israel. "Sin of Israel" is apropos since it revealed the notorious nature of their impiety. This evil place along with many others will be overthrown and laid waste in short order.

Also, **"thorn and thistles shall grow up on their altars."** These altars are those of the high places—flat platforms attached to these shrines to facilitate sinful activity. The growth of thorns and thistles on the altars indicate that they will be abandoned for an extensive spell while the people are in exile since judgement has come into full effect.

Furthermore, **"they shall say to the mountains 'Cover us' and to the hills 'Fall on us'."** Such depression will overwhelm them that they will implore the mountains and hills to crush and slay them, terminating their misery and suffering. Seasons will be so horrendous that, to the populace, life itself will fail to be valuable and they will relinquish it to escape such astounding cruelties. To their disappointment, however, they will be obligated to endure the pain and torture of exile and slavery.

Similarities abound with those who will, one day, meet everlasting damnation. The agony of doom will be so atrociously dreadful and unimaginable that its occupants will yearn to die a second time. Incalculable shrieks for mercy or annihilation will be heard. Yet, that reality will have no expiration date or cut off point. Consequently, today is the day to seek pardon and now is the time to accept the hope given through Jesus Christ, God's substitute. Are you God's child? Have you received Jesus Christ? Are you trusting in His work alone for salvation from eternal travail and trouble? Now is the time to accept the opportunity while the door to repentance remains yet open. The Lord Jesus receives all who call upon His name for rescue and forgiveness.

Hosea progresses with (vs. **9**) **"from the days of Gibeah you have sinned O Israel."** This verse highlights the events of Judges 19-21 where, yet again, Gibeah is the focal point. It was a city of unbridled lust, homosexuality, rape, abuse, violence, and murder—a city that made Sodom and Gomorrah look like amateurs. Almost every evil imaginable took place in that locale, and the worst of Israel's sinful past is brought back to the fore and presented to them. This is not arbitrary but purposeful. **"There they have continued"** refers to Gibeah's situation of the past. "They have continued" illustrates what "now" Israel persists in doing. Hosea connects Israel's past to its present, in that their conduct, then, matches to their conduct now. The more things changed the more they remained the same. Homosexuality, rape, abuse, violence, murder yet run rampant in Jewish society and the nation is, again, in the same spiritual valley as it was at the end of Judges.

Tragic it would be for those who profess to be God's seed to wallow unchanged in the same sinful state they abode in prior to salvation. To be "born again", in New Testament Greek, literally means to be "born from above" or "born from a higher place" (John 3:3). Christ's elect have both a new heart and new spirit inserted within that impedes them from operating predominantly by their pre-conversion, Adamic nature (Ezekiel 36:26-27). Christian conversion is comparable to monetary conversion. A pound (£) is not the same as a euro (€). We cannot claim to be the children of God if our lives have not seen the fruit of change. Even Paul told professed believers in 2 Corinthians 13:5 to "Examine yourselves, to see whether you are in the faith. Test yourselves. Or do you not realize this about yourselves, that Jesus Christ is in you?—unless indeed you fail to meet the test!"

The text continues with **"shall not the war against the unjust overtake them in Gibeah?"** In this rhetorical question the "unjust" refers to the sinful acts of Israel by which they violate the covenant of their God. Gibeah is brought into the equation to connect sinful Israel of the past with sinful Israel of the present. The word "war" is used to describe the pending invasion of their land by the enemy. The gist of the sentence is that judgement is imminent for Israel now just as it was imminent for Israel then.

The God that judged sin under the old covenant is the same God that will judge sin under the new covenant. Modern-day Christians should not delete God's attribute of holiness while simultaneously overemphasizing His attribute of love. Both elements must be held in balance if we desire to be faithful to Scripture and even to the New Testament. To not embrace both of these attributes—the holiness of God and the love of God—in unison is to have an understanding of God that is both unbiblical and dangerous. We must not overlook what happened to Ananias and Sapphira when they lied to the Holy Spirit (Acts 5:1-11). Neither must we forget Paul's warning to believers to not partake in the Lord's Supper unworthily as it can produce sickness or even death (1 Corinthians 11:29-30). Also, the Book of Revelation tells of the outpouring of God's wrath upon the earth which is still yet to take place. To erase the concept of a God who judges sin is to create a false idol. That God is just as realistic as a hot snowflake.

Verse 10 retorts that **"when I please I will discipline them."** The Lord will bring chastisement to the nation of Israel when He deems it appropriate to do so; when His desire is fulfilled, then the hatchet will fall.

Even now, the godly and faithful frequently wait for rescue and vindication from their current circumstances as they long to see God's hand of justice. We must learn to wait until God is pleased to exercise such justice on our behalf. We must wait while enduring the torture of a lying coworker. We must wait for justice to be served in an unfair business deal. We must wait for an offending criminal to be apprehended and charged. We must wait for a tyrannical, oppressive dictator to be cut off as head of the nation. Patience is an admirable virtue for the Christian because God does bring reproof, but He does it when He pleases. Thus, there are occasions when we will have to wait longer than we expect before God's faithful hand of justice moves.

The following phrase adds **"and nations shall be gathered against them."** The source of Israel's punishment is the Sovereign Lord, and the means through which this punishment is executed is through the godless nations which invade them. It's intriguing to apprehend that God even uses ungodly nations as His instruments in judgement. The Assyrian Empire specifically was a useful tool in the hand of the Almighty.

Isaiah 10: 5-6,

> *⁵ Woe to Assyria, the rod of my anger; the staff in their hands is my fury!*
> *⁶ Against a godless nation I send him, and against the people of my wrath I command him, to take spoil and seize plunder, and to tread them down like the mire of the streets.*

Wicked Assyria will be used by God to bring judgement to His own people.

This answers an important query that people usually have concerning the Old Testament. As most are aware, God occasionally instructs Israel to perform much violence on His behalf. Once specific instance was at the time when Israel first entered the Promised Land, and the Canaanite people groups were dedicated to destruction. How could a good God demand such horrendous action? Well, God was using Israel not only to possess the Promised Land but also as a tool to penalize the Canaanite nations. The Canaanites were evil in conduct and sorely depraved; hence, God used His own nation, Israel, as His tool to bring about destruction upon the Canaanites.

Contrariwise, in this script, we see the inverse happening. God uses the currently vile heathens to bring a beating upon Israel because they have violated the covenant. As God used Israel to judge other nations, He used other nations to judge Israel. The crux of the matter is that God is just and always does right. Whenever we observe in Scripture God using a nation to massacre another, the Lord is only using human tools to accomplish His will and those who are destroyed (in this case Israel) are getting exactly what they deserve.

This is done **"when they are bound up for their double iniquity."** The phrase "bound up" makes clear that the people will be arrested and dragged as prisoners from their land. It is not clear what is meant by the term "double iniquity" as Old Testament scholars have divergent views on the term and seldom do two scholars agree. In my opinion, the best explanation of the term "double iniquity" is Israel's worship of false gods and also it's partnering with ungodly allies politically. Of all the offenses committed against the covenant by Israel, these two seem to have been infringed upon most frequently.

> Discuss

1. Give two examples from the Bible where God judged someone powerful.

2. Excluding the locations mentioned in this chapter, give two examples from the Bible where God judged specific places.

3. How may a Christian effectively defend God's character when challenged about the bloody massacres that took place on God's behalf when Israel first conquered Canaan?

4. Practically speaking, how may a church keep the attributes of the holiness of God and the love of God in balance in its teaching ministry? (hint: lectio continua)

5. Have you ever waited longer than anticipated to see God's hand of justice prevail in a particular situation? Relate the story.

19

THE FOLLY OF FALLOW GROUND
10:11-15

¹¹ Ephraim was a trained calf that loved to thresh, and I spared her fair neck; but I will put Ephraim to the yoke; Judah must plow; Jacob must harrow for himself. ¹² Sow for yourselves righteousness; reap steadfast love; break up your fallow ground, for it is the time to seek the Lord, that he may come and rain righteousness upon you. ¹³ You have plowed iniquity; you have reaped injustice; you have eaten the fruit of lies. Because you have trusted in your own way and in the multitude of your warriors, ¹⁴ therefore the tumult of war shall arise among your people, and all your fortresses shall be destroyed, as Shalman destroyed Beth-arbel on the day of battle; mothers were dashed in pieces with their children. ¹⁵ Thus it shall be done to you, O Bethel, because of your great evil. At dawn the king of Israel shall be utterly cut off.

I will never forget my first visit to Germany. Having arrived on a Monday for a week-long conference, somewhere around Tuesday morning, I developed a toothache that got progressively worse throughout the day. A tooth filling I received several years prior, had eventually eroded.

By Tuesday night, the nerves of that tooth were being exposed, and I got a throbbing headache. That night was the worst night of the entire trip as I had gotten no sleep. I was unable to lay down flat because the more flatly my body was positioned, the more intense the pain became. Instead, I spent the entire night/morning sitting up in bed with my back against the wall.

As morning began to break and a speck of light peaked over the horizon, my mind was fixated on one thing—the need to get to a dentist immediately. I could bear the pain and discomfort no more! Not another night would be spent under torture. It was of necessity that I located a dentist and correct the problem immediately.

In the current text, Israel has an immediate need—the need of repentance. This could not be put on hold because the dam of God's judgement was at its breaking point and would burst at any time. Repentance is always an immediate need for those who live in rebellion.

The Past Situation

Verse 11 states **"Ephraim was a trained calf that loved to thresh."** In Jewish culture, when grains were harvested from fields, they were, subsequently, laid on a large stone floor, after which, a cow was brought in and made to walk over those grains. The purpose was to release the edible part of the grain from its attached straw, thus making them two separate entities. In eras previous to Hosea's, the nation of Israel was like a well-taught cow, obedient to its master. Tension between farmer and beast was much less thick than it is at present.

God informs **"and I spared her fair neck."** "Fair" means delightful. "Sparing Israel's neck" expresses that God, the farmer in this imagery, need not tighten the cow's braces to direct her because she performed what was required, satisfying the farmer. The applying of pressure to her neck was unnecessary due to the absence of waywardness. However, in the present circumstance, that has all changed. The verse presses forward with **"but I will put Ephraim to yolk."** The Northern Kingdom now has a burden placed upon its neck. In agriculture, a yoke is a wooden beam fastened across the necks of two animals who were attached to a plough that they would pull together. Instead of working in peace and freedom, Israel is obligated to pull along a weighty load because of its sin.

Sometimes disobedience makes our load in life heavy. Sin, although sweet at first, often turns sour and the more we drive ourselves into it, the heavier the burden upon our shoulders. Think about the individual who tells a lie. Eventually, he must reciprocate additional dishonest statements to conceal the initial lie and, overtime, will have to keep track of which lie he told in which context. The consequence is an unmanageable burden. What's best (and easiest) is honesty from the outset, to evade enduring an encumbrance upon our necks like the "cow" Ephraim.

Yet, not only will the North be placed under a yoke, the South will encounter the same. **"Judah must plough"** is the assertion of the text designating the Southern Kingdom, whose capital city was Jerusalem, implying that both kingdoms will be yoked together under the same weight of work. Both Ephraim and Judah are "cows" put under restraint because of scandalous conduct.

Next, **"Jacob must harrow himself."** Jacob, the national patriarch, historically, had his name changed to "Israel" (Genesis 32:28). Hence, "Jacob" here is another substitute label for the Northern Kingdom. A harrow is a farming device that consists of a solid frame with teeth attached so as to be dragged over already-plowed land to break up clumps, extract weeds, and cover seeds with top soil. The gist is that the entire Kingdom (North and South) must prepare itself the way soil is prepared for the lodging of seeds. No farmer casually drops seeds onto the ground and presumes the land will bear fruit; but rather, the soil must be cultivated and primed prior to embedding seeds into the earth.

The Present Need

God's command is to **"sow for yourselves righteousness."** Verse 12 seems to continue the thought of the previous verse, so now that the soil has been plowed and harrowed, the seeds are set to be planted. To "sow" is to plant seeds but what is significant is the identity of these seeds. God instructs them to sow "righteousness". What is righteousness? This Hebrew term literally means "rightness". It is to do what is just, act in the right manner, and do the right thing. He doesn't demand anything new; all He requires is obedience and holiness. This is the foundation of the covenant He made with the whole nation at its inception. When Moses charged the people to obedience, he declared in Deuteronomy 11:1, *"You shall therefore love the Lord your God and keep his charge, his statutes, his rules, and his commandments always."*

God required such of His people then, and He requires such of His people now. Are we currently sowing seeds of righteousness? Are we pursuing right thought patterns, right words, and right actions? Our Creator is immutable. In today's world, many—even some of which are professed Christians—would try to change who God is. Still, the Lord has not altered His nature and He unceasingly demands obedience to what He has decreed in Holy Scripture. Are you seeking obedience and holiness? Or are you diving deep into the oceans of sin? How is your language? Are you foul-mouthed? Do you entertain lustful thoughts? Are you living a sexually immoral lifestyle? Do you cheat on exams? Do you steal at work? Our lifestyles should be that of sowing righteous seeds; necessity is placed upon us to be upright farmers.

Furthermore, the command is to **"reap steadfast love."** Whenever something is sown, something will be reaped. Hosea assures them that sowing seeds of righteousness reaps steadfast love. The Hebrew word for "steadfast love" is *hesed*, referring to an unfailing kindness, generous mercy, and whole-hearted benevolence. In summary, if Israel plants seeds of righteousness in their lives, they will reap the unfailing kindness of God, this being consistent with the essence of the covenant ethos from the nation's beginning. Deuteronomy 30:15-16 reveals this well by stating,

> *[15] See, I have set before you today life and good, death and evil. [16] If you obey the commandments of the Lord your God that I command you today, by loving the Lord your God, by walking in his ways, and by keeping his commandments and his statutes and his rules, then you shall live and multiply, and the Lord your God will bless you in the land that you are entering to take possession of it.*

On the condition that Israel sowed righteousness, they would experience an ocean of God's overwhelming kindness.

It is, nevertheless, imperative to note that since New Testament Christians do not operate under the same covenant system as the Old Testament Jews, this dynamic cannot be claimed for the former. Our righteous seeds do not automatically translate into God's showers of unfailing kindness in the form of material blessings as it was for Old Testament Israel. However, under the new covenant we have blessings that transcend.

Firstly, those who have believed on Jesus Christ to be saved already have the seeds of righteousness sown within through the power of the indwelling Holy Spirit of God, resulting in the capacity to generate external righteousness (Gal. 5:22-23). The only remaining need is to cultivate those seeds by keeping them in rich soil, watering, and shedding sunlight upon them. Practically speaking, the cultivation of seeds occurs through Scriptural study and meditation, confession of sin, and constant prayer. All opportunities for spiritual growth must be intentionally seized, including faithful church attendance, the consumption of wholesome, biblical literature, and fellowship with the saints. These disciplines and more can be practiced to further nurture the indwelling righteousness.

Second, followers of Jesus Christ reap His steadfast love now and for all eternity, not implying that they will meet material blessings—although in specified seasons, God does give material blessings—but that we are always accepted and loved by Him in a way that other human beings will never experience. Christ's disciples are the apple of His eye, and He loves them immeasurably now and will manifest the completeness of that love in the glory of the eternal state.

Ephesians 2:4-6,

> *⁴ But God, being rich in mercy, because of the great love with which he loved us, ⁵ even when we were dead in our trespasses, made us alive together with Christ—by grace you have been saved— ⁶ and raised us up with him and seated us with him in the heavenly places in Christ Jesus, ⁷ so that in the coming ages he might show the immeasurable riches of his grace in kindness toward us in Christ Jesus.*

Since, Israel sowed unrighteousness and would, in turn, reap the fury of God, Hosea gives them a boisterous warning to **"break up your fallow ground."** "Fallow ground" refers to farmland left untouched for an extensive period of time to restore fertility back to its soil. During this season, the top soil becomes coarse and hard rendering it impossible to plant seeds without plowing the soil first. To "break up fallow ground" is to utilize tools, like a plow, and dig into the soil, breaking up the hard clumps, and transforming it to tillable land where seeds can be planted. Even if weeds had grown upon the land, the breaking up of the earth turns the soil bringing richer soil to the surface.

Fallow ground, in this setting, describes the people's stubborn will and ungodly disposition which detests being impacted by the seed of God's Word. It is the stony, rugged heart of Israel produced out of their rebellion and worldliness and just as soil left untilled becomes thick and impervious, their hearts left untilled had become the same. Therefore, Hosea urges the nation to stick the plow into its own spiritual apathy and stubborn ungodliness and turn it continually until the soil of their hearts had become soft and permeable, ready to receive the word of the Lord.

Equally, there comes seasons in our own lives when we need to break up our fallow ground as Christians, because we can become indifferent, unmoved, and desensitized to iniquity. We may go days or weeks without praying or reading Scripture. We may become loose in our language or cold and inconsiderate of others. We may become dangerous in what we watch or foolish in what we listen to, ignoring the voice of God's Spirit so much that it becomes nothing more than a faint whisper. The solution to all such dilemmas is to drive the plow deep into our hearts and turn it, turn it, turn it, until sensitivity and softness returns.

The text further reveals that **"it is time to seek the Lord."** The root word for "seek" in the original language means "to tread" or "trample with the feet". Imagine a dirt or a track road formed after people have consistently walked through that area overtime. Inherent in the word "seek" is the concept of frequency and repetitiveness alluding that seeking God is spending time with Him consistently. A way of life is the goal rather than a one-hit wonder.

It is incumbent upon God's people to make time to seek Him regularly. Once-a-week church attendance is not sufficient, as we must be communing with Him through the week as well. This qualifies as seeking the Lord because we are constantly coming before Him. Do you spend time seeking the Lord, or does your spiritual life rise and fall on Sunday worship only? If it does, then you are most certainly spiritually malnourished. You would never settle for feeding yourself only once a week, physically. So why settle for feeding yourself only once a week, spiritually?

How should the Lord be sought?

1. By studying and washing ourselves in Scripture because it is the avenue through which God speaks to His children. The Word of God is exactly that—the word *from* God.

2. By spending time in prayer which is the primary manner in which we speak to God. Prayer is our channel of communication with the Father—the telephone connection to which God is at the other end. These two disciplines alone make up the lion's share of what it means to seek the Lord and both are equally important to the process.

Charles Spurgeon perfectly captured the importance of both disciplines when he made the following remark: "When asked what is more important: praying or reading the Bible? I ask what is more important: breathing in or breathing out?"

These disciplines complement one another and one should never be abandoned in favor of the other.

Yet, both principles (breaking up the fallow ground and seeking the Lord) are the chief ingredients in bringing about a spiritual revival in the life of individual believers and in the life of a church corporately. Churches, young and old, must abide firmly in both realms if they desire to maintain spiritual health. To be clear, the New Testament fully supports these principles as well.

James 4:7-9,

> *7 Submit yourselves therefore to God. Resist the devil, and he will flee from you. 8 Draw near to God, and he will draw near to you. (Seek the Lord) Cleanse your hands, you sinners, and purify your hearts, you double-minded. 9 Be wretched and mourn and weep. Let your laughter be turned to mourning and your joy to gloom. (Break up your fallow ground)*

Thus, both concepts are adjacent to each other in the New Testament. Even church history has born testimony that these two principles executed in unison can shake the spiritual foundations of entire nations.

What is the result when both principles are carried out? It is **"that he may come and reign righteousness upon you."** Firstly, God will come and make His presence felt and known; He will be in the midst and it will be impossible to overlook Him. This applies both to the life of the individual believer and to the life of the church corporately. Secondly, He will rain righteousness upon His people. The mention of rain in this verse conveys the image of that which falls, soaks, and seeps into an object. This is not a passing incident with little to no impact, but is a state of being overwhelmed by something, in this case righteousness. To paraphrase, the Lord Himself will come and will effectively produce the rightness, godliness, and holiness that is so desperately lacking among Israel. Their hearts will be changed along with their actions. Rightness of living will become the fruit of their lives, and that fruit will come in abundance. The downpour will be torrential.

This was the desperate need of Israel in Hosea's day, and is also the desperate need of the Church today. Staggeringly difficult it is to put into words just how far Christianity has drifted off course even among those who claim to be Bible-believing. There is a great neglect—even disdain—for holy living. "Churches" openly disobey the clear teachings of Holy Scripture and compromise the tenets of the Christian faith. In many locations, there is little to no zeal for evangelizing the lost. Believers place more confidence in politicians than they do in prayer. Even though

God's Church across the globe is at varying degrees of spiritual maturity, by and large, Christianity worldwide is in need of a spiritual renewal. These two principles are the only means to which revival has ever happened in the past or will happen in the future.

The Present Rebellion

Hosea voices to Israel (vs. 13) **"You have plowed in iniquity; you have reaped injustice."** Observe the contrast to what the prophet sought after in verse 12 when He urged them to "sow righteousness" to, in turn, "reap steadfast love". Currently, Israel walks contradictory to what Hosea desires. Plowing in this verse is the practice of sowing the seeds and pushing them underground with a plow. Essentially, sowing and plowing are identical activities in this context and what they are sowing is moral wickedness and wrongdoing. Their wickedness produces the consequential fruit of "injustice" illustrating the neglect of treating people the way they should be. Hosea gives little details of the injustices of his day, but one problem to recall is the moving of landmarks revealed in Hosea 5:10, which says,

The princes of Judah have become like those who move the landmark; upon them I will pour out my wrath like water.

Moving landmarks was a method of stealing property—an injustice in the highest and purest sense.

Today, injustice is just as prevalent and toxic and we must keenly strive to do right by every individual rather than take advantage of others because of personal bias or prejudice. Fairness and impartiality must reign in our homes with our children, on the job with colleagues, in school with classmates, and even in transactions with the unconverted. It is seldom difficult to perceive when injustice occurs, and it leaves a bad taste in the mouth of the one who has been offended, especially if he is an unbeliever. As Jesus is called the "righteous Judge", His progeny must bear an identical testimony.

Furthermore, it is revealed that **"you have eaten the fruit of lies."** Mark the progression: they plowed, then they reaped, then they ate the fruit. "Eating the fruit" illustrates enjoying the result of what they have sowed which, from the beginning of the process, was lies and deceit. Fraudulence and manipulation was deeply embedded into the social culture of the day.

The similarities to the 21st century are glaringly obvious since contemporary culture is chock-full of scams and fraudsters. Internet, cell phone, mail, money, relationship, and marriage scams have proliferated in recent years and the more prevalent they become the more they trumpet the rottenness of humankind. Tricksters are not concerned in the least with whether someone has food for tomorrow, nor is there sympathy for the one stranded in a foreign land without money. So what if they trifle with your most intimate emotions then leave you high and dry! May no one who calls himself a child of God be caught up in such devious activities, and may Christians be vigilant of those who lie in wait to cuckold and fleece them of hard-earned money. God's wisdom is crucial to navigate the days and times in which we live.

The verse continues with **"because you have trusted in your own way and in the multitude of your warriors."** Israel has a misplaced trust; its confidence is in military power and might rather than in the Lord. The expression "your own way" perhaps alludes to war room, military strategies. Israel should have known better because its history is inundated with instances of the fragility of military might as the deciding factor in the triumph of God's people. Manifold are the Old Testament cases of how small numbers overcame large armies, evidencing that the determining aspect always started and ended with their God. Their trust in God (or lack thereof) was telling of their spiritual condition.

This begs introspection because we often have misplaced trust as well. Even saints have a way of believing in the most futile things to sustain us futuristically. Placing confidence in jobs, economic stability, and family connections to secure us is a conventional exercise, while, unhappily, those blessings can be as steady as a coconut tree in a Category-5 hurricane. Our faith must be in God and in Him alone! If King David was alive in Hosea's generation, he would have cried out, according to Psalm 20: 7, that "Some trust in chariots and some in horses, but we trust in the name of the Lord our God." "In God We Trust" was not engraved upon the coin of Israel's heart.

The Future Consequences

The 14th verse commences **"Therefore the tumult of war shall arise among your people."** The Hebrew word translated as "tumult" literally means "a loud noise" or "a roar". Although they exercised faith in their many warriors, they would be vanquished by the invasion of the enemy in their own country. Perilous times are afoot for Israel, and since they have ditched their God. Nothing can spare them.

Also, **"all of your fortresses shall be destroyed."** Such fortresses are places of refuge from which they will wage war. Fortresses are structures built from the sturdiest materials in high locations in order to oversee the surrounding area with the goal of outlasting enemy attack. If the fortresses are destroyed, everywhere else has already been obliterated, as fortresses are the last stand and final barrier to keeping the enemy at bay. This dilemma, for Israel, will morph into a devastating catastrophe. The verse proceeds to illustrate the horrific nature of the situation when it declares **"As Shalman destroyed Beth-arbel on the day of battle."** Uncertainty surrounds the identity of "Shalman" but there are two prospects.

1. Shalman may be an abbreviated name for Shalmaneser III, an Assyrian king from the 9th century.[xi] This monarch was the king to whom Hoshea, king of Israel, paid tribute in 2 Kings 17:3-4.

   > *³Against him came up Shalmaneser king of Assyria. And Hoshea became his vassal and paid him tribute. ⁴But the king of Assyria found treachery in Hoshea, for he had sent messengers to So, king of Egypt, and offered no tribute to the king of Assyria, as he had done year by year. Therefore the king of Assyria shut him up and bound him in prison.*

2. Shalman, according to some commentators, is Salamanu, a king of Moab. However, his absence from Scripture is a challenge, as he is only mentioned in some ancient writings.[xii] Although this option is not impossible to believe, it is less likely.

It is articulated that Shalman destroyed a site called "Beth-arbel". This location is not cited anywhere else in Scripture, but modern scholarship asserts it to be where the modern-day city of Irbid is located in the country of Jordan.[xiii] Thus, a battle previously took place at Beth-arbel and the city was destroyed by, the conqueror, Shalman.

The verse explains the horrendous nature of the destruction with **"mothers were dashed in pieces with their children,"** aiming to expound this battle's savagery since the bodies of mothers were sliced in pieces along with their young ones. Generally, when we contemplate war and battle, we imagine men losing their lives and rarely envision women and children being ravaged. Hosea's implication is that this identical viciousness is nearing Israel's door with mothers and their precious children butchered.

Sin is deeply offensive to God and its increase angers Him. While earthly realms can never be void of sin, the onus of Christians is to stand against the rolling tide of godlessness in their generation and to continue to be salt and light in an age that loves to revel in evil and call it harmless. The day the Church of Jesus Christ loses sight of God's holiness and hatred of sin is the day the entire world is doomed.

"Thus it shall be done to you, O Bethel" is the warning of verse **15**. The prophet foretells precisely what will occur in Israel, specifically in the city of Bethel. Face to face with the same scenario, they should either repent or prepare to confront the wrathful hand of God.

Bethel is singled out **"because of your great evil."** Evil, apparently, was ubiquitous in the land. The designation of the evil as "great" is likely due to the golden calf worshiped there. This city has already made several appearances in Hosea's prophecy, so its activity must have angered God. Note God's ability to direct His judgement to definite places. Also, **"at dawn the king of Israel shall be utterly cut off."** Hosea sticks to his guns without changing his message that the flame of the nation's leader will be doused. Twice in the 10th chapter, he made the same assertion.

Hosea 10:3,7,

> ^{3} *For now they will say: "We have no king, for we do not fear the Lord; and a king—what could he do for us?" ^{7} Samaria's king shall perish like a twig on the face of the waters.*

The distinct message of God's manservant must never transfigure into something more palatable to his audience. Hosea remained steadfast in speaking truth as it was received from the hand of God. Many 21st century churches have altered their message to make it appetizing to a sinful generation and have given into the lie that to speak truth is to be hateful. However, God's flock must profoundly grasp that truth will be categorized as intolerable to those who hate the truth. If we ever permit the world to dictate the parameters surrounding what we can proclaim, then soon we will have freedom to proclaim nil. Consequently, we must cleave ardently to the Holy Scriptures like a drowning man to a life jacket and never be embarrassed by its assertions because it is, indeed, the word of the living God.

> Discuss

1. Why do you suppose Hosea uses farming illustrations so frequently in his prophetic ministry? What might a contemporary minister learn from his example?

2. What might moving landmarks be comparable with in today's culture?

3. Practically, how might Christians break up their fallow ground?

4. "Churches openly disobey the clear teachings of Holy Scripture and compromise the tenets of the Christian faith." Give a present-day example that supports this assertion.

5. Why is once-a-week church attendance not sufficient to sustain the entirety of one's spiritual life?

20

TORN BY LOVE

11:1-7

¹When Israel was a child, I loved him, and out of Egypt I called my son. ²The more they were called, the more they went away; they kept sacrificing to the Baals and burning offerings to idols. ³Yet it was I who taught Ephraim to walk; I took them up by their arms, but they did not know that I healed them. ⁴I led them with cords of kindness, with the bands of love, and I became to them as one who eases the yoke on their jaws, and I bent down to them and fed them. ⁵They shall not return to the land of Egypt, but Assyria shall be their king, because they have refused to return to me. ⁶The sword shall rage against their cities, consume the bars of their gates, and devour them because of their own counsels. ⁷My people are bent on turning away from me, and though they call out to the Most High, he shall not raise them up at all.

Parent/child relationships can be challenging. Almost nothing drains the life out of a parent like a strained relationship with a child. The feeling of being shunned after decades of love, nurture, care, and investment can be debilitating and damaging. Some have even claimed that the only emotional pain worse than an estranged relationship is the death of the child altogether.

Yahweh, the God of the Bible, knows this pain all too well. This text of Scripture clearly sets forth how His son, Israel, spurned His perfect, parental love.

God Loves His Children

The 1st verse begins **"when Israel was a child."** "Child" conveys the notion of a youthful individual who is subservient and dependent on another for his provision, hinting to a time Israel was still in infancy. Israel was not always the powerhouse it was in Hosea's era. As a matter of fact, previously the nation did not reside on its own land as Israel was nothing more than a small family nucleus that multiplied over the millennia. Nevertheless, in this elementary state, God declared that **"I loved him."** The Hebrew word for "love" here literally means that He "breathed after" them expressing His desire and delight towards Israel.

God's feelings toward His New Testament church, the "called-out ones", are identical. *Eccleisia* (pronounced Ek-lay-see-a), the New Testament Greek word for "church", denotes those who have been called out of the world's system to a life consecrated and committed to Jesus Christ, and God has that same yearning and gladness in His church. Romans 8:35 asks the question, *"Who shall separate us from the love of Christ? Shall tribulation or distress or persecution or famine or nakedness or danger or sword?"*

Verse 37 retorts *"No, in all these things we are more than conquerors through him who loved us."* 1 John 4:19 sets it more succinctly with *"We love because he first loved us."* God first initiated love, and we only responded in kind. Do you know beyond the shadow of a doubt that you have been born again and are God's child? If the answer is affirmative, then you are a specimen of those who are loved unconditionally by the living God—eternally by the Creator and Sustainer of the universe. Although seasons may prevail when you doubt the love of your family, close associates, or even fellow saints, rest assured that no matter what, God's love for you, His child, is immutable.

The verse continues **"and out of Egypt I called my son."** Historically, Israel, as a family, lived in Egypt as subservient slaves until God called them out of that location. "Called" carries with it the notion of addressing a person by name and summoning him to a certain direction. Israel's call is evidenced by Exodus 4:22-23. God tells Moses,

> [22] *Then you shall say to Pharaoh, 'Thus says the Lord, Israel is my firstborn son,* [23] *and I say to you, "Let my son go that he may serve me." If you refuse to let him go, behold, I will kill your firstborn son.'"*

Firstly, He called Israel out of Egypt from under Pharaoh's rule. Secondly, He beheld the entire nation as offspring by referring to them as "son". Also noteworthy is that, often in Scripture, Egypt is symbolic of worldliness which is opposed to the God of heaven and in this clause He calls His son out of Egypt.

Again, this runs parallel to the core definition of the church since the term points to those addressed by name and summoned to forsake the world's philosophy. As God, in the Old Testament, called Israel out of Egypt, God in the New Testament, calls the church out of the world. Is that your testimony? Have you separated yourself from the world's way of thinking and acting? Is your distinction from the world recognizable or do you camouflage with ease? Is your kindred aware of your profession of faith in Christ? Do your neighbors know your claim to Christianity? Is involvement in sin and compromise your delight? Not everyone that enters a church building is a part of the actual Church. The body of Christ are the ones called out of darkness into light (Ephesians 5:7-11).

Evangelist Billy Sunday took the position that "Going to church doesn't make you a Christian any more than standing in a garage makes you a car."

The 2nd verse starts **"the more they were called."** Obviously "they" refers to Israel, but who they were called by is less apparent. The most astute conclusion is that they were called by God's prophets. Repeatedly, God sent His spokesmen to convince them of disobedience and call them to repentance. Even in Hosea's prophecy, the role of the prophet graces the fore on a number of occasions.

Hosea 6:5,

Therefore I have hewn them by the prophets; I have slain them by the words of my mouth, and my judgment goes forth as the light.

Hosea 9:8,

The prophet is the watchman of Ephraim with my God; yet a fowler's snare is on all his ways, and hatred in the house of his God.

Hosea 12:13,

By a prophet the Lord brought Israel up from Egypt, and by a prophet he was guarded.

God's voluminous prophets called the people to be faithful to the covenant ethos, and it was their duty to call Israel out on the carpet when they transgressed.

Today, the prophets of God still speak concerning His already-revealed revelation. They speak from the authority of the Bible—their mandate and playbook as they invite people to repentance. Duty remains to have the truth of God told forth as written in His Word. Unbiblical "Christianity" would have you believe the pastor's only purpose is to assist in conjuring up decent feelings about oneself. He exists solely as a motivational speaker who works in a church setting. Such contemplations have no scriptural foundation. Sure, there are times when encouragement is necessary; however, there also comes occasions when he must call people to repentance. Sinners must be called to repent and believe the gospel, while saints ought be called to continuous and daily repentance from sin. The Old Testament prophets called men to repentance. The New Testament apostles called men to repentance. Today, the directive to repent still remains.

Still, **"the more they were called the more they went away."** Israel, called by God's prophets to be faithful to the covenant, strayed from the covenant instead of yielding to it. Rather than submitting, they rebelled. Rather than repenting, they roamed. They pushed away from Jeremiah's preaching, rejected Isaiah's words, and counted Ezekiel as a fool. Amos was nothing more than a clanging cymbal. Maybe, today, you imitate the same pattern. The more you are called to draw near to God, the further you run away; the clearer the beckoning to repentance, the deeper you dive into sin. If this describes your current condition, you are at a dangerous cliff edge. To reject God's teachings is to reject God Himself! I urge you to soften your rebellious heart and submit to the Lord in accord with Hebrews 3:7-10,

> [7] *Therefore, as the Holy Spirit says, "Today, if you hear his voice,* [8] *do not harden your hearts as in the rebellion, on the day of testing in the wilderness,* [9] *where your fathers put me to the test and saw my works for forty years.* [10] *Therefore I was provoked with that generation, and said, 'They always go astray in their heart; they have not known my ways.'"*

Oh my friend, now is the time to draw nigh to God, not steer away from him.

The text explains their going astray saying, **"they kept sacrificing to the Baals and burning offerings to idols."** Israel had a penchant for submerging themselves in idolatry. Again, note that both "Baals" and "idols" is plural due to their acts of whoredom with multiple objects. Egregious offence to Yahweh was made by not giving Him the prime position in their lives as God. Fearfully were they warned about the dangers of such prior to their conquest of the Promised Land.

Deuteronomy 6:4-5,

⁴ *Hear, O Israel: The Lord our God, the Lord is one.* ⁵ *You shall love the Lord your God with all your heart and with all your soul and with all your might.*

Deuteronomy 6:14,

¹⁴ *You shall not go after other gods, the gods of the peoples who are around you.*

The Lord was a jealous God then and He has not altered His disposition. Thus, we must investigate whether anything in our lives would drive Him to that emotion. Is there anything with which we are smitten more than Him?

He Cares for His Children

According to the verse 3, **"yet it was I who taught Ephraim to walk."** The metaphor of the beloved son continues in this verse. The concept of walking gives the idea of movement and progress explaining that it was God Himself who gave Israel progress as a nation. When did He teach them to walk? He's probably highlighting the season in which He cared for them while they wandered in the wilderness. This conclusion can be realized because their being called out of Egypt has already been established. Progress in their journey and identity was solely the result of their God. He taught His son, Israel, to walk.

Next, **"I took them by their arms but they did not know that I healed them"** furthers the metaphor of Israel as a beloved son. Every parent knows the joy of taking up their child by the arms as the young one looks up at you from below with outstretched arms. To rise up and be held in your warm embrace is what they yearn. Yahweh did the same for His son Israel; He picked him up and held him tight during the wilderness wanderings, not leaving the elect nation to perish. The Father preserved them securely in their journeying until they reached the designated land.

Unfortunately, they failed to perceive how their God healed them by refusing to recognize and acknowledge His care. God brings to their recollection His protection, provision, and forgiveness in the wilderness. Israel was not flawless in the wilderness as there were challenges, failures, and sin. Nevertheless, God remained faithful to them.

We commonly resemble those wilderness Jews having personal challenges and major defects. We engage sin more than we would dare to admit, but, thank God, He never discards or abandons His children. He will not trade us in for a better stock. May all God's children shamelessly testify, like those wilderness Jews, that He is indeed faithful.

As the hymn writer, Thomas Chisholm, spoke:

"Great is Thy faithfulness, O God my Father
There is no shadow of turning with Thee
Thou changest not, Thy compassions, they fail not
As Thou hast been Thou forever wilt be
Great is Thy faithfulness, great is Thy faithfulness
Morning by morning new mercies I see
All I have needed Thy hand hath provided
Great is Thy faithfulness, Lord, unto me."

God stated, in verse 4, that **"I led them with chords of kindness with bands of love."** Some scholars contend the image of a beloved son continues into verse 4; others have determined that the verse starts a new illustration—the farmer with his animals. I side with the latter option because of specific words used. God steered Israel with both "chords of kindness" and "bands of love", the terms explaining how cords used in animal training are drawn by the Lord upon Israel in tenderness. Divine love is still the emphasis of verse 4.

Accurately this illustrates the manner in which God loves His children—with kindness and tenderness. His affection for His begotten is enduring and everlasting. Even when He chastens His children it is out of love. Be reminded of Hebrews 12:5-6,

> [5] *And have you forgotten the exhortation that addresses you as sons? "My son, do not regard lightly the discipline of the Lord, nor be weary when reproved by Him.* [6] *For the Lord disciplines the one He loves, and chastises every son whom He receives."*

As God's child, you might be undergoing a season of chastening in your life. Take comfort that God loves you no less than another believer. Conversely, it is because of His affection that He disciplines as an earthly father should discipline his son if he truly loves him.

Commentary continues with **"and I became to them as one who eases the yoke on their jaws."** Since particular words are used, it is more plausible that the imagery is of a farmer with his animal. There is little evidence, even in ancient cultures, that yokes were put on the necks of children. The easing of the yoke on the animal's jaw means the burden will decrease or be removed altogether. Historically, God transported His people out of the wilderness and, eventually, brought them into the land flowing with milk and honey. Moreover, despite their time in the wilderness being much longer than was necessary, they, in due course, walked into a season when their burden was loosed from their backs and the pressure of their trying circumstances was released.

On occasion, the trials we endure seem to be endless. This may accurately describe your current condition. You see no light at the end of the tunnel. You've been trotting this dark road for a while. This burden has weighed down your shoulders for longer than you can remember. Take comfort in knowing that, at times, God does lighten the load, answers the prayer, removes the trial, and gives joy again. Don't quit! Don't throw in the towel! Don't raise the white flag of surrender! Like Franklin D. Roosevelt once remarked, "If you've reached the end of your rope, tie a knot, and hold on!" Psalm 30:5b encourages that "Weeping may tarry for the night, but joy comes with the morning." Yet, if that trial is never removed, remember this fleeting life will soon be ended, and the child of God can affirm as the Puritan Thomas Watson, did when he stated, "We spend our years with sighing; it is a valley of tears; but death is the funeral of all our sorrows."

Next, God reveals **"I bent down to them"** like a farmer bends down to his resting animal showing humility and care. He **"fed them"**, providing manna and quail every day to sustain Israel in the desert. Equally, God has the resources to sustain and keep His people today; therefore, we must prioritize seeking Him for those resources.

He Disciplines His Children

The 5th verse declares that **"they shall not return to the land of Egypt."** At first glance, this statement seems to contradict what Hosea has already said earlier in Hosea 8:13,

"As for my sacrificial offerings, they sacrifice meat and eat it, but the Lord does not accept them. Now he will remember their iniquity and punish their sins; they shall return to Egypt."

Recall as well Hosea 9:3,

"They shall not remain in the land of the Lord, but Ephraim shall return to Egypt, and they shall eat unclean food in Assyria."

Hosea, twice, stated they will return to Egypt, but in verse 5, he reverses by insisting they will not return to Egypt. Should this be tagged as an example of a scriptural contradiction? No. The Bible never contradicts itself. If instances ever appear when the Bible seems to refute itself as in the present example, one must merely dig deeper into the meaning and (historical/grammatical/literary) context of the passage to untie that knot. During the aforementioned verses, when Hosea speaks of Israel returning to Egypt, he was not communicating they would literally return to Egypt. He uses the title Egypt as a metaphor for bondage and slavery because of what they previously suffered in Egypt. His goal, though, was not to infer they would return to physical Egyptian territory; he insinuated Assyria would become their new "Egypt" through their defiance. It was all figurative language. In verse 5, the text explicates that they will not return to the land of Egypt which is literal Egypt and not a metaphor. By and large, they will not as a nation return to that land proper, although Scripture does uncover that a miniscule group of them did in time go back to that land. Moreover, it must be understood that the Bible never contradicts itself although it may appear to on the surface. The rebuff of laziness and a deeper dive into Scripture always makes the murky waters clear.

In the place of them factually returning to the land of Egypt, the text discloses **"but Assyria shall be their king."** The God of heaven, Yahweh, was to be their sovereign and because they have excluded Him, as such, another realm will have mastery over them.

This is emblematic of all people on our planet. Everyone has a king. Either Creator God is king or something/someone else is king, but everyone has a king. If your king is not the God of the Bible, then it might just be yourself, your money, good looks, clothing, or maybe even your country. Nonetheless, make no mistake about it, everyone has a king! Who or what is your king? What is it that has mastery over you, controlling the manner in which you reason and function? Soul searching must be engaged to not be deceived concerning who we truly worship. Assyria will be their king **"because they have refused to return to me."** Note that God is devastated most, not by their drifting away, but by their staying there after incalculable warnings from His prophets. An astute gentleman once said "Men don't drown by falling into the water, they drowned by staying there."

My friend, none are faultless or sinless as we all drift off course during seasons of weakness. Yet, do you return to the Lord after He sends out His warning through His Word? When through Scripture our errors are exposed, do we return to shore or stay adrift in the ocean? When we've discerned that our associations are ungodly, or that we've not been good stewards of our finances, or that our minds ponder ungodly fantasies, what is our response? Do we remain dormant and leave things as is or is there remorse and change? Are we turned to God?

"The sword shall rage against their cities" according to verse 6. When the Assyrians enter the land, deadly fighting will befall the nation and countless lives will be cut off. The word translated as "rage", in the original Hebrew, bears the impression of "a spinning" or "a whirling" communicating the manner in which the population will be overwhelmed by an insurgence of violence. Furthermore, it will **"consume the bars of their gates"**. In Ancient Near Eastern cultures, the gates of the cities was the location of administrative offices where leadership and civic duties were fulfilled. The sum of these kinds of activities will be brought to destruction and the very lifeblood of the cities will be smothered. Yahweh will **"devour them because of their own counsels."** Political and military planning would be to no avail since no one sought God's face. Traditionally, He was at the helm of the nation's victories and strategies throughout most of the Old Testament, but this generation does not embrace God in their preparations.

Under the Old Covenant, God required Israel to include Him in their groundwork, and seek Him in the decision-making process. He still expects the same courtesy from us today. Do we seek God in the major decisions of our lives? Do we desire His wisdom or do we operate based on our own limited knowledge? We must be actively seeking God's guidance before making major decisions. Neglecting to do so would be as foolish as Israel who deliberated martial action without God's involvement.

Verse 7 continues with **"my people are bent on turning away from me."** "Bent" gives the idea that this is what Israel adheres to as their habitual practice. Gone are the days when they possessed some sensitivity to God and the word of His prophets. Their default position is that they have defected from being loyal to their Maker.

Are you "bent" on turning away from God? This is not the individual who has made a blunder, but someone whose default setting is turned away from God's path. When it comes to God, your switch is on "off"! You want nothing to do with God! You have no interest in spiritual things. I humbly urge you to make a change and turn to the Lord through Jesus Christ, His Son, before the flame of your life goes out. Either you will face God in repentance now, or you will face Him in torment later. Your stubborn refusal to acknowledge the truth doesn't make that truth any less truthful. Jesus affirmed in John 14:6 that *"I am the way, and the truth, and the life. No one comes to the Father except through me."*

However, **"though they call out to the Most High he shall not raise them up at all."** There's coming a time when these Jews will cry out for help, but by then time would have expired; their fate would have been sealed making it impossible to escape the coming downpour of God's judgement.

Every sinner needs a Saviour and Jesus Christ, God's sinless lamb, is the only one qualified to forgive sin and declare a guilty sinner as righteous. Now is the time to plead to the Lord for salvation. Days are coming when innumerable persons will shriek under the fury of God's judgement upon iniquity, but by then it will be too late. The time to seek the Lord for rescue is now, while the door to the ark of safety yet remains open. When the Assyrians arrive, God will allow these Jews to be swallowed whole; and when Hell fire comes, God will ensure unforgiven sinners to be swallowed whole.

> Discuss

1. What does the Greek word for "church", *eccleisia* suggest about the Christian's relationship to worldliness?

2. How does God's immutable love for His children comfort the believer's heart?

3. If God loves His children, why does He punish them?

4. Practically, how can we seek God's face before making major decisions?

5. "His affection for His begotten is enduring and everlasting." Excluding the verses referenced in this chapter, give two examples from different books of the Bible to support this truth.

21

MERCY MULTIPLIED

11:8-11

⁸ *How can I give you up, O Ephraim? How can I hand you over, O Israel? How can I make you like Admah? How can I treat you like Zeboiim? My heart recoils within me; my compassion grows warm and tender.* ⁹ *I will not execute my burning anger; I will not again destroy Ephraim; for I am God and not a man, the Holy One in your midst, and I will not come in wrath.* ¹⁰ *They shall go after the Lord; he will roar like a lion; when he roars, his children shall come trembling from the west;* ¹¹ *they shall come trembling like birds from Egypt, and like doves from the land of Assyria, and I will return them to their homes, declares the Lord.*

Charles Spurgeon once made the statement that "God's mercy is so great that you may sooner drain the sea of its water, or deprive the sun of its light, or make space too narrow, than diminish the great mercy of God."

The text under examination certainly underscores that statement. Hosea's prophecy thus far contains many threats of the judgement of God. Nevertheless, the theme of mercy is present within it as well, and because of God's great mercy the ultimate goal of retribution is restoration.

A Reluctance

This section commences at verse 8 with **"How can I give you up, O Ephraim?"** and is highly emotional for the Lord as if the cup of His feelings is overflowing. Theologically, God's speech in this section is an anthropopathy which means that human feelings are ascribed to something or someone non-human. In this case that someone is God.[xiv] The phrase "give you up" carries a military connotation, and it is often used when one group of individuals is transmitted to their enemies to do as they please.[xv] Therefore, although a question is asked in this verse, in reality a statement is being made. God does not anticipate an answer from Israel; rather, He desires that Israel apprehend this assertion. In essence, He says "although you have been increasingly disobedient to me O Israel, I can't give you up and I won't give you up. I won't completely obliterate you from the face of the earth although you deserve it."

The next clause expresses the same idea. It is **"How can I hand you over, O Israel?"** "Hand you over" expresses a mirroring notion to "give you up" painting the picture of a military transaction. Again, the Lord is making an assertion. "I can't hand you over, and I won't hand you over" is His mindset as He is still enamoured with Israel despite their vileness. He still has in mind verse 1 of Chapter 11 when He loved Israel, even as a child, and called Him out of Egypt.

God will always adore those who are truly His children notwithstanding our shortcomings, failures, sins, and weaknesses. He never abandons a son or daughter once they are a part of His family. The exclamation of the author of Hebrews on God's behalf is this: *"I will never leave you nor forsake you"* (13:5). If that verse were translated into the Hosean vernacular, he would say "I will never give you up; I will never hand you over." The saints of God shall most assuredly not meet eternal torment nor will His Holy Spirit vacate our physical frames (Romans 8:9-11; Ephesians 4:30). Always present in you will be the Spirit of truth, to convict, guide, and comfort you, and then transfer you at the end of this present life into life everlasting. Furthermore, this implies that true, born-again Christians can never be demon-possessed. 2 Corinthians 6:14b enquires, *"What fellowship does light have with darkness?"* To assert that the Holy Spirit and a demon could dwell together in the same individual is borderline blasphemic. If Christians could be demon-possessed, it would mean that God has "given them up" and "handed them over", the Holy Spirit having submitted to an evil spirit—nothing short of a travesty. Contrary to popular belief, however, God never allows the devil to occupy the bodies of His saints.

Emotions continue to pour forth with **"How can I make you like Admah? How can I treat you like Zeboiim?"** Admah and Zeboiim are two locations that most Bible readers would be unfamiliar with; however, it is likely that there would be familiarity with two other cities that those towns are allied with in Scripture. Deuteronomy 29:22-23 discloses the popular cities linked to those townships.

> *²² And the next generation, your children who rise up after you, and the foreigner who comes from a far land, will say, when they see the afflictions of that land and the sicknesses with which the Lord has made it sick— ²³ the whole land burned out with brimstone and salt, nothing sown and nothing growing, where no plant can sprout, an overthrow like that of Sodom and Gomorrah, Admah, and Zeboiim, which the Lord overthrew in his anger and wrath—*

Thus, Admah and Zeboiim were destroyed the same time and in the same way as Sodom and Gomorrah and—highly likely—for the same cause, which was the pervasiveness of the sin of homosexuality. God wiped them off the map in unison with Sodom and Gomorrah because of their gross depravity. They were no more. Yet God explains, here in Hosea, that although Israel has transgressed recurrently and committed the same sins as Admah and Zeboiim, it will not draw the same end result. Yes, they will still face divine indignation, but they shall not be annihilated from the face of the planet like these two cities. Why does God not treat Israel as Admah and Zeboiim?

It is because **"my heart recoils within me."** Yahweh—not having a literal heart— is using human language to make Israel understand His emotional disturbance. The word translated "recoils" in the original language means "to overturn" or "overthrow". That is to say, God's heart has been turned over and changed toward Israel. This is the exact word used to describe what transpired in Exodus with Pharaoh after he came to the realization that he had liberated Israel out of servitude to the Egyptian kingdom. Exodus 14:5 informs that *"When the king of Egypt was told that the people had fled, the mind of Pharaoh and his servants was <u>changed</u> toward the people, and they said, 'What is this we have done, that we have let Israel go from serving us?'"*

The word translated "changed" in the Exodus verse is the same word translated "recoiled" here.

If that were not enough, He also says *"my compassion grows warm and* **tender,"** explaining the kind of change that has taken place in God's heart. It moves from anger and wrath to compassion, warmth, and tenderness; He makes a 180 degree turn when it comes to Israel. The question could be raised "Why did His heart change for Israel and not for Admah and Zeboiim, and by extension Sodom and Gomorrah?" Why were they wiped off the map but not Israel? All three locations were enthralled in rebellion, and the same kind of rebellion. Why such diverse treatments?

1. It was God's wish to treat them differently. He is not entitled to operate by human expectations or inputs, but, rather, functions by His own desires. Whatever God does is blamelessly right. If He purposes to extend greater mercy to some than to others, that is entirely His prerogative because He is sovereign.

2. The nation of Israel was/is God's elect people with whom He made a covenant thousands of years beforehand. He promised that they would be great, and through Israel all other nations of the world would be blessed. Scripturally, no indication is ever given that Israel would be expunged from the world as a people. Therefore, it was unlikely that Israel would ultimately meet the same demise as Admah and Zeboiim.

God always keeps His promises. He kept His promises in the ancient era, and that consistency remains even up to our present time. Every assurance that God has made to you and I as His New Covenant people, He will firmly retain. Although we cannot claim all the promises of the Old Testament because we are not Israel, we can certainly claim all the promises of the New Covenant. Don't ever give suspicion to any promise God has made to His children.

A Repeal

Verse **4** states that **"I will not execute my burning anger."** This clause does not imply that God has no right to be angry, because He has every right to be irate due to the people's constant rebellion. Yet, He is free to decide not to act on that anger.

This is a lesson to you and I as well. There will be times in life when we will have every right to be angry but that does not necessitate that our burning anger must be unleashed. Thank God that He doesn't always execute His burning anger and neither should we. If God, who is perfectly just, can mitigate His indignation to the showing of mercy, then certainly we who are imperfect and sometimes unjust can also show mercy negating the opportunity to be slaves to our emotions which can cause us to sin. Emotions are part and parcel of being human, but they must not always dictate our behaviour.

The verse continues **"I will not again destroy Ephraim."** Observe that God does not assert that Ephraim would not be destroyed, cancelling His judgement. The word "again" is important, emphasizing that it would not be repeated. Furthermore, they will never be disposed of as God's people, as the Lord will keep His promises.

Likewise, believers must not assume that an unchangeable relationship with their Saviour impedes them facing God's disciplinary procedures. Such an outlook despises the grace of God rather than honors it. Genuine converts must not interpret eternal security as a license to sin freely (Romans 6:1-2). To contravene in this way is to put ourselves in grave danger of facing the discipline of the Father. Rather, God's keeping power should make us overzealous to please Him and elevate our level of worship. Paul relates it this way in Romans 6:1-4.

> [1]*What shall we say then? Are we to continue in sin that grace may abound?* [2] *By no means! How can we who died to sin still live in it?* [3] *Do you not know that all of us who have been baptized into Christ Jesus were baptized into his death?* [4] *We were buried therefore with him by baptism into death, in order that, just as Christ was raised from the dead by the glory of the Father, we too might walk in newness of life.*

The grace of God is no license to sin.

The Lord launches further with **"for I am God and not a man"** to demarcate His separateness and distinction from His creation; therefore, it should not be assumed that God would function in the manner that man would. Because His thoughts and plans surpass anything we could comprehend, no one should witness this situation and presume that God is unjust by eventually handing Israel mercy, then not being generous to Admah and Zeboiim. Grasping the ways of God is far beyond human reach (Isaiah 55:8-9).

Neither should anyone today conclude God is unjust by drawing some to eternal salvation and not others—mercy to a few, but not to all (Romans 9:14-16). As a matter of fact, were God to perform justice upon every soul in the world, none would escape punishment in everlasting hell. No one would receive mercy. Personally, I prefer the opportunity for mercy which is exactly what God has done. Select citizens of earth are not perishing all due to the sheer grace and mercy of God (Titus 3:5). This is the grace that is truly "amazing".

In addition, He is **"the Holy One in your midst."** "Holy", when used in reference to God, explains His absolute purity and cleanliness, making Him free from all defilement and untainted by anything profane. The Godhead is the solitary personality in the universe that can claim impeccable holiness; therefore, anything or anyone else is only able to do so because it is derived from God. Case in point, the Ark of the Covenant was a holy artifact to the Jews, but only because the presence of God upon the Ark made it holy. Nothing was holy concerning the gold used to construct it. God's children are called a "holy nation" as well, due to the presence of God living within by way of His Holy Spirit. Therefore, only God holds intrinsic holiness—the precise reason why the clause singles out God as the "Holy One". His transcendence is being emphasized since the Creator's attributes go far beyond human attainment.

Nevertheless, the clause also states that He is "in your midst" to articulate that God's presence is with His people. The Lord is not afar and aloof, unaware of or unconcerned about the daily undertakings of our existence. Instead, He is present with regard to everything taking place. In this phrase, the transcendence of God is juxtaposed against the imminence of God. He is entirely otherworldly and yet also near and involved in our lives moment by moment. God holds the billions of galaxies under the fingernail of His thumb, but is nearer to us than the clothes on our backs. Yahweh, the God of the Bible, is both transcendent and immanent. Psalm 138:6b succinctly captures this balance when it states *"For though the Lord is high, he regards the lowly..."*

Both aforesaid qualities of God must be held in equal equilibrium. Some Christians lean too heavily on His transcendence, the disadvantage being He always seems far away. He is unapproachable and impersonal. Other believers lean too heavily on His imminence. God is brought so low as to make Him colloquial. He is nothing more than another "homeboy". There is a lack of respect and awe of the Creator. The biblical mandate is to honour both equally. We must stand in awe of Him, and yet we must be in love with Him. He is royalty as well as family.

The script continues **"and I will not come in wrath,"** reiterating what was said from the start of the verse. God's anger for Israel will not reach its fullest expression as it did for Admah and Zeboiim. Retribution will not be as horrendous as God has the power to make it, calling to mind the cry of the prophet Habakkuk in 3:2b which humbly pleads *"in wrath remember mercy"*. This is precisely the heart of God in Hosea 11. Even in His anger, He has mercy on His people.

No one alive should imagine that what he/she is facing personally is the full extent of God's wrath. This is not to imply that the situation is not painful, nor the burden heavy, nor the challenge overwhelming. Yet, regardless of your predicament, God is exercising mercy in some way, shape, or fashion. We are not enduring the worst, and our burden is still not as heavy as our God has the ability to make it. Slices of God's mercy are yet wrapped up in our packages of personal suffering, and as Habakkuk suggests, even in wrath, God remembers mercy.

A Return

Verse 10 begins **"they shall go after the Lord."** A potentially confusing clause, it does not imply they will pursue the Lord in antagonism as the phrase "go after" often suggests. It communicates they will go behind God or follow after Him; He will take the lead and His people will follow suit. The verse explains the statement's meaning when it says **"he will roar like a lion."** The metaphor changes from God as a caring parent to, once again, the image of a lion. So far, such imagery has been used negatively (Hosea 5:14), but, in this instance, the image is used in a fairly positive manner. For the first time, the actual roar of the lion is underscored, emphasizing the power and territorial reign of that creature. God's roar symbolizes that He is dominant over the land of Israel.

The result is that **"when he roars his children shall come trembling from the west."** A lion's roar alerts its own offspring, so when God sees fit, His children will return in fear of Him. Furthermore, (verse 11) **"they shall come trembling like birds from Egypt and like doves from the land of Assyria."** The metaphor quickly shifts again from a lion to two different types of birds. Although the metaphor is different, the verb "trembling" remains unchanged indicating the manner in which these Jews will return from their various places of exile. This echoes what was earlier acknowledged in Hosea 3:5,

⁵Afterward the children of Israel shall return and seek the Lord their God, and David their king, and they shall come in fear to the Lord and to His goodness in the latter days.

Could it be that you have turned away from God and are in exile because of disobedience? Today, I urge you to come back trembling in fear of the Almighty. Return in repentance and seek the Lord of afresh.

The end of the verse declares that **"I will return them to their homes declares the Lord."** God will restore His people to the very land from which they were driven. After His wrath came mercy, and Israel will be permitted to go back to their former abode.

The Jews will return to their homeland, not because they deserve it, nor because somehow sin has been eradicated from their bodies, but because God shows His mercy. He will not stop loving them. God loved Israel as a child and that love has never changed. Even though God sometimes punishes His children, the ultimate goal is always to, one day, restore them.

> Discuss

1. Where else in Scripture does God use anthropopathic speech?

2. Excluding the references in this chapter, give Scriptural support for the Holy Spirit's presence in every believer?

3. Why is the grace of God not a license to sin?

4. What does God's mercy in the midst of wrath reveal about His character?

5. Do you successfully keep the transcendence and imminence of God in balance? Which are you more likely to gravitate towards?

22

U-TURN
11:12-12:6

¹² Ephraim has surrounded me with lies, and the house of Israel with deceit, but Judah still walks with God and is faithful to the Holy One. ¹Ephraim feeds on the wind and pursues the east wind all day long; they multiply falsehood and violence; they make a covenant with Assyria, and oil is carried to Egypt. ² The Lord has an indictment against Judah and will punish Jacob according to his ways; he will repay him according to his deeds. ³ In the womb he took his brother by the heel, and in his manhood he strove with God. ⁴ He strove with the angel and prevailed; he wept and sought his favor. He met God at Bethel, and there God spoke with us– ⁵ the Lord, the God of hosts, the Lord is his memorial name: ⁶ "So you, by the help of your God, return, hold fast to love and justice, and wait continually for your God."

Roundabouts are common occurrences in nations where there is a history of significant British influence. One major advantages of roundabouts is that it facilitates the ability to perform a U-turn with ease.

U-turns are necessary because undoubtedly there will be occasions when one must turn to begin traversing the opposite direction. Roundabouts make this need a much less dangerous and daunting task.

There are also times in life when a spiritual U-turn is necessary. At this juncture in Israel's history, they are in need of such action; thus, Hosea urges them to turn around and proceed in the reverse direction.

In the Hebrew Bible (Masoretic Text), the last verse of the 11th chapter (in English translations) is the first verse of the 12th chapter. Thus, the Hebrew Bible has an additional verse in Hosea's writings which accounts for the dissimilarity. Should this discrepancy be counted as problematic for the integrity of Scripture? Does it expose chinks in the armour of the biblical text? Not at all. It must be remembered that chapter and verse designations of Holy Scripture were added by biblical scholars overtime. However, the initial prophetic manuscripts included no such designations. Nothing is lost by a variance in verse count since all the information is still extant.

National Corruption

The 12th verse begins **"Ephraim has surrounded me with the lies."** The nation's character is not upright by any stretch of the imagination as they are relentlessly dishonest in a variety of ways. Naturally, there is intrigue surrounding who "me" in the verse refers to. Does it point to Hosea or God? In the opinion of this author, it is more plausible that "me" refers to God than the prophet. Nevertheless, because Hosea was God's mouthpiece and representative at this juncture in Israel's history, the effect is still the same. As God stands in their midst (or Hosea as God's ambassador) everywhere there is falsehood. The text presses further with **"and the House of Israel with deceit."** "Deceit" also carries the indication of fraudulent activities reiterating the initial clause of verse 12. From everywhere and every angle, God perceives the culpability of Israel due to their daily dishonest lifestyle as a populace. It is vigorous evil in His sight.

Believers must take inventory of their personal lives to ensure they do not entertain the sin of dishonesty. Fairness in business deals must be the uncompromising standard. None must be swindled out of their due. Christians must never steal goods and services, but conduct the entirety of our lives in trustworthiness and evenhandedness, steering clear of purchasing items through the "back door". Bootlegs and falsifications should not be an option for the people of God. We must endeavor to be honest and we must work the expected time span without shortcuts, being truthful in all dealings and associations.

In contrast, **"Judah still walks with God and is faithful to the Holy One."** Across the border, the Southern Kingdom of Judah was not a sinless kingdom, but a better kingdom. Because their fellowship and obedience to God was more admirable than

Israel's, the Lord took note. God is brought to the fore as "the Holy One" in this verse to highlight the expectation upon His nation—both North and South; however, the South was more faithful in adhering to the standard since the imagery of walking with God symbolizes closeness and submission.

This potently illustrates God's concern for our "walk with Him" and obedience to Him in spite of imperfections. Although sinlessness will never be attained in this life, God expects His seed to persevere in fellowship with Him. We can never give up in the battle against sin and complacency. We can never throw in the towel. Just as Judah delighted God more than the Israel of Hosea's day, some Christians are more successful in delighting their Heavenly Father than others. Yes, God loves all believers the same, but the truth of the matter is, not all believers love God the same and He is aware of these actualities. He is concerned about how well we conduct our lives in His presence; our performance as Christians matter to Him. Therefore, persistence is required in walking with God as Judah, thus being faithful to the Holy One.

The 1st verse of chapter 12 states that **"Ephraim feeds on the wind"** using imagery to show the unprofitability of Israel's lifestyle. To "feed on the wind" is to attempt to achieve sustenance and satisfaction by something that has no substance. The wind is nothing more than a movement of air that will leave the nation famished; all of Israel's efforts and activities are useless. It is reiterated that Israel **"pursues the east wind all the day long"** painting a visual of Israel following after the east wind. Again, this is a pointless endeavour because the direction of the wind cannot be controlled, since it is guided by God's hand. Notice the specific mention of "the east wind" which was often destructive to vegetation as it brought in hot air from the desert-like regions. This is confirmed later in Hosea 13:15 which declares,

"Though he may flourish among his brothers, the east wind, the wind of the Lord, shall come, rising from the wilderness, and his fountain shall dry up; his spring shall be parched; it shall strip his treasury of every precious thing."

Thus, not only was it pointless to run after the wind, but the east wind, in particular, was harmful and damaging. Israel was wasting its time and hurting itself in the process.

Similarly, many people today are pursuing the east wind, aimlessly running after things that won't permanently satisfy like money, fame, possessions, drugs, sex, prestige, and the list goes on. Yet, not only will these things neglect to satisfy them, but hunting those obsessions will be injuriously scorching like the east wind.

Pursuing satisfaction in these vices rendered many wounded on the riverbanks of ruin.

Only Jesus Christ is worth feeding on and pursuing. Nothing deadly or destructive is produced out of trusting your life to Him. If you have not yet committed your life into His care, you merely waste your time in pursuits that are of no true value. Israel should be pursuing God, but their hearts were as far from His affections as the East is from the West.

The verse goes on to articulate that **"they multiply falsehood and violence."** "Falsehood", again, brings attention to the lies and deception that was all too common for the nation. Repetitiveness of the allusion to falsehood means that by now it was widespread, commonplace, and embedded in their sinful DNA. The resulting citing of violence is unsurprising since lies and treachery often begets violence in some form. A scarcity of honesty in any context—both ancient and modern—leads to conflict among people that regularly causes bloodshed. Lies and violence have a cause/effect relationship with each other; only a culture of integrity and truthfulness has the ability to elicit a peaceful livelihood.

Moreover, **"they make a covenant with Assyria and oil is carried to Egypt."** This covenant is a binding agreement between two nations: Israel and Assyria. The nature of the agreement is not bared explicitly, but it is of minimal significance since God had previously instituted a more excellent covenant with Israel. This covenant had been ratified on several occasions in Israel's history. Since Assyria was a pagan state, it was nonsensical for Israel to establish covenants with that realm. The desire of the nation to make alliances with Assyria could only be the result of their lack of faith in Yahweh to guide, protect, and provide. The "oil" is believed to be olive oil—a commodity Israel possessed in abundance—and would have afforded them the opportunity to export to other nations according to the demand.[xvi]

Negotiations occasioned contractual agreements with Egypt, an "off limits" activity from God's point of view since the more they became entangled in Egyptian affairs, the greater the likelihood that they would be sinfully influenced. Israel was to separate from ungodly nations and trust God for their material provisions, not their ability to bargain with pagans.

Likewise, it is an act of treachery for Christians to compromise their morality for the cause of financial gain. When God's people disregard trusting in Him to provide for their needs, there is no limit to the depths to which they will stoop to achieve monetary cushion. Such fall prey to the trap of pilfering from their workplace or gambling away their paycheck. Another byproduct is the Christian who lacks faithfulness in giving to the Lord's work; they doubt their ability to survive if they place money into the offering box. Do you trust God to take care of and provide for your needs? If you don't, then it is highly probably that, even now, you are compromising your financial stewardship in some way by not handling your finances with a godly perspective. Israel's relationship to God was so withdrawn, they could not even fathom depending upon Him. Bidding them to place their confidence in God was comparable to asking them to fly. The saint's ability to believe God for His provision is a barometer of his spiritual maturity. Our exercising of faith does not stop at conversion; we continue to grow in faith throughout our spiritual journey.

Jacob's Transformation

Verse 2 pronounces that **"the Lord has an indictment against Judah"** with the term "indictment" transmitting the impression of a contentious matter or a legal dispute. The identical Hebrew word translated in English as "controversy" in Hosea 4:1, is translated as "indictment" here in verse 2. Observe, however, that the indictment is against the nation of Judah, the same kingdom God has just affirmed "walks with Him". How could this be? Was there dishonesty on God's part?

By no means was Judah a sinless nation since they were morally challenged as well. Though not as robust in their rebellion as Israel, there remained iniquitous faults making it crucial that they hear the voice of God. It was compulsory that they be informed regarding where God's displeasure with them arose, as only that could delay their mutation into a "second Israel".

No one who walks planet Earth is faultless as we all possess the capability of becoming wayward in our morality, regardless of the length of time, we have hitherto walked with God. Perpetually, it is essential for the Christian to hear God's truth expounded recurrently. Despite Judah's more fortunate spiritual condition, Yahweh did not neglect to confront them; and, as such, neither should we abandon occasions to be confronted by God's Word. To detach ourselves from this conviction is to put ourselves in grave danger, even if we have been a member of God's family for longer than we can remember.

The verse continues **"and I will punish Jacob according to his ways; He will repay him according to his deeds."** The challenge is to distinguish who the term "Jacob" makes reference to. Possibly, it refers to Israel alone and functions as parallel to Judah or it may also refer to Judah and Israel together. No matter the conclusion, it is certain that Israel is, somehow, included in the term "Jacob" since Judah has already been referenced. Moreover, the Lord has condemned the iniquity of the people and promises that judgement will ensue.

The entirety of verse 2 squarely demonstrates God's clash with all of humanity. The issue is that we all have defied a holy and righteous God. Romans 3:23 discloses that *"all have sinned and fall short of the glory of God."* To use Hosean terminology, God has an "indictment" against all humanity. Accordingly, we must be punished according to our ways and repaid according to our deeds. That penalty is to be cast into Hell for all eternity, according to the Bible, which is what we justly deserve (Revelation 20:15). Yet, God graciously provided the sole avenue of escape—fleeing to Jesus Christ to receive mercy through His substitutionary death when He was crucified, buried, and rose again after three days. Anyone who receives unto himself that sacrifice by faith, will gain eternal life and be shielded from the future hand of God's just wrath. Such is the only provision by which corrupt humanity can escape being "punished according to our ways" and "repaid according to our deeds".

Hosea, then, proceeds to use the inspiring example of Jacob's life as a model for repentance. The oracular speech carries on with **"in the womb he took his brother by the heel"** recalling the birth narrative of Jacob and his twin brother Esau. Although Esau, the oldest brother was born first, Jacob exited his mother, Rebecca's womb with his hand clutched to Esau's heel. Personally, I am convinced this action was predictive of Jacob's character as his very name translates as "supplanter", "deceiver", or "cheater". Scripture unveils the account in Genesis 25:24-26 when it records,

> [24] *When her days to give birth were completed, behold, there were twins in her womb.* [25] *The first came out red, all his body like a hairy cloak, so they called his name Esau.* [26] *Afterward his brother came out with his hand holding Esau's heel, so his name was called Jacob. Isaac was sixty years old when she bore them.*

Jacob appeared destined to commit folly even from his mother's womb. Hosea's adds, **"and in his manhood he strove with God. (vs. 4) He strove with the angel and prevailed."** The setting changes to Jacob's struggle with the angel of the LORD at Peniel recorded in Genesis 32:22-32, where Jacob wrestled with a being believed to be a theophany, an Old Testament appearance of God in human form. This conclusion is made because, although the Scripture labels the individual a "man" in verses 24 and 25, He is also called "God" in verses 28 and 30. Jacob "strove" with God, wanting desperately to receive a blessing and would give every fiber of his being to accomplish that task. The point of the interaction does not exalt Jacob's physical strength above that of his Creator, as that could never accurately portray reality. Rather, the focal point is his willingness to pursue God with all of his capabilities for as long as he was physically able; the outer struggle of the flesh exhibiting the inner struggle of the heart which, despite its flaws, was in pursuit of God. Jacob's character was changing. He was not the same infant born grasping his brother's heel, or the same man that robbed Esau's of his blessing. The patriarchal figure was aware of his desperate need for God and would stop at nothing to gain Yahweh's favour.

Then, it is revealed that **"he wept and sought his favor."** It is best to assume Jacob is the individual referred to as weeping in this clause. The more difficult question is whose favour did he seek? There are two potential answers:

1. It refers to his struggle with the Angel at Peniel.
2. It refers to what transpired when he lovingly reunited with his brother, Esau, for the first time after an extensive season of familial conflict.

At first glance, it would appear more reasonable to choose the former interpretation. However, upon deeper investigation, I submit that it is preferable to consider the phrase a reference to his meeting with Esau even though he is not named in the biblical text. The logic that cloaks this reasoning is that both "weeping" and "seeking favour" are mentioned in the account of the meeting of the two siblings, whereas neither is mentioned in the narrative of Jacob wrestling with the angel.

Genesis 33:4,

But Esau ran to meet him and embraced him and fell on his neck and kissed him, and they wept.

Genesis 33:8,

Esau said, "What do you mean by all this company that I met?" Jacob answered, "To find favor in the sight of my lord."

Since both the weeping and seeking of favor are mentioned in the Genesis 33 account, this latter half of verse 4 must refer to Jacob's reunion with Esau after a number of years.

The text adds that **"He met God at Bethel."** Most certainly this marks the occasion that Jacob encountered God in a dream at Bethel, chronicled in Genesis 28:10-22. There, God revealed Jacob's lineage would be gifted a definite plot of land and would be blessed with innumerable offspring. The vivid drama of this encounter left such an impression that Jacob erected a memorial stone to commemorate the experience. Theologically, this is the climax of Jacob's transformation. The scene of his life in this passage moves from a child born as a deceiver, to a man who wrestles with God; a broken brother restored to the one whom he beguiled, to the patriarch who encountered God and was blessed by His Almighty hand. In short, he has been broken and renewed.

Brilliantly does Jacob's life illustrate conversion to Christ Jesus. Brokenness must occur before the flood of renewal can spread abroad. We must be humbled by our sin, seeing ourselves as out-and-out hopeless under God's all-seeing eye before we can receive the blessing of His redemption. No one's ark has rested upon the mountain of true salvation until they have first been shattered by their own mutiny against God. Many around God's globe contend they will enter eternal Heaven by reason of their moral behaviour. There is no brokenness, no conviction, and no mourning over innate depravity. In its place is pride, arrogance, self-dependence, and self-sufficiency. Brokenness over sin will always precede the blessing of salvation. If you're convinced you deserve salvation, it is a tell-tale sign that you possibly don't even have it.

God's Expectation

The verse continues **"and there God spoke with us."** Hosea connects God's past communication with Jacob to His present communication with the people of Israel to affirm that Jacob's life story was not to be consigned to the chains of the past; it was advantageous for all his seed which would come after him. It was for all of Israel—both the person and the people.

The same is applicable to God's modern people. The transcript of Holy Scripture is not only to inform of what God communicated to the people of the past; it was written because God speaks to us through it as well. Although the Bible was not written to us, it was certainly written for us that we may glean from it and grow thereby. Thus, Paul explained to Timothy that *"All scripture is breathed out by God and profitable for teaching, for reproof, for correction, and for training in righteousness that the man of God may be complete equipped for every good work."*[xxvii] There is not one single book in the Bible through which God does not speak to His people today. The whole Bible makes the whole Christian. No section of God's Word is "off limits" when it comes to the Christian individually or the church corporately. From *"In the beginning"* in Genesis to the last *"Amen"* of Revelation, all of the between is to profit God's flock.

The 5th verse functions almost as a doxology when it proclaims, **"the LORD, the God of hosts, the LORD is his memorial name."** Hosea leaves no speculation regarding who spoke to Jacob and, accordingly, who was speaking to the children of Israel in Hosea's generation. His "memorial name" is one that must be remembered for all time. In the English Bible, it is transcribed as LORD. In the Hebrew language, however, it is the name Yehovah often pronounced "Jehovah" in English. The name literally comes from a root word that simply means "to be" or "to exist". In layman's terms, He is "the Existing One"—the only being in the universe whose existence is not dependent upon another. He is unequivocally eternal and self-sufficient. This is the God of Jacob, the God of the nation Israel, and the God of every saint who has been purchased with Christ's blood. The sheer concept of existence protrudes out of God and God alone.

Therefore, anything that subsists in the cosmos today is extant because God has allowed it to be—all things, living and non-living, all people, from darkest to lightest complexion, and all beings, from Michael the archangel to Satan the deceiver. All of it survives because the Lord has mercifully brought it into existence. God created the very tongues of those who curse Him. He created the very brains of those who claim by self-deceived, false intelligence that there is no God. The wood of the cross on which He was crucified was spoken into existence by His own breath. Everything that has life and everything that is, is at the mercy of that one Creator. What thoughts do you have in mind when you pray to God or ponder His being? The greatness of God should give passion to our prayers and our praises alike. We must always be mesmerized by the God who is.

In addition to being "the Existing One", the verse appeals to Him as the "God of hosts". Because "hosts" denotes an organized army, it speaks to the mass army of angels at His disposal. No physical army can ever begin to approach the greatness of God's army (2 Kings 6:15-17). The prophet is heaping upon Israel's shoulders, an understanding of the supreme majesty of God. How ought they respond to the God that Hosea has just presented to them?

Verse 6 begins **"so you."** Now that the example of Jacob's conversion has been perused, and the majesty of God has been put on full display, what follows is God's current expectation for Israel. The phrase **"by the help of your God"** identifies that God must assist Israel to be the people they should; it is He who must turn them around as they cannot merely do it of their own accord.

Likewise, believers in Christ today need God's enabling power to live in the manner to which we are called. The victorious Christian life cannot be achieved by our own strength; there must be an unbroken reliance upon God and an enabling by Him to fulfill the mission He has for us individually. Are you disastrously attempting to live godly in your own strength, or are you seeking the divine assistance of the one who called you unto Himself?

Furthermore, this clause "by the help of your God" echoes that sinners cannot come to repentance unless God activates it from within. David Hubbard opined, regarding this verse, that the statement "is a reminder that even repentance is impossible without the divine grace that enables it".[xviii]

The next word in the text is an imperative—**"return"**—and it implores Israel to turn back to God in repentance. They must turn away from their despicable lifestyles.

Maybe you have need to turn from your evil ways as Israel did. If that adequately describes your current situation, please find solace in the fact that the door to God's office is never shut. He is ever seated at His desk waiting to receive anyone who will turn to Him.

Furthermore, they must **"hold fast to love and justice."** Both of these qualities were lacking in the nation during the period of Hosea's ministry. "Love" here is an affection for both God and each other prompting them to wholesomely dwell together in a manner satisfactory to Yahweh. "Justice" indicates that Israel would make fair decisions and treat one another justly as Scripture commanded. Their repentance would be evidenced by their conduct.

Likewise, true, salvific repentance will be evidenced by the deportment of an individual's life. If there has been no change, there has been no repentance.

The final part of the verse is **"and wait continually for your God."** Typically, when the word "wait" is imagined in English, we think of someone sitting by idly. However, in Hebrew, the word carries a greater edge of expectancy and anticipation. They are to expectantly wait repeatedly for their God. What are they waiting for? If they return to the Lord and take heed again to love and justice as He expects from them, then God promised He would heal the land and restore them to former glory. They should obey the call to repentance and obedience, and when the nation yields, God's glory will return and fill the land with His presence and blessing. Nowhere else in Holy Writ has this truth been made clearer than in 2 Chronicles 7:14.

If my people who are called by my name humble themselves, and pray and seek my face and turn from their wicked ways, then I will hear from heaven and will forgive their sin and heal their land.

If Israel repents and turns back to love and justice as God demands, He will eventually show up once again with a mighty harvest of blessing upon the nation.

> Discuss

1. How might believers naively be guilty of the sin of dishonesty today?

2. How might a Christian compromise morality for the cause of financial gain today?

3. Why is it important to hold fast to both love and justice as a Christian?

4. "The sheer concept of existence protrudes out of God and God alone." What implications does this have for all of humanity?

5. Why do believers need God's help to live the victorious Christian life?

23

ONE AND THE SAME

12:7-14

⁷ *A merchant, in whose hands are false balances, he loves to oppress.* ⁸ *Ephraim has said, "Ah, but I am rich; I have found wealth for myself; in all my labors they cannot find in me iniquity or sin."* ⁹ *I am the LORD your God from the land of Egypt; I will again make you dwell in tents, as in the days of the appointed feast.* ¹⁰ *I spoke to the prophets; it was I who multiplied visions, and through the prophets gave parables.* ¹¹ *If there is iniquity in Gilead, they shall surely come to nothing: in Gilgal they sacrifice bulls; their altars also are like stone heaps on the furrows of the field.* ¹² *Jacob fled to the land of Aram; there Israel served for a wife, and for a wife he guarded sheep.* ¹³ *By a prophet the LORD brought Israel up from Egypt, and by a prophet he was guarded.* ¹⁴ *Ephraim has given bitter provocation; so his Lord will leave his bloodguilt on him and will repay him for his disgraceful deeds.*

In electrical circuits, the term "conductor" alludes to any material or object that is used to transmit the flow of electricity. Although the metal itself is not the electricity, the force of the electricity can be felt through the metal when the circuit is switched on.

Likewise, God's prophet is the conductor of God's message and although the prophet himself is not God, God's force can be felt through the message of the prophet. For this reason, the voice of the prophet is the voice of God.

The Denial of Iniquity

Verse **7** launches with the reference to **"a merchant."** Broadly speaking, a merchant is an individual that buys and sells goods in large quantities. Hosea cites the nation here, many of whom were merchants. As a matter of fact, even in the modern world, Jews are known as a people skilled in operating small businesses and large companies alike. Interestingly, the word "merchant" stems from the identical Hebrew word which can also be translated as "Canaanite", a reference to the people of the land of Canaan whom the Jews were ordered to drive out of the Promised Land when they first entered. Disappointingly, they failed in their mission resulting in a resurgence of that heathen population. By the prophet's day, they had successfully seduced Israel into idolatry. Some scholars contend that the word "merchant" is a play on words as Hosea shrewdly insinuates that the nation of Israel is just as wicked as those godless Canaanites; they resemble a pagan society, not God's people.[xix]

What do we resemble: paganism, secularism, or God's holy nation? Today, the Christian church is becoming increasingly secular as practices and belief systems once shunned are now commonplace. It is considered intolerable to call iniquity by its name. Core doctrinal beliefs are being thrown to the dogs. Francis Schaeffer made an accurate assessment in his own day when he said "Tell me what the world is saying today, and I'll tell you what the church will be saying in seven years." What an appalling state of affairs! Nevertheless, the solution starts with each believer, individually, and the local church, corporately. We must hold fast to saturating ourselves in Scripture and committing to exhibiting its tenets through daily living. In addition, agonising, fervent, heartfelt prayer must be restored to primacy. This is the singular Bible-proven, historically-tested method to anti-paganize and anti-secularise post-modern depravity. It originates always with individual Christians first, then moves to the wider church body, then impacts outward society. Therefore, the church can never expect change in the world if that organism is not unabashedly resolute and fervently committed to the entirety of its God-given mandate.

The verse further describes this "merchant" as one **"in whose hands are false balances."** The balances are the scales used to weigh items and goods that were bought and sold. According to the text, Israel, during this period, possessed a plethora of faulty scales. They strategically found avenues of getting the scales to produce incorrect readings; much stealing and thievery occurred. Amos, whose prophetic ministry was performed at the same time as Hosea's, gives clearer insight into the nation's exploitation.

Amos 8:4-6,

> ⁴ Hear this, you who trample on the needy and bring the poor of the land to an end, saying, "When will the new moon be over, that we may sell grain? And the Sabbath, that we may offer wheat for sale, that we may make the ephah small and the shekel great and deal deceitfully with false balances, ⁶ that we may buy the poor for silver and the needy for a pair of sandals and sell the chaff of the wheat?"

Amos' account is that they minimized the ephah measurements while maximizing the shekel measurements. In the Old Testament era, wheat was measured using the ephah as a unit and the shekel was a measure of valuable coins like gold or silver; hence, merchants measured wheat by the ephah and received the due amount in silver weighed by the shekel. Making the ephah lesser and shekel larger was deception times two since the buyer would acquire less grain while, simultaneously, giving a larger sum of silver. In addition, they vended the chaff of the wheat—the shell that covered the outside of that grain. Presumably, they mixed chaff in bags that were to contain pure wheat alone. Chaff was not to be sold, only discarded. Selling the chaff of wheat is like selling the husks of corn. Downright robbery was taking place in the season of Hosea and Amos' ministries.

Today, stealing is the pastime of many, taking place in literally hundreds of forms, both physically and electronically. It is incumbent upon God's people to shun involvement in any such practices of deception and theft. However, precaution must be taken not only against stealing from others, but in opposition stealing from God as well. What a tragedy it is that God's own progeny can abandon—and at times even despise—their responsibility to fund the fulfilling of His Great Commission, despite all He so freely and richly provides! Such miserliness forced the prophet Malachi to counteract by exclaiming,

> ⁸ Will man rob God? Yet you are robbing me. But you say, 'How have we robbed you?' In your tithes and contributions. ⁹ You are cursed with a curse, for you are robbing me, the whole nation of you. ¹⁰ Bring the full tithe into the storehouse, that there may be food in my house. And thereby put me to the test, says the Lord of hosts, if I will not open the windows of heaven for you and pour down for you a blessing until there is no more need."ˣˣ

To be clear, giving is not bound to the Old Testament dispensation; it is a New Testament principle as well. The apostle Paul vowed to the Corinthian believers that *"Whoever sows sparingly will also reap sparingly, and whoever sows bountifully will also reap bountifully. Each one must give as he has decided in his heart, not reluctantly or under compulsion, for God loves a cheerful giver."*[xxi] While not engaging theft from our fellow man, the Christian must, too, take pains to not indulge stealing from the Lord. Since God has abundantly blessed us with His provision, we should not feel hard-pressed to bless Him with a portion of ours.

It is further written that **"he loves to oppress."** Ephraim "oppresses" people, a term that literally means "to press upon". It is analogous to taking advantage of others or banishing them to unjust treatment. Observe that he "loves" to do this, hinting at Israel's accustomed way of life. It is manifestly malicious for someone to be a tool of oppression to another. Our objective should be to handle every sole individual justly and fairly, regardless of age, gender, socioeconomic standing, nationality, or ethnicity. The statue of prejudice must fall as we toil to do right by others simply by reason that they are image-bearers of God.

According to verse 8, **"Ephraim has said, 'Ah, but I am rich; I have found wealth for myself; in all my labors they cannot find in me iniquity or sin'."** Currently, Israel appears drenched in financial prosperity. Because the hammer of God's judgement had not fallen as yet, they still maintained some of God's blessings. Furthermore, the nation engaged in trading treaties with powers like Egypt, to whom they traded oil to receive goods and services. Thirdly, widespread theft occurred rendering many in the nation wealthy. Therefore, in their irresponsible pride the nation claims "I am rich". The most contagious virus that can infect those who experience material success is a haughty spirit. Nothing is inherently wrong with monetary success, but those that will encounter such blessings must plead to God for special grace in order to keep humbly dependent upon Him. Few things cause a believer to roam like a dense bank account.

In addition to pride, Israel is in a state of denial as the text declares **"in all my labors they cannot find in me iniquity or sin."** The Jews were strangers to the truth. During this season, they proliferated in corruption more zealously than any other period of Jewish history, including the dark period of the judges. Nevertheless, what's dissimilar to the aforesaid season is that the prophetic ministry (as far as Scripture records) was quite minimal. Military leaders were the primary means through which God delivered Israel from oppression. Current Israel had the presence of faithful prophets whose voice they failed to heed. Most certainly, this generation was more steadfast in their rebellion. Nevertheless, their false claim was that no one could charge them with iniquity.

Denial of the truth does not make it any less truthful.

Furthermore, **"I am the LORD your God from the land of Egypt."** Yahweh reminds the nation that His eye and care was upon it from inception, and His relationship with them was extant before the conquest of Canaan. I reckon this response includes a stench of rebuke for their state of denial; God tolerates none of it. The plot is comparable to a young lad attempting to hoodwink his mother and she retorts "Boy! Don't you ever think you can pull the wool over my eyes. I knew you before you were born." God was not only aware of their sinful condition, He could recall every transgression they committed since Egyptian slavery.

Neither can anyone pull the wool over God's eyes today as He knew every sin we would commit even before He spoke the world into existence—whether it be an offense of thought, word, or deed. Yahweh cannot be swindled.

The auxiliary threat is **"I will again make you dwell in tents, as in the days of the appointed feast."** "Dwelling in tents" is an allusion to the Feast of Tabernacles, termed also the Feast of Booths, which was commemorated annually by the Jews. The event reminisced upon God's guidance of His people through the wilderness after the exodus, and during the feast they resided in tents/booths for seven days until its completion. Information regarding this appointed festival can be sourced in Leviticus 23:33-36.

> *^{33} And the Lord spoke to Moses, saying, ^{34} "Speak to the people of Israel, saying, On the fifteenth day of this seventh month and for seven days is the Feast of Booths to the Lord. ^{35} On the first day shall be a holy convocation; you shall not do any ordinary work. ^{36} For seven days you shall present food offerings to the Lord. On the eighth day you shall hold a holy convocation and present a food offering to the Lord. It is a solemn assembly; you shall not do any ordinary work.*

Verse 42-43,

> *^{42} You shall dwell in booths for seven days. All native Israelites shall dwell in booths, ^{43} that your generations may know that I made the people of Israel dwell in booths when I brought them out of the land of Egypt: I am the Lord your God."*

This is the feast being mentioned in verse 9, which infers the Lord will return them to a similar situation of dwelling in tents, not for the purposes of the Feast of Booths, however, but to dwell in Assyrian exile. The upcoming tent-dwelling will not be an occasion of celebration; it will be an occasion of suffocation. Their vigorous denial of sin and rejection of the Hosean proclamation will have disastrous consequences.

As there were disastrous consequences for Israel when they were recalcitrant in sin denial and rejected the word from God, there are devastating costs today for those who pursue an equivalent pattern.

The Need for Prophecy

When it comes to the Bible, and specifically the Old Testament, two major features of prophecy exists. The first is fore-telling—the prediction of future events by the reception of direct revelation from Yahweh. This aspect of prophecy is lesser when frequency is the measuring rod. Regrettably, in modern Christianity—largely because of the influence of Pentecostalism and the Charismatic/Apostolic movement, most people envisage this feature when they hear "prophecy" or "prophet". Yet, this is the miniature aspect of prophecy. The lion's share of prophecy in the Scriptures is that of forth-telling—the telling forth and proclamation of God's already-revealed truth. The Old Testament prophets called Israel to commit and recommit themselves to God's covenant in the *Torah* more than thrice as often as they forecasted the future and encountered visions. Thus, the term "prophet" or "prophecy" should yield thoughts of forth-telling first, and fore-telling second, instead of the reverse. Failure to grasp this dynamic leaves one's perspective on prophecy rather distorted.

Markedly, Verse 10 begins **"I spoke to the prophets."** These five words define everything that is true of biblical prophecy. It is God speaking *to* men and *through* men—nothing more, nothing less. Miracles are not the foundation for biblical prophecy as not all prophets performed miracles. As a matter of fact, the bulk of Old Testament prophets did not accomplish miracles. Excluding Moses, Elijah, and Elisha, it would be onerous to find a named miracle-working prophet. Visions are not the foundation for biblical prophecy as not all the prophets saw visions—Hosea being the nearest specimen. The unaccompanied criteria for prophecy is that God has spoken to men and, thus, has caused them to speak. Everything else is supplementary—the icing on the cake. I deem the quintessential verse on biblical prophecy in all of Holy Writ to be 2 Kings 17:13.

Yet the Lord warned Israel and Judah by every prophet and every seer, saying, "Turn from your evil ways and keep my commandments and my statutes, in accordance with all the Law that I commanded your fathers, and that I sent to you by my servants the prophets."

In short, a prophet urges people to turn from sin and keep the laws of God.

Therefore, those who preach God's Word today, essentially qualify as prophets since they implore individuals to turn from sin and keep God's edicts. Prophecy is not only an Old Testament phenomenon, but a New Testament phenomenon as well, resulting in the terms "prophecy" and "prophet" also occurring in the second covenant, as it predominantly occasions the forth-telling aspect.

The Lord confirms that **"it was I who multiplied visions."** Constructing upon the pre-established foundation, God adds that He afforded the prophets visions. Broadly speaking, this indicates that some of the prophets saw divine revelation from the hand of God. In many cases, God allowed Old Testament prophets to peer into the end times. However, in the interest of full disclosure, it is often difficult for students of prophecy to discern the minute eschatological elements of prophetic texts.

The verse continues **"and through the prophets gave parables."** "Parables" relates the idea of a similitude—using an illustration to compare one thing to another. A prime example is our prophetic case study, Hosea. He marries Gomer, the prostitute, to exemplify the relationship between God and Israel. Recall that such similitudes are known as "sign acts". Performed by various prophets, sign acts are examples of similitudes, or as the text calls them, "parables". Hence, even sign acts, standing alone were gifted the prophets by the hand of God.

"If there is iniquity in Gilead, they shall surely come to nothing" is the assurance of the 11th verse. Despite the appearance of a conditional sentence, Hosea, in all probability, aims for it to be received as a declarative one. It's similar to announcing "If you're not going to study for the test, then you should not expect a good grade." This company of words confirms already that Gilead is guilty of sin.

Hosea 6:8,

Gilead is a city of evildoers, tracked with blood.

It was identified that much murder and violence was in the city, so Gilead will certainly come to nothing. They will be ruined and destroyed.

Vital is the observation that God often puts specific locations in Scripture under the magnifying glass. This is done because these places were extraordinary in their sin. While the whole of Israel lived in a sin-soaked culture, immorality was particularly concentrated in certain areas. Gilead was singled out due to a high homicide rate, and since murder is a heinous evil, one of the worst sins a man can commit, God had a special eye of judgement toward that city.

People who perpetrate murder today, will not evade God's everlasting fury except they repent and flee to Jesus Christ for wholesome forgiveness and cleansing. Often such tyrants suppose they are big, bad, and bold, but the day of judgement draws nigh when the tide will shift and a frightful reckoning must be faced.

He singles out another location with **"in Gilgal they sacrifice bulls."** Gilgal, too, is a location previously cited in Hosea's prophecy.

Hosea 9:15

Every evil of theirs is in Gilgal; there I began to hate them. Because of the wickedness of their deeds I will drive them out of my house. I will love them no more; all their princes are rebels.

This place is also noted as a place of wickedness. Verse 11 tells of their bull sacrifices; thus, their error must have been syncretism in animal sacrifices. They mingled heathen worship with Jewish worship—false religion with true religion—error with truth. Yet, God did not merely skimp over their colossal blunder in appreciation of the fact that they were, at least "religious". He demanded worship that was pure and undefiled.

If you make claims to being a follower of Christ, you must follow Him exclusively, to the rejection of every other religious ideology. You cannot be both a biblical Christian and a Muslim. You cannot be both a Christian and a Hindu. Neither can you be Christian and Buddhist, Christian and Sikh, or Christian and Rastafarian. A New Age devotee cannot be Christ's disciple as well. Those who follow Jesus Christ must worship and serve Him exclusively. Merging the worship of a risen Christ with anything/anyone else is egregious syncretism and insulting to the Most

High God. So distasteful was this activity that the city of syncretism was singled out just as the city of murder. It was not a lightweight matter to Yahweh.

In addition, **"their altars are like stone heaps on the furrows of the field."** The stone heaps are simple piles of rocks. Hosea makes jest of the altars they made because, apparently, they did not seem sensibly or tactfully constructed. Their idolatrous altars resemble a pile of rocks left in a vacant field by a farmer without structure or beauty to their makeup. Their worship is offensive and ugly simultaneously. This is a far cry from how beautifully and meticulously Jewish worship was organized and fulfilled.

"Jacob fled to the land of Aram" is the assertion of verse 12. Hosea is not finished with the patriarch, Jacob, as, again, he takes center stage. The beginning of this verse marks the time when Jacob fled to a place known fully as Paddan-aram for two purposes. Most importantly, he arrived there to flee Esau's rage after stealing his blessing (*Genesis* 27:43-44). The second reason was that he was directed to find a wife among Laban's daughters (Genesis 28:1-2).

Furthermore, **"there Israel served for a wife and for a wife he guarded sheep."** "Israel" here refers to the single individual, Jacob, and not the nation since Jacob's name was ultimately changed by God to Israel. Jacob worked for a wife (Rachel) for 14 years instead of the original 7 years he was promised. The guarding of sheep well-illustrated the manner in which God guarded His sheep, Jacob. The point is that although the patriarch was in a taxing situation, he was cared for and molded by the mighty hand of God.

God's children, too, are cared for and molded by God's hand, even in the most irksome circumstances. The Lord never leaves His children and is always purifying and sanctifying them to mold them into the image of His Son. Purposefully, James 1:2-4 encourages believers to

> ² *Count it all joy, my brothers, when you meet trials of various kinds,* ³ *for you know that the testing of your faith produces steadfastness.* ⁴ *And let steadfastness have its full effect, that you may be perfect and complete, lacking in nothing.*

God used this situation to convert Jacob into the manner of person He wanted him to be.

Our Creator performs the same actions in my life and in yours. The unforeseen circumstances that Jacob endured are typical of what must happen with us if we will be complete and whole in our spiritual maturity. Diamonds are produced under pressure. Gold is refined through fire. Even so, God's children must endure trying times. To the exclusion of iniquity, your current trial is sovereignly ordained by the will and hand of God.

According to verse 13, it was **"by a prophet the Lord brought Israel up from Egypt."** Because the prophet's identity is not unveiled, we must conclude it is Moses since Moses led Israel out of Egypt. With rarity do people fancy Moses a prophet. However, he fits the bill of a prophet as defined by that quintessential verse on biblical prophecy (2 Kings 17:13). He frequently compelled the people of God to turn from evil and keep the commands and statutes of the God-given law. Moreover, Moses dubbed himself a prophet. In Deuteronomy 18:15, Moses foretold of the coming prophet who would be like Moses in His ministry. This anticipated prophet Moses prophesied concerning was Jesus of Nazareth. Moses reveals in the text.

The Lord your God will raise up for you a prophet like me from among you, from your brothers—it is to him you shall listen—

Hence, Moses ratified that he himself was a prophet. The case that Moses is the prophet whom Hosea references in verse 13 is built upon reliable evidence.

It presses forward with **"and by a prophet he was guarded."** Moses both led the people out of Egypt and guarded Israel through the wilderness. Notice the connection of how "guarding" is mentioned twice. It is in verse 12 and 13 consecutively. As Israel (the person) guarded sheep, so God would, eventually, guard Israel (the nation) who were His sheep. "Guarded" in both instances can be accurately substituted with the word "preserved". In other words, God's care and concern for the Jews was expressed through the ministry of the prophets. The Lord gave them as gifts to guide His people in a God-ward direction.

Hosea makes a sharp point in this stanza of the discourse. God used a long line of men to guard Israel throughout the nation's history. Hosea—the prophet of the present day—fit clearly and squarely into that tradition. The elephant in the room is this, "Will Israel allow Hosea, God's current prophet, to now guard them?" Such was the prophetic purpose; to preserve and guard them and to sound the alarm whenever Israel strayed off course.

This is precisely the reason that, in our day, God still calls men to mount pulpits across the globe to open the Word of God—the "more sure word of prophecy" (2 Peter 1:19-20 KJV)—and lift up their voices to cry aloud that which God has already confirmed.

With what spirit do we receive the words that God declares through His mouthpieces today? What is our attitude toward public declarations from the Holy Scriptures? The Israel of Hosea's day was stubborn, unyielding, and intransigent. Their stance will force them to face full-on destruction. God's modern flock must give incredible effort to repudiating their example.

Lamentably, Israel will not respond in travail and repentance as urged but will bellow forward headlong and headstrong in a despicable direction.

"Ephraim", according to Hosea's assessment of the matter, **"has given bitter provocation"** (vs. 14). Israel does not learn from the life of Jacob after whom it was named. Jacob's testimony is that he began in a deviant manner, but his journey concluded under considerably improved character. Although imperfect, he was a changed man. Israel, unfortunately, would not follow his model. Israel not only offended the Lord, he offended Him immensely by exercising no caution or restraint.

God detests all sin; yet, He is notably infuriated by sin that is draped in an absence of moderation or control. Morality does not rescue from eternal doom, but it still benefits society at large by tapering off God's wrathful vengeance. Moral restrictions and laws are a blessing to every generation of humanity. The less God is provoked, the healthier human existence will be.

The result is **"so his Lord will leave his bloodguilt on him."** Unsurprisingly, "bloodguilt" is the state of being guilty of shedding blood: murder is what God has on His mind. The fact that this vice is continually brought to the fore demonstrates that it particularly annoys him. The more something angers you the more intensely you think about it. That is where God is presently.

The only viable response is that he **"will repay him for his disgraceful deeds."** "Disgraceful" denotes a scornful reproach— something shameful. This is how God perceives their sin and they will receive the due reward for their shameful activities.

> Discuss

1. "Tell me what the world is saying today, and I'll tell you what the church will be saying in seven years." Do you think Francis Shaffer's assertion is typical of much of the modern church? Why or why not? What can be done to remedy this situation?

2. What are the dangers of associating the word "prophecy" with fore-telling more than forth-telling?

3. Briefly survey the major prophetic figures of the Old Testament. For each person decide whether fore-telling or forth-telling is more prevalent in the individual's ministry. Overall, which figures predicted the future more than they boldly proclaimed God's already-revealed covenant truth? Which prophetic element was more prevalent overall?

4. Under the Old Covenant, what was to be the response to a self-proclaimed prophet whose prophesy did not come to pass? Use Scripture to support your answer.

5. Could the desire to engage fore-telling today indicate a lack of faith in God? Why or why not?

24

DEAD MAN WALKING

13:1-8

¹When Ephraim spoke, there was trembling; he was exalted in Israel, but he incurred guilt through Baal and died. ² And now they sin more and more, and make for themselves metal images, idols skillfully made of their silver, all of them the work of craftsmen. It is said of them, "Those who offer human sacrifice kiss calves!" ³ Therefore they shall be like the morning mist or like the dew that goes early away, like the chaff that swirls from the threshing floor or like smoke from a window. ⁴ But I am the LORD your God from the land of Egypt; you know no God but me, and besides me there is no savior. ⁵ It was I who knew you in the wilderness, in the land of drought; ⁶ but when they had grazed, they became full, they were filled, and their heart was lifted up; therefore they forgot me. ⁷ So I am to them like a lion; like a leopard I will lurk beside the way. ⁸ I will fall upon them like a bear robbed of her cubs; I will tear open their breast, and there I will devour them like a lion, as a wild beast would rip them open.

Matthew Henry, a biblical commentator and preacher, once quipped, "When the sins of a people reach up to Heaven, the wrath of God will reach down to earth."

The Northern Kingdom of Israel is in severe danger of God's wrath. They have refused to heed the prophet's message and repent of their wickedness. In this passage of Scripture, God uses vivid imagery to explain the horrors of this judgement. It is certainly a fearful thing to fall into the ocean of God's wrath.

The Nation's Folly

Verse 1 commences **"when Ephraim spoke there was trembling; he was exalted in Israel."** In this instance, "Ephraim" designates the individual tribe itself, rather the Northern Kingdom holistically. This phraseology references a time when this specific tribe was powerful, prosperous, and well-established amongst the other 9 tribes of the Northern Kingdom. They were influential and commanded much respect politically and militarily. Interestingly, this use of "trembling" in its Hebrew form is a hapax legomenon—the only time this particular word is used in the entire Hebrew Bible (Masoretic Text). The Hebrew transliteration is *retheth* and it literally means "a terror". Tribal Ephraim struck fear in all the other clans of Israel during their golden years.

However, **"he incited guilt through Baal and died."** The tribe of Ephraim incriminated itself by sharing in the worship of the false god, Baal. The ill-fated outcome is that Ephraim "died". Physical death is not the intention of the term, but rather spiritual death. They lost their ability to play their role in God's design, and, as a result, judgement awaited them. Derek Kidner interpreted the situation well when he affirmed "at that point Ephraim died as surely as Adam did, although like Adam, he went on living to all outward appearance".[xxii]

Ephraim is no exception, however, as all of God's human creation incur guilt due to sin and, so, have died spiritually. Romans 5:12 captures the situation vividly with this proclamation: *"Therefore, just as sin came into the world through one man, and death through sin, and so death spread to all men because all sinned."*

Our situation is calamitous like Ephraim's. Not one stands spotless before the High Court of Heaven. Sin is regarded as whatsoever we think, say, or do that breaks God's law at any point in our existence. Even a momentary instance of lying, cheating, stealing, foul language, or immoral lust makes us culpable for all eternity. Nevertheless, the good news is that God sent His only perfect Son into the world to drink the cup of God's wrath for sin and to be punished—without guilt—when all mankind should have been punished. Romans 5:18-21 comments that,

> [18] *Therefore, as one trespass led to condemnation for all men, so one act of righteousness leads to justification and life for all men.* [19] *For as by the one man's disobedience the many were made sinners, so by the one man's obedience the many will be made righteous.* [20] *Now the law came in to increase the trespass, but where sin increased, grace abounded all*

> the more, ²¹ so that, as sin reigned in death, grace also might reign through righteousness leading to eternal life through Jesus Christ our Lord.

Only through Jesus Christ, God's sinless substitute, can one be made righteous and also receive eternal life. I implore you to trust fully in Christ alone for the removal of you sin-burden. Call upon the name of the Lord Jesus and receive pardon through His name; otherwise, you remain in your guilt resembling the tribe of Ephraim.

Nonetheless, (vs. 2) **"now they sin more and more."** *Chata*, the Hebrew word translated "sin", has the meaning of "to miss the mark" or "to err from the mark" portraying an archer using a bow and arrow to hit a target. This definition of sin is uncharacteristic to what we would ordinarily envision. Usually, we think only of egregious and flagrant acts as sin. Indeed, sin is often flagrant; yet, sin is not always as striking as one might assume, and this definition makes that point obvious. Missing the mark equates to not measuring up to God's expectation in every area of your life, every day of your life. Many surmise that only individuals that fall into the category of murderer or thief qualify as sinners, but sin is missing God's standard of pure perfection. As an example, James 4:17 makes this assertion,

"So whoever knows the right thing to do and fails to do it, for him it is sin."

Therefore, sin qualifies not only as doing the wrong thing, but neglecting to do the right thing in any situation. Prayerlessness, neglect of church attendance, silence concerning evil—all these actions qualify as sinful as well.

Thus, for someone to claim sinlessness is to simultaneously claim divinity and to put oneself on the same character level as the everlasting God. Doing so borders on sacrilege, but many effortlessly engage this mindset daily by refusing to acknowledge their sin-guilt. Such folk have rejected the Gospel since the Gospel is only "good news" if the bad news has first been acknowledged. Are you still in denial about your impure standing before a holy God? Agree with God's assessment of your condition because it is the truth that will set you free.

Returning to the text, it says **"they sin more and more"**. This comes as no surprise because the nation has already died spiritually. When the New Covenant is examined, spiritual death always produces more depravity rather than less (Ephesians 2:1-3). Decrease in sin only comes from being converted to Christ, which prompts inward transformation. Are you sinking continually deeper into the black ocean of sin? The glorious Gospel of Jesus Christ is the only lifeline that can lift you back to the surface and renew your deadening lungs with a burst of fresh air.

Not only do they sin more, they **"make for themselves metal images"**, an activity expressly forbidden from the establishing of the Mosaic law. It was a transgression of the second commandment.

Exodus 20:4-5,

> [4] *"You shall not make for yourself a carved image, or any likeness of anything that is in heaven above, or that is in the earth beneath, or that is in the water under the earth.* [5] *You shall not bow down to them or serve them, for I the Lord your God am a jealous God, visiting the iniquity of the fathers on the children to the third and the fourth generation of those who hate me,*

The Second Commandment (as with all the commandments) were foundational to Jewish society. Even if the Jews failed to recall most of the 316 commandments contained within the entire Mosaic Law, it was quite unlikely they would forget this particular directive. Their barefaced disregard for the simplest of God's laws shows they did not honour God in the least. Israel was content in its defiance.

Do we care for God's laws? Are we concerned about the clearest and most basic regulations He has set forth in His Word? It is not uncommon for Christians today to say "Yes, I know what the Bible says, but...." Ignorance of what Scripture teaches is one thing; but knowing what Scripture demands and choosing to do things our own way is just as offensive to the Lord as these Jews who made metal images. Yet, although these Jews disregard God, there ultimately came a day when God would disregard them, despite their need for Him.

Likewise, modern Christians must beware of disregarding God's will because there may come a day when He decides to disregard us. Ashamedly, many who title themselves the "people of God" want nothing to do with the will of God.

The script further reads **"idols skillfully made of their silver, all of them the work of craftsmen"**. The images they deified were constructed by the efforts of meagre human beings. They honoured and worshipped what was prepared by their own hands. That is no different than you worshipping the plate of food you cooked for Sunday dinner. How foolish!

Sin always diminishes our intelligence rather than increases it. The further a person, church, or nation falls into sin, the less rational they become. Iniquity makes us silly, less discerning, and often unaware of our state.

Furthermore, **"those who offer human sacrifice kiss calves!"** Human sacrificing, in particular child sacrifice, was a common ritual the Israelites espoused when they became ensnared by the false Canaanite gods. This practice was often done to the false god, Molech. Examples of this can be located in the Scriptures. It can be assumed that the practice was popular in Hosea's day. Jeremiah 32:35 gives an account of the shameful ritual.

35 They built the high places of Baal in the Valley of the Son of Hinnom, to offer up their sons and daughters to Molech, though I did not command them, nor did it enter into my mind, that they should do this abomination, to cause Judah to sin.

This further confirms the earlier proposition that sin robs people of basic discernment: it made Israel so silly that mothers and fathers watched their children burn alive in agony. Their commitment to idolatry persuaded them to annihilate future generations of their own people.

Nonetheless, further idolatry is extant in this verse. The text says they "kiss calves" referring to the nation's shrines erected at Bethel and/or the metal images concocted for personal use. Kissing these cows was symbolic of loyalty to the god it represented, in this case Baal (1 Kings 19:18).

Who are we, the Lord's elect, "kissing"? Who do we pledge loyalty to? The world's system entices us daily to kiss the many idols of this godless age. There's no lack of things we can kiss. The Bible, however, commands us to kiss the Son. Psalms 2:12,

Kiss the Son, lest he be angry, and you perish in the way, for his wrath is quickly kindled. Blessed are all who take refuge in him.

The "Son" is God's Son, Jesus of Nazareth, the risen King. Are we kissing the Son or the house that we own, our social media image, and our Netflix subscription? The Son is where our ultimate love and loyalty should always lay.

The third verse commences, **"Therefore, they shall be like the morning mist or like dew that goes early away."** Israel is compared, first of all, to a cloud of mist that rests on the surface of the earth in the early hours of the day. The "dew that goes early away" portrays a related idea of the condensation that rests on the leaves of plants but quickly evaporates as the morning progresses.

The next comparison is that it is **"like the chaff that swirls from the threshing floor."** "Chaff" is the dry outside shell of grains which was separated when a large beast such as an ox, cow, or horse walked over the grain on the threshing floor cracking the seeds. The chaff, being light, would float into the air especially in windy weather. The next comparison is **"like smoke from a window."** It's not certain what this phraseology proposes, but it could probably be the situation of someone cooking food near an open window where smoke escapes. What do all of these situations have in common? They all represent items that are transient. Mist, dew, chaff, and smoke are all fleeting and never lasting. God undoubtedly submits that because of Israel's depravity, they will vanish away from their land: since they have done away with God, God has done away with them.

The Nation's Father

God affirms (vs. 4) **"But I am the LORD your God from the land of Egypt"** echoing precisely what he communicated to the nation immediately before they were endowed with the Ten Commandments. He said in Exodus 20:2,

"I am the Lord your God, who brought you out of the land of Egypt, out of the house of slavery."

Yahweh was their God then, and He was still their God now. The allusion to the "land of Egypt" is a staple reminder of where they were and what they endured before God delivered them. If it was not for His heroic hand of rescue, they would be void of hope. Yet, their only source of deliverance has been abandoned.

Humanity often finds itself in an equivalent predicament. When spells of tribulations come, and the Lord delivers us out of them, we sometimes forget His acts of mercy. We forget about the times we laid on our sickbeds—or perhaps our deathbeds. We fail to recall how we almost became homeless. We don't remember how God saved our marriage or delivered our children out of dangerous situations. It's quite easy to forget these graces and turn our backs on God—the same God that brought us hope when there was none. Have you forgotten God's blessings upon your existence? Are you like these Jews who are unable to remember when they were slaves in Egypt? It is regrettable that our memory is often just as fleeting as the aforementioned dew.

Furthermore, **"you know no God besides me."** "Know" here is a term of intimacy and communion that explains how they were mandated to be in exclusive union with God just as human marriage is exclusive. He freely chose them of His own sovereign grace, and that demanded loyalty. He adds **"and besides me there is no savior."** God assures them that He only can rescue and deliver them. This information will be important because of the judgement they will encounter when they are taken into bondage by the Assyrian state. God, speaking through Hosea, has already foreseen their judgement take place. Only the Almighty Father can deliver them from the judgement that is quickly approaching, but before they can be rescued they must repent. By now, Hosea's countless calls to repentance resemble a scratched record. He has repeated himself over and over and over again. Why does he continue his efforts? It is for two main reasons.

1. The people have not yet repented.
2. The judgement has not yet fallen.

When either of these options comes to pass, Hosea's need to prophesy will terminate. However, until that day, Hosea must continue preaching in God's name and call people to change their minds.

Those of us who carry the Gospel message today must halt our exertions only for either of those two reasons. Either the person has repented and believed on Jesus or eternal judgement has already ensued. Until then, we must continue to unashamedly proclaim Gospel truth even if we appear to others a scratched record like Hosea.

However, the point must not be overlooked that God made clear He was the sole being who could save these people from judgement. He alone could save from the coming judgement, then, and He alone could save from the coming judgement now. Anyone in the world can only be saved from eternal punishment through believing on the Lord Jesus Christ. The location of an individual's birth, his ethnicity, or religious background has no bearing upon His eligibility to enter heaven's gates. Eternal life and everlasting peace comes exclusively through taking hold of the lifeline offered by Jesus Christ, God's Son.

Acts 4:12,

And there is salvation in no one else, for there is no other name under heaven given among men by which we must be saved."

Hosea's prophecy, in verse 5, continues with **"It was I who knew you in the wilderness in the land of drought."** Again, the term "know" comes up signifying intimacy with Israel and His choosing of them for a relationship with Him. God elected this nation in a vulnerable state in their wilderness wanderings with nothing but His provision. Formerly, they were not a prestigious or prosperous people, but they had God and He was all they needed.

If you have God, you have all you need. It is better to know God and have little (or what you perceive to be little) than to not know God and have much. Proverbs 15:6 makes this potent point when it declares, *"Better is a little with the fear of the Lord than great treasure and trouble with it."*

"But when they had grazed, they became full" is the accusation of **verse 6**. "Grazed" carries with it the sense of a flock feeding on pasture land showing that God gave the nation greater provision and they were satisfied with their feeding. But **"they were filled and their heart was lifted up."** Their material satisfaction made them haughty and proud with an exalted sense of self-importance.

Believe it or not, sometimes success is not good for us—especially financial success as it can make some of us haughty and conceited like Israel. It's often said that money changes people, but I reckon that financial success is an effective tool which pushes to the surface what is already laid hidden.

What is the result of all this? It is **"therefore they forgot me."** The nation's Father, Yahweh, was no longer important to their existence. Israel had no excuse because God had specifically warned about the dangers of forgetting Him.

Deuteronomy 8:11-18,

> [11] *"Take care lest you forget the Lord your God by not keeping his commandments and his rules and his statutes, which I command you today,* [12] *lest, when you have eaten and are full and have built good houses and live in them,* [13] *and when your herds and flocks multiply and your silver and gold is multiplied and all that you have is multiplied,* [14] *then your heart be lifted up, and you forget the Lord your God, who brought you out of the land of Egypt, out of the house of slavery,* [15] *who led you through the great and terrifying wilderness, with its fiery serpents and scorpions and thirsty ground where there was no water, who brought you water out of the flinty rock,* [16] *who fed you in the wilderness with manna that your fathers did not know, that he might humble you and test you, to do you good in the end.* [17] *Beware lest you*

say in your heart, 'My power and the might of my hand have gotten me this wealth.' ¹⁸ *You shall remember the Lord your God, for it is he who gives you power to get wealth, that he may confirm his covenant that he swore to your fathers, as it is this day.*

Believers must seriously adhere to God's warnings in Scripture because He is infinite in wisdom and is 100% accurate in everything He sets forth. Exaggerations are not a part of His repertoire; every caution from God is warranted and must be strictly heeded. He knows our frames and to what temptations we are most susceptible. If God declares the possibility of danger, we would be fools not to believe Him.

The Nation is Frightened

Dreadfully, God responds (vs. 7) **"So I am to them like a lion."** Lions are large, fearless, ferocious beasts that can overwhelm almost every other beast on the earth— a terrifying force which God has already used to illustrate His judgement upon Israel. Also, **"like a leopard I will lurk beside the way."** The leopard, also brought into the picture, focuses on the act of lurking. The root word for "lurk" means "to go around something" or "to spy out" articulating lying in wait for an opportunity to pounce on the hunted animal.

According to verse 8, **"I will fall upon them like a bear robbed of her cubs."** Understandably, a female bear would terrorize anyone who removes her young ones from her presence. Nothing could ever be done to agitate the she-bear more than this blatant act. God pictures this as how violently He will treat His own people. Then He adds, **"I will tear open their breasts."** "Breasts" focuses upon the chest cavity that encloses the heart. God will ensure every bit of life is drained from them. They won't be able to simply recover from God's attack on His people. He promises **"and there I will devour them like a lion, as a wild beast would rip them open."** After draining the life out of Israel, He will consume every bit of their flesh. This judgement leaves no stone unturned. "Wild beast" is a synonym for all the previously mentioned animals (lion, bear, and leopard) which are the kind of beasts that shepherds protected their flocks from being ravaged by. Israel is God's flock whom He would normally protect. However, the tables have turned and He is on the attack since they hate repentance.

This image of God is rarely depicted in churches today. The contemporary God, in most congregations, is nothing more than a genie in a bottle. Rather, the God of the Bible is a fierce, overwhelming being who should not be taken for granted. The unfortunate situation of Christendom today is t hat the pendulum has swung so far in the opposite direction that, to a large extent, fear of the God of the Bible is desperately lacking. Biblical Christianity begs that the love of God and the wrath of God be kept in balance, not neglecting one attribute over the other, but establishing them both as indispensable elements in comprehensively understanding the Almighty Creator. Satan has skillfully used a scandalous negligence of the Old Testament by modern Christians to foster a culture of iniquity and evil that has permeated most of western society. The world is forcefully shoving the church down an ungodly pathway. The true Church of Jesus Christ must be returned to a biblical balance if we will successfully live and serve in the manner that God has designed. Otherwise, we will find ourselves shipwrecked on a distant reef—ineffective, unproductive, defeated, and dead.

> Discuss

1. "Therefore, sin qualifies not only as doing the wrong thing, but neglecting to do the right thing in any situation." Does this magnify your understanding of the concept of sin? How?

2. Would James 4:17 make an individual more likely or less likely to be guilty of sin?

3. What makes idolatry an evil act?

4. Mist, dew, chaff, and smoke are all transient objects. Name another image Hosea could have utilized to make the same point?

5. Excluding Hosea, give two instances in Scripture where God is portrayed as a lion. One should be negative and the other positive.

25

DEMOLITION DAY

13:9-16

⁹ He destroys you, O Israel, for you are against me, against your helper. ¹⁰ Where now is your king, to save you in all your cities? Where are all your rulers—those of whom you said, "Give me a king and princes"? ¹¹ I gave you a king in my anger, and I took him away in my wrath.¹² The iniquity of Ephraim is bound up; his sin is kept in store. ¹³ The pangs of childbirth come for him, but he is an unwise son, for at the right time he does not present himself at the opening of the womb. ¹⁴ I shall ransom them from the power of Sheol; I shall redeem them from Death. O Death, where are your plagues? O Sheol, where is your sting Compassion is hidden from my eyes. ¹⁵ Though he may flourish among his brothers, the east wind, the wind of the LORD, shall come, rising from the wilderness, and his fountain shall dry up; his spring shall be parched; it shall strip his treasury of every precious thing.¹⁶ Samaria shall bear her guilt, because she has rebelled against her God; they shall fall by the sword; their little ones shall be dashed in pieces, and their pregnant women ripped open.

Vacant, derelict high-rise buildings are often an eyesore. They can decrease the value of neighbouring properties, become a breeding ground for criminal activity, or, quite frankly, become an unofficial dump for unwanted objects. In addition, if the building has already been deemed structurally unsound, the death dye has been cast, and it, most certainly, is a lost cause.

Then comes the wrecking ball. A large circular steel object weighing thousands of pounds is plowed through the walls of the structure reducing it to merely a rubble of rocks to be carted away and put to some favourable use.

Within a few short hours, the several-story building is reduced to its foundation and an enormous gaping space appears at that site. The structure has been annihilated.

This imagery accurately depicts God's immediate plans for Israel as their devotion to sin has left Him no choice but to demolish the whole country by His own awful, crushing power. When His judgement is complete, not one block of concrete will be standing upon another. From this section of Hosea, it is made clear that judgement suits those who rebel against God.

No King

The 9th verse of this chapter commences with **"He destroys you, O Israel"** carrying on the concept from the prior verse where God was described as a wild beast who would rip open His own people. This brutal beast will rain upon the Northern Kingdom mayhem and ruin as they feel the brunt of His wrath as never before. The cause of their destruction is **"for you are against me."** The nation is in opposition to God.

There are only two kinds of people in this world—those who are for God and those who are against Him—the saved and the lost—the converted and the unconverted—the Heaven-bound and the Hell-bound. The contemporary lie of Satan is to convince people that they can somehow be in neither of these categories and dwell in the middle without deciding. Nevertheless, if you have failed to decide, then you reside in the camp of those who will endure the unquenchable fire unless you come to genuine repentance and seek rescue through the divine person and finished work of Jesus Christ, God's substitute, who alone retains within Himself the hope of endless life. There is no neutral territory when it comes to the condition of the soul. You are firmly and exclusively in one camp or the other. Are you against God or for Him? I implore you to call upon the name of the Lord Jesus even now to receive eternal forgiveness.

Furthermore, it discloses that they are **"against your helper."** It was Yahweh who gave assistance and provided for the needs of the people of Israel. He was the sole individual responsible and no one else could take credit for being Israel's helper. Thus, the Psalmist acknowledged in Psalm 121,

> *¹I lift up my eyes to the hills. From where does my help come? ² My help comes from the Lord, who made heaven and earth. ³ He will not let your foot be moved; he who keeps you will not slumber. ⁴ Behold, he who keeps Israel will neither slumber nor sleep. ⁵ The Lord is your keeper; the Lord is your shade on your right hand. ⁶ The sun shall not strike you by day, nor*

> the moon by night. *⁷ The Lord will keep you from all evil; he will keep your life. ⁸ The Lord will keep your going out and your coming in from this time forth and forevermore.*

The Lord was Israel's Helper.

Who is your helper? The moment you get into a difficult situation, personally, what's your first reaction? Who does your mind rest upon? On a wider scale, it appears that increasingly modern Christianity is becoming decreasingly dependent upon God. In many jurisdictions, God's church is putting its heart into the hands of ungodly politicians. What a recipe for disaster! The last time I checked, Jesus Christ was Lord! That affirmation rolls off the tongue with ease, but do we honestly believe that? If God is your helper, you will not seek illegitimate means to accomplish goals. God was Israel's helper, but because they ignored Him so copiously, the nation will face a judgement during which His services would not be available.

"Where now is your king, to save you in all your cities?" is the inquiry of verse 10. The "king" is brought into the discussion because he is who the nation trusted to be their helper. They had placed their confidence in kingship rather than in God in a number of locations. "In all your cities" signifies that in all places in the country, they put trust in an earthly king above the Heavenly One.

Again, we must inspect our own hearts to determine who we are trusting to safely navigate us through the challenges of life. Some put faith in their money and assets, while others put dependence upon family members or their ability to negotiate. For the child of God, ultimate confidence must be placed in the Lord.

The text asks **"Where are all your rulers—those of whom you said 'Give me a king and princes'"?** Essentially, Hosea asks "Where did all your national leaders go?" This echoes the sentiments of Hosea 10:3,

For now they will say: "We have no king, for we do not fear the Lord; and a king—what could he do for us?"

An admission has already been made that the nation was lacking a king presently, but take note that there was an occasion in the past when the nation begged "give me a king and princes". When did this appeal occur? The answer rests in 1 Samuel 8:1-9.

¹When Samuel became old, he made his sons judges over Israel. ² The name of his firstborn son was Joel, and the name of his second, Abijah; they were judges in Beersheba. ³ Yet his sons did not walk in his ways but turned aside after gain. They took bribes and perverted justice. ⁴ Then all the elders of Israel gathered together and came to Samuel at Ramah ⁵ and said to him, "Behold, you are old and your sons do not walk in your ways. Now appoint for us a king to judge us like all the nations." ⁶ But the thing displeased Samuel when they said, "Give us a king to judge us." And Samuel prayed to the Lord. ⁷ And the Lord said to Samuel, "Obey the voice of the people in all that they say to you, for they have not rejected you, but they have rejected me from being king over them. ⁸ According to all the deeds that they have done, from the day I brought them up out of Egypt even to this day, forsaking me and serving other gods, so they are also doing to you. ⁹ Now then, obey their voice; only you shall solemnly warn them and show them the ways of the king who shall reign over them."

The above passage discloses the time in which Israel requested a king. God's original intent was for them to never have an earthly king because He was to be their king, ruling by Himself. Israel was set up as a theocracy. The prefix of the word "theocracy" is "theo" which comes from *theos* that, in New Testament Greek, refers to God. Quite frankly, it was to be a God-ruled nation, literally—the only theocracy in the history of the world. In asking for a king, sadly, they renounced God who was their King and He, without protest, gave them the desire of their hearts. Israel discarded the garments of a theocracy and, consequently, became a monarchy. They traded in God-rule for man-rule.

The clear lesson for today is that sometimes what we imagine is the best situation for us may not really be such. 1 Samuel 8:20 advises that Israel wanted a king to follow the paradigm of the heathen nations which encompassed them. In addition, they wanted a king to judge them and fight their battles. Although Israel originally had the perfect king, they supposed a human king would be superior. Saul would be Israel's first king—an utter disappointment.

To be clear, God would, in due course, use the monarchy to fulfill His plans for redemption (try figuring that one out!). However, it was not His original objective and the repudiation of God as king brought consequences. What Israel thought was best for them turned out to be a gigantic mistake. Often, what we assume to be the best path for ourselves is not so. We reckon we should seek a certain career, attend a particular school/university, live in a specific country, or date a certain person; all the while, God, knowing that if we had accomplished specific goals, our lives would have been demolished. An anonymous friend of wisdom once stated that "one of the greatest blessings in our lives is that of unanswered prayer". If those prayers were answered, we would not be where we are today. Hence, we must beg God to lead us in the right path and saturate the major decisions of our lives in prayer. Seeking godly advice from mature Christians is an additional step of wisdom. These are all barriers of protection against bad decisions and big mistakes.

"I gave you a king in my anger" is the affirmation of the 11th verse referring to the first earthly king of Israel, Saul. Saul was not who God wanted to be their king because He was to be their king; nevertheless, He granted them a king in anger. There are times when God will grant us our requests and permit us to face their ensuing consequences. The current Christian falsity that's taught among many congregations which says "God will always have your back no matter what" is simply not true. God will not have your back if you're running contrary to His will or consistently bucking against the clear teaching of Holy Scripture. Instead, you're riding out as a Lone Ranger bereft of God's support. After Israel received the king they begged for, they were forced to endure all of his ungodly flaws and failures. The consequences of their actions were quite more than they bargained for.

In addition, **"I took him away in my wrath."** Disagreement exists among Bible commentators concerning the identity of "him" here. Some naturally believe it refers to Saul since the preliminary part of the verse refers to Saul, and Saul also died in unfortunate circumstances (1 Samuel 31:4). However, others contend that Hoshea is the king referred to. Hoshea was the last reigning king of the Northern Kingdom before Israel was taken into exile by Assyria.

2 Kings 17:6,

In the ninth year of Hoshea, the king of Assyria captured Samaria and deported the Israelites to Assyria. He settled them in Halah, in Gozan on the Habor River and in the towns of the Medes.

Therefore, "him" could be the first king of Israel or the last king of Israel. I'm not fully convinced of one option above the other, but that is inconsequential since both kings were eradicated from their rule through the sovereign hand of God.

No Birth

It is revealed that **"the iniquity of Ephraim is bound up"** according to verse 12. The phrase "bound up" indicates that something is pressed or cramped in a narrow situation. Additionally, **"his sin is kept in store."** "Kept in store" is one word in the original and it suggests something is hidden and concealed, touting the language of pregnancy. Israel holds on to keeping its wickedness safe just as a mother's womb keeps the child safe. Sin and iniquity is dear to the nation's heart and Israel will not part ways with it.

As God's people, we must be on mission every day to eject sin from our lives. Iniquity is always dangerous to our existence and we must be on the offensive to gain ground against our sinful desires. Never should it be embraced as near and dear to our hearts like a precious unborn child. Rather, it must be treated like a cancer that eats us alive which we would do anything to effectively extract from our bodies lest it kill us. One of the main reasons Hosea's prophetic voice was scorned and the people were so hardened in sin by this time was because sinful lifestyles were precious to them. Progression was made from "bad" to "not so bad"; from "OK" to "I really like this".

Next, (vs. 13) **"the pangs of childbirth come for him."** Labor pains now converge on the womb; pressure is being applied. Personally, I reckon these labor pains are the verbal proclamations of Hosea and other prophets like him. These clarion voices apply spiritual pressure to Israel—who has set up blockages to protect its deviant lifestyle—all in an effort to push Ephraim's iniquity down the birth chamber and out of its system. Alas, **"he is an unwise son"** who is not intelligent nor has the discernment to know what he should do.

It is because **"at the right time he does not present himself at the opening of the womb."** Childbirth can be extremely risky. When a mother is in labour, a specific order of events should transpire to safeguard a secure delivery for the infant. Issues along the birth canal may present danger for both the child and the mother's life. Surely, in Old Testament seasons, countless women and children died during this process, since there was such a lack of modern-day technology and equipment to safeguard against these occurrences. This illustration should have potently struck a chord with Hosea's audience; the prophet basically says "if you don't let go of your sinfulness as a nation, you will die in the birth canal". The unwise son remains in the womb with his sin and dies, but the wise son pushes out of the womb along with the sin he once held securely.

No Compassion

The Lord asks (vs. 14) **"Shall I ransom them from the power of Sheol? Shall I redeem them from Death?"** Differences of opinion occur in Bible translations concerning how the beginning of verse 14 should be interpreted. One option is to view this part of the verse as an affirmative statement: "I shall ransom them from the power of Sheol. I shall redeem them from Death". The alternative is to view them as rhetorical questions as conveyed presently in the *English Standard Version*. Which is the correct understanding? I believe it is the rhetorical question. This conclusion is determined because of the verse's literary context. All of chapter 13 thus far has peddled a negative connotation as will the remainder of the chapter. This segment of verse 14 would be the sole positive outlook of the chapter if it is to be understood affirmatively. Although not impossible, it would be awkward for the author to include a positive outlook in such a negative stretch of text. Also, the last clause of the verse is clearly negative. Thus, I believe these phrases are rhetorical questions, not affirmative statements.

The terms "ransom" and "redeem" have similar meanings, both suggesting the paying of a price for an item to retrieve it again. The terms "Sheol" and "Death" also have similar meanings. Sheol, in the Old Testament, generally designates a subterranean location where all the dead were located. Hence, both of these questions mirror each other; rhetorically, God is asking "Shall I rescue them from the death they will encounter in the birth canal?"

Then comes the exclamatory question, **"O Death, where are your plagues?"** A plague is any kind of pestilence that brings destruction, whether it be an animal, natural, or spiritual plague. The ten plagues that came upon the Egyptians when Israel lived in Egypt is what should come to our minds.

The next question is **"O Sheol, where is your sting?"** The term sting means "destruction" or "extermination" which expounds upon what comes about as a result of the plagues.

Again, it must be determined how these statements should be understood. Are they to be understood as glorious and triumphant as Paul uses them in 1 Corinthians 15:55, "*O death, where is your victory? O death, where is your sting?*" Or are they to be understood as Hosea invoking Death and Sheol to bring "plagues" and a "sting" respectively to Israel? Again, the answer must be decided by the context of the passage. Since the context of the passage is adverse, these statements must be recognized as derogatory. Hosea is invoking Death to bring its plagues and Sheol to bring its sting so that these people can be annihilated. "Do it and do it now!" is God's cry. The reason the apostle Paul uses the identical phraseology positively and triumphantly in 1 Corinthians is because he resided on the other side of Calvary's cross, and had received the blessings of what Jesus Christ accomplished in the New Covenant.

The cross of Jesus Christ is the only lens that has the power to convert the darkness of death into the brightness of life. It only has the power to overturn the spiritually bankrupt state in which all humankind is cemented. Paul cites this verse of death as a verse of triumph due to what was accomplished through the death, burial, and resurrection of God's sinless sacrifice.

Neither will there be any triumph, hope, or forgiveness for you, the reader, unless it is through the combined person and work of the Lord Jesus. Have you accepted the Lord Jesus by faith? Have you cast your life upon His once-for-all payment for sin? You must do so, otherwise you will face the plagues and the sting of eternal death.

It is also told that **"Compassion is hidden from my eyes."** Nothing can move God to pity any longer. Mercy is nowhere to be found; He has had enough of their foolishness. Compassion is no longer in His sight-line as if it doesn't even exist.

"Though he may flourish among his brothers" is the commencing of verse 15. Ephraim, the tribe alone, is probably being singled out since it was last mentioned in verse 12 and presently the verse claims that there are brothers (plural). This northern tribe, apparently, was the apex of prosperity and prestige since the entire Northern Kingdom was regularly referred to by this tribe's name alone. Even though they possessed military and political superiority over the other northern tribes, judgement was speedily approaching.

Never be mistaken in presuming that success and prosperity is necessarily a sign of God's blessing. Just because someone prospers financially does not mean they have God's endorsement. As a matter of fact, it can mean the contrary. Matthew 5:45b says,

"For he makes his sun rise on the evil and on the good, and sends rain on the just and on the unjust."

God doesn't reserve His blessings for believers only; He allows unbelievers to receive the same. Never peg a person's spirituality on their possessions or lack thereof, and never measure your own spirituality by that yardstick. Because someone flourishes now, does not mean they will not be under the oceans of God's wrath in the near future.

The verse continues with **"the east wind, the wind of the Lord, shall come rising from the wilderness."** This is the second occasion of the east wind's mention in Hosea, the initial instance being Hosea 12:1. The east wind was hot and destroyed vegetation in the land as it came off the desert regions. Several Scriptures mentioned the east wind such as Ezekiel 19:12.

But the vine was plucked up in fury, cast down to the ground;
the east wind dried up its fruit; they were stripped off and withered. As for its strong stem, fire consumed it.

Jonah 4:8 also references the east wind.

When the sun rose, God appointed a scorching east wind, and the sun beat down on the head of Jonah so that he was faint. And he asked that he might die and said, "It is better for me to die than to live."

Two unquestionable observations can be made about the east wind.

1. It was extremely hot.
2. Often, it was God's tool of judgement.

Both facts are evident in the verse under examination.

Additionally, **"his foundation shall dry up; His spring shall be parched."** Fountains and springs are locations where refreshing water is found. If they dry up, there is no location where citizens can refresh themselves when thirsty. Israel will incur a desert-like experience although they currently live in the Promised Land, the land flowing with milk and honey. The result is that **"it shall strip his treasury of every precious thing."** A treasury was a place where items of value were stored like corn, food, and precious metals such silver or gold. Even today "treasury" is the term used to designate where a nation's finances are held for safekeeping. That this scorching hot wind makes its way into the storehouses and removes its most precious belongings leads us to assume that the east wind is metaphorical rather than literal. Even though God, at times, sent a literal east wind to reprimand His people, it is more than likely that this east wind was a figurative east wind representing the Assyrian army.

The following verse gives supplementary evidence for this as it says (vs. 16) **"Samaria shall bear her guilt because she has rebelled against her God."** Samaria was the capital city of the Northern Kingdom but was representative of the entire country. It represents the location where sin has converged in large numbers, yet this affirmation does not exclude the rest of the country. Because of her disobedience, the effect is that the capital will bear the weight of her own sin, a reasonable, anticipated outcome of this kind of situation. Samaria, and by extension, Israel, is getting exactly what she deserves.

Yet, this is precisely what makes the message of the Gospel of Jesus Christ so uniquely spectacular since the Gospel says that although we have been defiant 'scallywags', someone else was willing to bear the weight of our guilt. This someone was Jesus of Nazareth as He hung high on Golgotha's hill with the immense weight of iniquity on His shoulders—iniquity that He did not commit and had no associations with. Still, He bore that load of sinfulness receiving the due punishment so that wicked sinners could escape the ordeal. Every breathing soul on God's green earth is in one of two positions. Either you are bearing your own guilt like Samaria, or Jesus Christ has already shouldered your guilt through His work of atonement. If you fail to seek God's pardon through His Son, then right now, you are bearing your own guilt and will be punished like Samaria. Escape the coming wrath by calling upon the name of the Lord Jesus to rescue you (Romans 10:13).

The consequences of Israel's sin, however, is that **"they shall fall by the sword."** This is symbolic of death by violent means. They will not die of natural causes since many of them will have their lives taken away. Also, **"their little ones shall be dashed in pieces."** The Assyrian army will cruelly take precious little babies and slaughter them by inhumanely throwing them against rocks and stones. The definition of cruelty and godlessness is when people are comfortable with slaughtering children in such a horrific manner. The nation should have never gotten over the fact that God was its only true helper. However, it is clear that God was not exaggerating when He said compassion was hidden from His eyes.

Furthermore, **"their pregnant women"** were **"ripped open."** There's no limit to the cruelty that the Assyrian army used against children out of the womb. In addition, mothers will perish with their children as their stomachs are cut open with the sword. To be clear, this was not metaphorical language but literal as these cases are found in Scripture.

2 Kings 8:13,

And Hazael said, "What is your servant, who is but a dog, that he should do this great thing?" Elisha answered, "The Lord has shown me that you are to be king over Syria."

Some would wonder why a good God would allow His nation to endure such viciousness. The reason is that the people never repented of their sinful ways. Their hearts were as hard as rocks. God gave them His Word and sent His prophets, but they still would not return to covenant faithfulness. The outcome is that He will give them over to every single evil imaginable. Most people can somewhat discern deep down inside that sin brings judgement, but not everyone cares enough to do something about it. May we as God's people never fall into that category, but always desire to live in accordance with the commands of our God who is a consuming fire.

> Discuss

1. "There is no neutral territory when it comes to the condition of the soul." Do you agree or disagree? Why?

2. Is there a prayer you are thankful God never answered because you came to realize later that it would have been detrimental to you in some way?

3. Excluding the words "theocracy/theocratic", give 3 others word in the English language that begins with the prefix "theo" along with their definitions.

4. Can adverse weather conditions sometimes be a sign of God's judgement? What in this chapter hints at that fact?

5. Why can't anyone bear his/her own guilt before the Creator God without facing the consequences?

26

HOMECOMING
14:1-9

¹ Return, O Israel, to the LORD your God, for you have stumbled because of your iniquity. ² Take with you words and return to the LORD; say to him, "Take away all iniquity; accept what is good, and we will pay with bulls the vows of our lips. ³ Assyria shall not save us; we will not ride on horses; and we will say no more, 'Our God,' to the work of our hands. In you the orphan finds mercy." ⁴ I will heal their apostasy; I will love them freely, for my anger has turned from them. ⁵ I will be like the dew to Israel; he shall blossom like the lily; he shall take root like the trees of Lebanon; ⁶ his shoots shall spread out; his beauty shall be like the olive, and his fragrance like Lebanon. ⁷ They shall return and dwell beneath my shadow; they shall flourish like the grain; they shall blossom like the vine; their fame shall be like the wine of Lebanon. ⁸ O Ephraim, what have I to do with idols? It is I who answer and look after you. I am like an evergreen cypress; from me comes your fruit. ⁹ Whoever is wise, let him understand these things; whoever is discerning, let him know them; for the ways of the LORD are right, and the upright walk in them, but transgressors stumble in them.

Homecomings are usually synonymous with food, fun, and fellowship, and although they may differ in purpose, they all express one unifying theme. Homecomings bring people back to their roots. Whether the attachment is a school, hometown, or family reunion, all homecomings are engineered to summon nostalgia and cause people to reminisce about the way things used to be. Celebrants are urged to return to locations that shaped their destiny. In this final segment of Hosea's prophecy, Yahweh is calling Israel home. Home, in this instance is not a place, but a person. God desires that His people begin to seek Him afresh and return to being faithful to the covenant He made with them from the nation's inception.

The Call to Repentance

The final chapter of Hosea's prophecy commences with the words (vs. 1) **"Return, O Israel."** "Return" means to turn back. It is as if Israel has set sail on a journey and drifts away from home in the open ocean. The demand is that Israel go back to home base because that is where she should be. There is no reason why she should be lost at sea in a distant land; only danger and destruction is available there.

Maybe you need to return to God. Church attendance does not confirm that one is walking with God. Just because you sing songs on Sunday does not mean you are in love with the Saviour; fellowship with the saints does not indicate fellowship with God Himself. When I was in Bible college, a guest preacher spoke at our college's chapel my freshman year. He made a startling statement that I found difficult to believe at the time. He said one of the easiest places in the world to fall away from God was at a Christian college where young men and women are being trained toward godliness. Initially, I thought the idea was an exaggeration. However, then came my sophomore year, junior year, and senior year. Looking back on those years, I've concluded that he was right. Over that time, I saw many fall away from God while at a Christian college, and if it could occur there, it can happen anywhere. Do you need to return to God?

Hosea also acknowledges who they should return to: **"the Lord your God."** For the last time in this prophecy, he emphasizes possession using the word "your". It is not Israel who owns Yahweh, it is Yahweh who owns Israel. They are Yahweh's bride, possession, and people who belong exclusively to Him.

The same applies to those born of His Spirit. If you profess to be a child of God, then you are exactly that, God's child, and He demands the ownership of your life. You are His possession before you are anyone else's. You may be someone else's child or spouse but your primary relationship is your relationship to God. Therefore, before anyone else has precedence, He has precedence. Is that the reality of your life? Do you live like He has proprietorship of you or do you live like you own yourself and have no higher authority? Many professed believers today only give lip service to Christianity and they may be successful at misleading others—and probably even themselves—but they will never fool God. 2 Timothy 2:19 reveals the following,

But God's firm foundation stands, bearing this seal: "The Lord knows those who are his," and, "Let everyone who names the name of the Lord depart from iniquity."

The word "his" refers to His possession and people. God knows the identity of His children, and it is impossible to bamboozle Him.

The text adds **"for you have stumbled because of your iniquity."** The word translated "stumbled" means literally "to totter or waver from side to side." This should conjure up images of an intoxicated individual. Because the legs are feeble, they cannot walk upright and straight ahead; they are here, there, and everywhere spiritually. There is no firmness and stability all because of their disobedience and transgression. It's not just one sin, but all the sins: drunkenness, stubbornness, pride, sexual immorality, idolatry, lack of faith in God, etc.

The more we find ourselves engulfed in iniquity, the more we will waver from side to side aimlessly. Hence, daily purification and cleansing is requisite. We must plead alongside the hymn writer James Orr who said,

"Search me O God and know my heart today
Try me, O Saviour know my thoughts I pray
See if there be some wicked way in me
Cleanse me from every sin and set me free."

Verse 2 starts with **"take with you words and return to the LORD; say to him."** Hosea directs the nation on how to repent, even as far as telling them what to say. He attempts to make this process as easy as possible, especially since they may not know where to begin. He's putting the shoes on the bottom rack doing whatever necessary to assist them in reaching the goal.

That should resemble our hearts as believers, especially toward the unsaved. We must be willing to assist in whatever ways we can to help bring people into right relationship with God. Whether it be by presenting the Gospel directly, distributing a tract, baking a cake for an event, or giving money toward a Gospel-worthy cause. Paul retained the same mindset during his missionary journey. In 1 Corinthians 9:20-22, he determined that,

> [20] *To the Jews I became as a Jew, in order to win Jews. To those under the law I became as one under the law (though not being myself under the law) that I might win those under the law.* [21] *To those outside the law I became as one outside the law (not being outside the law of God but under the law of Christ) that I might win those outside the law.* [22] *To the weak I became weak, that I might win the weak. I have become all things to all people, that by all means I might save some.*

Paul was willing to break the box of his own comfort zone to make himself as effective as possible in presenting the Gospel of Jesus Christ to others. He met people where they were, but he did not leave them there; his goal was to connect them to the good news. Here, Hosea does whatever it takes to bring people to repentance, even if he had to provide a road map of what to say and how to start in order to make the journey to repentance traversable. Today, we should follow this model as well.

Their prayer is to ask God to **"take away all iniquity."** In other words, "wash us, cleanse us, purify us from our sins". The Almighty Creator holds the power and authority to forgive sin exclusively. This fact is underscored in the New Testament when Jesus healed the paralytic man in Mark 2. Jesus told the man in verse 5, *"son your sins are forgiven."* Verses 6 and 7 follow with *"now some of the scribes were sitting there questioning in their hearts, why does this man speak like that? He is blaspheming. Who can forgive sins but God alone?"*

Even the scribes knew that only God had the authority to forgive sins. However, where they went wrong was that they did not comprehend that Jesus was God, therefore He had the authority to say such to that man.

Jesus still holds that authority and power today. Do you feel dirty because of sin? Do you perceive yourself as wretched because of iniquity? Jesus Christ is the great sin-cleanser. That's why He journeyed to the Cross of Calvary and shed His precious blood. Yet, although His blood is red, it will wash as white as snow all who cling to His provision of eternal life. If you believe on the Lord Jesus Christ today, you will find yourself spotless before God the Father for all eternity. Another hymn writer, Elisha A. Hoffman to wrote,

Have you been to Jesus for the cleansing power?
Are you washed in the blood of the lamb?
Are you fully trusting in his grace this hour?
Are you washed in the blood of the lamb?

Chorus

Are you washed in the blood?

In the soul cleansing blood of the lamb?
Are your garments spotless are they white as snow?
Are you washed in the blood of the lamb?

Then, they must beg God to **"accept what is good."** When it came to confession and repentance, there were ceremonial expectations for the Jews. Several times in Scripture, they were forbidden to come to God empty handed (Exodus 23:15; Exodus 34:20; Exodus 16:16). Instead, they were to bring prayers, vows, and sacrificial gifts. So, Hosea urges them to plead with God to accept the gifts that accompany their repentance.

Furthermore, **"we will pay with bulls the vows of our lips."** A bull was a more expensive sacrificial animal in the Jewish sacrificial system. What is being communicated is that the vows they will make with their lips will match the worth of the expensive animals they will sacrifice. No more empty talking; they will be committed to these vows. What are these vows?

Firstly, **"Assyria shall not save us."** The kingdom must come to the realization that political alliances with the Assyrian nation will not benefit them despite their copious seeking (5:13; 7:11; 8:9). God is their singular Saviour and Helper (13:4,9). Moreover, the object of their trust must change, otherwise, it does not equate as genuine repentance.

Secondly, **"we will not ride on horses."** It is best to consider this statement a reference to Egypt since Egypt was significantly involved in the horse trade. Support for this notion can be found in Deuteronomy 17:16.

"Only he must not acquire many horses for himself or cause the people to return to Egypt in order to acquire many horses, since the Lord has said to you, 'You shall never return that way again'."

Israel found confidence in the military might of Egypt, but it was a misplaced confidence. Dependence upon horses was a common occurrence in the ancient world, which probably led David to exclaim in contrast that,

"Some trust in chariots and some in horses, but we trust in the name of the Lord our God." (Psalm 20:7)

Where does your trust ultimately lie? Is it in fleeting things? If our trust is in anything or anyone other than God, we will be sorely disappointed. Our trust should never lie in our finances, our family, or our freedoms. Trust must always be in God, first and foremost.

They also make another vow to God. It is that **"we will say no more 'Our God' to the work of our hands"** a vow that runs counter to their present idolatry. Idolatry is offensive in and of itself, but what makes it terrible for the Jews is that they were worshipping the very items they designed with their own hands. No right-thinking people would do this—worship the items they had constructed.

Naturally, that is the impact of sin. It makes one foolish, nonsensical, and blinds an individual to how stupid his actions are. Paul made the same observation in first chapter of Romans when he stated in verses 21-23,

> [21] *For although they knew God, they did not honor him as God or give thanks to him, but they became futile in their thinking, and their foolish hearts were darkened.* [22] *Claiming to be wise, they became fools,* [23] *and exchanged the glory of the immortal God for images resembling mortal man and birds and animals and creeping things.*

The description of that passage mirrors Hosea's day. He desires them to put off their idolatry and return to God. Those that will return to the Lord today must put off their idolatry as well. Anything in our lives that satisfies us more than Christ is idolatrous.

The prayer further affirms that **"In you the orphan finds mercy."** At first glance, it is difficult to understand why the orphan is catapulted into Hosea's prophecy. No comment on an orphan is extant anywhere in the most recent speech of Hosea. Why is the orphan cited?

It is because that term appropriately illustrates how distant and disconnected Israel was from their covenant commitment with God. In Chapter 11:1, God made it clear that Israel was His son. However, their sin has detached them from communion with their Father and, presently, their activity resembles an orphan rather than a son. Nevertheless, Yahweh has a biblical reputation of being favourable to fatherless children. Psalm 10:14b reveals that, *to you the helpless commits himself; you have been the helper of the fatherless.*

The word for "mercy" in the Hebrew text literally means "to be soft" conveying the idea of loving and cherishing someone. Although Israel has rebelled and now takes the disposition of an orphan, God is willing to show them tender loving care upon their return to Him.

He will do the same for anyone who comes to Him in repentance, regardless of previous mistakes and deep flaws. Even a Christian in deep sin who comes to God with a repentant heart, turning away from his iniquity and seeking God's mercy will be received by God in softness. The Lord wants all orphans to return home to Him as sons.

The Promise of Renewal

Next, (vs. 4) God informs His people that **"I will heal their apostasy."** "Apostasy" refers to their turning away and defection from God. "Heal" suggests that they have a wound that only God can stitch. Only by His grace and initiation will they be brought back to Him. Observe carefully that Israel does not accomplish this; it is God who moves in order to cure their defection from Himself.

Similarly, God must move within sinners if they are to be brought back into right relationship with Him. This is the effectual call of God. Peter made this point clear in 1 Peter 2:9-10 when he said,

> *⁹But you are a chosen race, a royal priesthood, a holy nation, a people for his own possession, that you may proclaim the excellencies of him who called you out of darkness into his marvelous light. ¹⁰Once you were not a people, but now you are God's people; once you had not received mercy, but now you have received mercy.*

Paul says in Romans 8:30 as well,

*And those whom he predestined he also **called**, and those whom he **called** he also justified, and those whom he justified he also glorified.*

God is the starting point and first cause of every believer's salvation— "the author and finisher of our faith". We love Him because He first loved us. If God had not regenerated us, we would be hopelessly perishing. Therefore, all glory belongs to God for our glorious, magnificent, and eternal salvation! Don't ever submit glory to yourself for being a Christian; you are only a Christian because God made you one, and if God had not called you unto Himself, you would be on your way to eternal damnation.

He further informs that **"I will love them freely."** In addition to healing, they will be loved by God. Israel should be immensely comforted since, in Hosea 9:15, God threatened that He would love them no more. Although, their judgement will make them feel unloved, that situation will one day change. The word "freely" means that the love is voluntary with a readiness of mind. God will not need to force Himself because love will gush forth naturally. Verse 5-7 will make this unmistakably clear.

Thankfully, all God's children are loved freely by Him. His affection is not fake or forced as it gushes unrestricted toward those He has redeemed with the precious blood of His Son. We must hold firmly to this truth because seasons in life will arise when we will feel unloved and alone, although surrounded by hundreds of people. We will be rejected, hurt, and abused. Nevertheless, may it be eternally stamped upon the souls of God's children that God adores us with an unending love—one that's deeper than the deepest ocean and higher than the highest mountain.

God's comfort continues with **"my anger has turned from them"**, explaining that fierce wrath no longer pursues His people. What occurs in verse 4-7 must be futuristic since that was not His disposition toward Israel in Hosea's era. During the time-span of Hosea's ministry, God's anger had not yet touched their soil. When the aforesaid period approaches, God's anger will be no more.

"I will be like the dew to Israel" is the 5th verse's affirmation. Previously, the Hosean mention of "dew" points to something fickle and fleeting—a negative assertion. In this case, however, "dew" is a favourable notion, speaking of the early morning dew that brings moisture to the dry farming season of the summer so that crops would not wither out in that time.[xxiii] Because of Him, the nation will be refreshed.

Furthermore, **"he shall blossom like the lily."** As a result of God's dew and refreshment, Israel, the lily, will receive moisture and flourish showing off its beauty and colour. This assessment is light years away from where the nation and its relationship to God is now. At the close of chapter 13, He threatened that their pregnant women would be ripped open.

Then, **"he shall take root like the trees of Lebanon."** Focus shifts from the shoot system (that which is above the ground) to the root system (that which is below the ground). Because of the moisture from God's dew, the roots will dive deep into the soil bringing about stability and firmness as a nation. Lebanon was/is a region in the northern part of Palestine blessed with fertile soil and, most particularly, large, beautiful cedar trees (Psalm 92:12; 104:16).

In the 6th verse, Yahweh reveals **"his shoots shall spread out; his beauty shall be like the olive."** Transitioning back above ground, the shoot's expansion demonstrates that God's dew will cause the plant to grow expectantly since there is sufficient nourishment. Olive trees are popular in that region as a source of food and especially because of the trading of olive oil. In short, much success and admiration will come to the nation.

Also, it is affirmed that **"his fragrance"** shall be **"like Lebanon"**. Again, this references that region where an amalgamation of cedar trees give off a sweet scent. In a time to come, Israel will give off a sweet scent metaphorically.

"They shall return and dwell beneath my shadow" is the cry of verse **7**. "Return" highlights a returning to God, emphasizing their future repentance. "Shadow" indicates a shade under which the nation will enter and dwell securely. Upon their return, they will be safeguarded and protected by the hand of their God in comfort and in peace. Moreover, **"they shall flourish like the grain; they shall blossom like the vine."** Yahweh reiterates the overwhelming success the nation will encounter during this season by using the metaphors of "flourish" and "blossom". He will reverse the curse of judgement that once sat squarely upon their heads.

"Their fame shall be like the wine of Lebanon." All the earth globally will be fully aware of the blessings of God's hand upon Israel and talk of them will be upon many lips.

Enquiring minds would want to distinguish when the sum of these events will transpire. From what is set forth in these three verses, it appears that such events have not yet come to pass. Most plausibly this occurs during the Millennial Reign of Christ. Much of the Bible testifies to the magnificent nature of that season. These events seem to coincide with what is expected during that period.

Wisdom to Remember

Verse 8 continues the prophecy with **"O Ephraim, what have I to do with idols?"** This is a rhetorical question. God emphasizes one final time that He is disgusted by their idol worship. Idolatry has no part in the nation He has birthed and loved.

They are nothing more than dumb, powerless objects. Furthermore, **"it is I who answer and look after you."** In contrast, with dumb idols, the living God, Yahweh, was the nation's Saviour and Keeper, and He alone.

Today that has not changed; the living God looks after His people. The Hebrew word translated "look after" means to walk around something inspecting it, which is precisely what God does. He is ever present and always observing His people whether we are aware of His presence or not. Yahweh is never absent from any situation. He is always present and involved, regardless of your emotional state. No matter the circumstance, God is always looking after His children.

Hosea affirms on God's behalf that **"I am like an evergreen cypress; from me comes your fruit."** This is the only location in the Old Testament, where God compares himself to being like a tree.[xxiv] Israel must understand one more time that anything beneficial they receive comes from the Provider. Bringing his prophecy to a close, Hosea says in verse 9 **"whoever is wise let him understand these things."** Notice the last sentence of Hosea's prophecy begins with "whoever" establishing that all that is written therein is not only for the Jews. It is written for anyone and everyone to read, study, and benefit from. As the book ends, it underscores that all of Scripture is God-breathed and written for the benefit of humanity. Yes, Israel's relationship to God was the primary thrust of the book, but this prophecy was recorded for every willing ear. The word translated as "understand" means "to separate mentally" or "to distinguish mentally". Thus, if someone is intelligent or skillful in thinking, he should ponder and contemplate meticulously the contents of this prophecy.

The believer in Christ must firmly engage this mindset with not only Hosea, but all 66 books of the Bible. Scripture demands this when it says in 2 Timothy 2:15,

Do your best to present yourself to God as one approved, a worker who has no need to be ashamed, rightly handling the word of truth.

Also, **"whoever is discerning, let him know them."** "Know" conveys the idea of becoming acquainted with something. In other words, the goal is not to only ponder and contemplate truths but to allow them to become a part of you. D.A. Carson said, "The goal is not to master the Word, but to be mastered by the Word." This must be the goal because **"the ways of the Lord are right."** The word translated as "right" literally means "straight", implying a lack of crookedness or perversion in what God's Word proposes. Where He leads is the direction mankind should go; God's path is the most upright.

Finally, the broken-hearted prophet asserts that **"the upright walk in them."** Those who are godly and righteous will live their lives according to the ways God has directed. They find delight in the ways of the Lord. Alternatively, **"transgressors stumble in them."** A transgressor is literally someone who "breaks away" or "falls away" from the right authority. This stumbling, again, recalls the image of one who wavers from side to side with weak legs. Those who are rebellious will not live according to the direction of God. Many today claim to be Christ's sheep but, godliness is determined by how one walks according to the ways of the Lord.

God's children must and will live according to God's will for their lives. In John 15:8, Jesus Himself testified that,

By this my Father is glorified, that you bear much fruit and so prove to be my disciples.

> Discuss

1. Is it possible that many who profess to know Christ today may not be truly converted?

2. According to 2 Timothy 2:19, what should those who belong to the Lord prioritize in their lives?

3. Why did Hosea seemingly make an obscure reference to an orphan in this text?

4. What informs the reader that Hosea's prophecy was not only written to benefit the Jews of that day?

5. How do Christians respond to the ways of the Lord? How do non-Christians respond to the ways of the Lord?

ABOUT THE AUTHOR

O'Neil K. Russell (M.Div., Liberty University School of Divinity) is a pastor-teacher, theologian, and writer who holds two consecutive theological degrees. His foremost passion is to see Christians anchored again to the foundation of God's Word. Although originally from The Bahamas, he now serves the Lord in the Republic of Ireland. He loves to watch sports, reading, and also enjoys holidays with his family. He is married to Kayvanna and has two sons, Zion and Julius.

---

[i] D. Martin Lloyd-Jones, *Preachers and Preaching* (Grand Rapids, Michigan: Zondervan Publishing House, 1972), 9.
[ii] David Allan Hubbard, *Tyndale Old Testament Commentaries: Hosea* (Downers Grove, Illinois: IVP Academic, 1989), 113.
[iii] J. Andrew Dearman, *Hosea: New International Critical Commentary* (Grand Rapids, Michigan: William B. Eerdmans Publishing Company, 2010), 174.
[iv] https://allthatsinteresting.com/port-royal
[v] Ibid.
[vi] M. Daniel Carroll R. ,Thomas E. McComisky, *The Expositor's Bible Commentary: Hosea, Amos, Micah* (Grand Rapids, Michigan: Zondervan, 2008), 132.
[vii] Hubbard, 167.
[viii] Carroll & McComisky, 135.
[ix] T. H. L. Parker, *Calvin's Preaching* (Louisville, Kentucky: Westminster/John Knox Press 1992), 40.
[x] Ibid.
[xi] J. Andrew Dearman, *The Book of Hosea: New International Commentary on the Old Testament* (Grand Rapids, Michigan: William B. Eerdmans Publishing Company, 2010), 273.
[xii] Carroll & McComisky, 151.
[xiii] Hubbard, 194.
[xiv] Dearman, 289.
[xv] Hubbard, 204.
[xvi] Dearman, 298.
[xvii] 2 Timothy 3:16
[xviii] Hubbard, 218.
[xix] Ibid.
[xx] Malachi 3:8-10
[xxi] 2 Corinthians 9:6-7
[xxii] Derek Kidner, *The Message of Hosea* (Downers Grove, Illinois: Intervarsity Press, 1981), 114.
[xxiii] Dearman, 341.
[xxiv] Dearman, 344.

Made in the USA
Columbia, SC
05 October 2021